Demokratie, Sicherheit, Frieden
Democracy, Security, Peace

herausgegeben von Prof. Dr. Michael Brzoska
Series Editor Prof. Dr. Michael Brzoska

DSF   Band 205
DSP   Volume 205

Eine Veröffentlichung aus dem Institut für
Friedensforschung und Sicherheitspolitik
an der Universität Hamburg

A publication of the Institute for Peace Research
and Security Policy at the University of Hamburg

Delia Rahmonova-Schwarz

Family and Transnational Mobility in Post-Soviet Central Asia

Labor Migration from Kyrgyzstan, Tajikistan and Uzbekistan to Russia

Nomos

For my children

Die Deutsche Nationalbibliothek verzeichnet diese Publikation in
der Deutschen Nationalbibliografie; detaillierte bibliografische
Daten sind im Internet über http://dnb.d-nb.de abrufbar.

Die Deutsche Nationalbibliothek lists this publication in the
Deutsche Nationalbibliografie; detailed bibliographic data
is available in the Internet at http://dnb.d-nb.de.

Zugl.: Bielefeld, Univ., Diss., 2009

ISBN 978-3-8329-7830-3

1. Auflage 2012
© Nomos Verlagsgesellschaft, Baden-Baden 2012. Printed in Germany. Alle Rechte, auch die des Nachdrucks von Auszügen, der photomechanischen Wiedergabe und der Übersetzung, vorbehalten. Gedruckt auf alterungsbeständigem Papier.

This work is subject to copyright. All rights are reserved, whether the whole or part of the material is concerned, specifically those of translation, reprinting, re-use of illustrations, broadcasting, reproduction by photocopying machine or similar means, and storage in data banks. Under § 54 of the German Copyright Law where copies are made for other than private use a fee is payable to »Verwertungsgesellschaft Wort«, Munich.

Contents

Acknowledgements		9
List of Tables and Figures		10
1.	Introduction	11
1.1.	Research Topic	11
1.2.	State of the Art	17
	1.2.1. Migrations in Central Asia	17
	1.2.2. Theories of International Migration and the Transnational Paradigm	20
	1.2.3. Transnational Migration and Development	24
	1.2.4. Migrations and Kinship	26
1.3.	The Present Research	29
1.4.	Outline	30
1.5.	Technical Comments	33
2.	Theories and Methods	34
2.1.	Theoretical Arguments	34
	2.1.1. Kinship as a Unit of Analysis: Institutional Approaches to Kinship in Transformation Studies	34
	2.1.2. Distinction of Kinship from other Formal/Informal Institutions and Organizations	37
	2.1.3. Structuration and Post-Soviet Transnationalization	40
2.2.	Methodology	42
	2.2.1. Data Collection and Data Analysis	43
	2.2.2. Fieldwork	46

Part One
From a History of Migrations and Mobility Control in the Soviet Union towards a Conceptual Framework for Post-Soviet Transnationalism

3.	Historical Overview of Migrations during the Soviet Period and in the Early Years of THE USSR's Dissolution	51
3.1.	The Genesis: The Early Years of Mobility Control in Pre-Soviet Russia	52

3.2.		Control of Movement through Labor in the Period before the 1917 Revolution	53
3.3.		Institutionalized Restriction on Movement of People under Stalin with a Focus on Soviet Central Asia	55
3.4.		Migration Patterns in the 1960s and 1980s	60
	3.4.1.	The Presence of the Slavic Population in Central Asia	60
	3.4.2.	Emigration of the Jewish Population	61
	3.4.3.	'Friendship of Nations' and Construction of a Multiethnic Soviet Society: Education Migration, Internationalization of the Division of Labor and Solidarity among Nations	63
3.5.		Migrations in the Late 1980s and the Demise of the USSR: Wither "Friendship of Nations" and "Brotherhood of Peoples"?	71
3.6.		Migration patterns in Central Asia and Russia in the 1990s: The Demise of the Soviet Union and Further Increase of Emigration and Mobility Rate	72
4.		Conceptualizing Post-Soviet Transnationalization	76
4.1.		A Framework for Understanding Post-Soviet Transnationalization	77
	4.1.1.	The Unusual Case of the Former Soviet Union	77
	4.1.2.	The Soviet Era and the Residuals of Sovietization Policies	80

Part Two
Analyzing Transnational Migrant Practices and Filial and Conjugal Relations in Kinship

5.		Sending Cash Home: Monetary Remittance Practices of Central Asian Transnational Migrants in Russia	91
5.1.		Informal and Formal Cash Transfer Mechanisms	92
5.2.		Monetary Transactions and Social Ties	93
	5.5.1.	Legal Status and Brokerage Practices of Women	94
5.3.		The Somewhat Different Collective Remittances	95
5.4.		Receiving Remittances	98
5.5.		Conclusion	101

6.	Toil in Russia to Tie the Knot: Weddings and Other Life Cycle Practices in the Context of Transnational Migration	103
6.1.	Labor Migration and Weddings	104
6.2.	'The Bridegroom Works in Russia': Representation of Migrant Workers in Marriage Arrangements and Wedding Negotiations	114
6.3.	Life-Cycle Rituals of Migrant Workers beyond Marriage	119
6.4	Conclusion	123
7.	Documenting Transformation and Transnational Migration: Filial Relations in Central Asian Families	124
7.1.	Transformational Factors of Labor Migration	124
7.2.	Migrants as Sons and Daughters	128
7.2.1.	The Eldest Son – The Rescuer of the family	128
7.2.2.	The Uneasy Situation of Youngest and Only Sons	132
7.2.3.	Daughters and their Search for a New Start	133
7.3.	Female-Headed Households: Introducing Gulruh and Shohistaxon	137
7.3.1.	Gulruh	137
7.3.2.	Shohistaxon	141
7.4.	The Impact of Changing Citizenship on the Kinship	146
7.5.	Conclusion	151
8.	Conjugal Relationships in a Migration Context: Interaction of Mobility and the New Mode of Life with Cultural Values and Mores	153
8.1.	The Struggle Against and Retaining the Virtue of a Docile Daughter-in-Law	153
8.2.	A New Chapter in the Life of a Married Woman	158
8.2.1.	A Path to Freedom from an Authoritarian Husband	159
8.2.2.	Situation in Dependent Families of Bread-Winning Wives	163
8.3.	Parents-in-Law and Their Leash of Morality	165
8.4.	Conclusion	172

9.	Transnational Polygamous Relations	174
9.1.	The Other Wife in Russia: A Typology of Extramarital Relationships of Labor Migrants	175
9.2.	The Institutional and Judicial Level	180
9.3.	Situational Analysis	183
9.4.	Transnational Polygamies in the Global Context and the Case of Central Asia	187
9.5.	Female Narratives at Both Ends of Migration: From Patience to Tolerance (or the Lack Thereof)	192
9.6.	Conclusion	195

Part Three
Kinship and Post-Soviet Continuity in Migrant Transnationalism

10.	Formalization of Migrant Kinship and Patronages: Emergence of Central Asian Migrant Organizations in Russia		199
10.1.	Central Asian Transnational Patronages		204
	10.1.1.	Relative Anonymity: Concealed Personal Identities and Activities	205
	10.1.2.	Authority/Pseudo-Parental Attitude of Patrons	211
10.2.	Asymmetrical Reciprocity		213
10.3.	The Base of Resources of Central Asian Patrons in Russia		215
10.4.	Conclusion		217
11.	Concluding Remarks		218
11.1.	Transnationalization and Continuity		218
11.2.	Transnationalization and Kinship		219
11.3.	Relevance to Migration-Development Paradigm and Transformation Discourse		222

Appendix

Selected List of Informants	229
References	232

Acknowledgements

I owe immense gratitude to a number individuals and institutions that assisted me during the four years of my PhD research, out of which this book has developed. I am deeply grateful to my research advisor Prof. Dr. Thomas Faist at Bielefeld University. Conducting this research would have been much less of a pleasure without his valuable scholarly advice, enriching discussions, moral support, responsiveness, encouragement and unfailing patience. I am very thankful also to my second advisor Dr. Markus Kaiser, whose regional and research expertise I appreciated at all stages of this work. Thanks are due to Dr. Wolfgang Zellner, Head of the Centre for OSCE Research (CORE) in Hamburg, for showing great interest in my initial thoughts and support for the publication of my research. I wish to thank my former colleague and friend Dr. Anna Kreikemeyer. And, I am very grateful to my editor Elizabeth Hormann for her valuable assistance. It was a pleasure to work with you.

The research was generously supported by the following institutions: First and foremost, I wish to express my utmost gratitude to the Evangelisches Studienwerk e.V. Villigst for providing me with a full two year scholarship and financing my field trips to Central Asia and Russia. For the first six months of my research I was also offered financial support within the framework of the Marie Curie Pre-doctoral Fellowship at the Université de Poitiers, France, where I enjoyed the research facilities of the migration research center MIGRINTER. I am indebted as well to the International Graduate School in Sociology (IGSS) and the members of its Executive Council. It was the IGSS and the admission to its PhD program that helped me make my research project a reality. Thanks are also due to my fellow doctoral students for reading parts of this work. I really enjoyed the circle of international PhD students, doctoral seminars and library facilities in Bielefeld.

My appreciation goes to my friends, colleagues and acquaintances from state institutions, NGOs, international organizations in Russia and Central Asia who helped me find people to talk to and places to visit. I am indebted to a great number of courageous individuals who were willing to be interviewed by me: men, women and adolescents who not only shared their lifestories but sometimes also the little food they had at their disposal. Thanks so much for your hospitality and generosity!

I wish to thank my family and friends for their continuing love and support. It would be impossible to list everyone here, but without you this book could not have been published. My deepest appreciation and heartfelt gratitude goes to Florian Schwarz for the assistance, support and encouragement he offered me sometimes across continents and many time zones. Thanks for everything, Florian – for preparing lovely meals, accompanying me home from libraries at late hours and helping me carry those heavy books. You were more helpful than you could ever have imagined.

List of Tables and Figures

Figure 1: Triadic Relations for Post-Soviet Transnational Spaces 39
Table 1: Regional Population Growth in the USSR, 1981-1985.
Source: Goskomstat SSSR 1988, 16-33, 160-69
(Gibson, 1991:146) 70
Figure 2: A list of items to be accumulated for the wedding of
an average peasant family in the Province of Khatlon (TAJ) 106
Figure 3: Genogram of Shohistaxon and her siblings 145
Figure 4: Genogram of a Polygamous Transnational Family 180
Figure 5: Abstract Situational Map 184
Figure 6: Relational Analysis Considering Married Migrant
Couple in the Center 186

1. Introduction

1.1. Research Topic

On a warm late-May morning I entered the house of a Tajik labor migrant's family in a small village in Southern Tajikistan to conduct an interview. This time I was welcomed cordially, not just by the migrant's family members living in the house, but also by a circle of six or seven women from the neighborhood who were sitting on the floor around some tea, homemade butter, and fresh-baked bread. "Yeah, so you are writing about *migraciia* (Rus. for 'migration')," said one of the women. "Right here in this room, we are all *migraciia*!" she said motioning with her hand, to her neighbors. Some of them looked at each other, perplexed by the meaning of this Russian word. "That's right!" she said to me, and pointed at every woman one by one. "Me, I am *migraciia*. Here – she is *migraciia*, that one over there – *migraciia*, that other neighbor – *migraciia*...and help yourself to bread and tea, girl...all of us here are *migraciia*! Do you want to write about all of us?" The women laughed, each of them repeating and trying to pronounce *migraciia, migraciia* in her own accent, and some of them, still laughing, asked bluntly, "What's *migraciia* anyway?"[1]

"Well, your husband is gone for work, so is my eldest son and that neighbor back there, her son, that's *migraciia*," others explained.[2]

By the time I heard family members of migrants in their homelands speak of migration in this way, it had become clear that, apart from being a process of movement from one geographic place to another, as the term *migration* suggests, in Central Asia it had come to signify a social phenomenon, a mode of life, an attribute with which a segment of the population associate themselves. In 2005, when this research began, labor migration from Central Asia to Russia had increased to such an extent that one could hardly find a

---

1   *Migratsiash chiyay?* (In Kulobi dialect of Tajik.) Field observations in Khatlon Province, April-May, 2007. In this respect my informants differ from Oaxacans surveyed by Cohen *et al.* who refer to their economically motivated movements as *migration* and actually use this word (2003:713). While the media in Central Asia applies the concept of migration, Uzbek, Tajik, or Kyrgyz equivalents (*muhojirlik, muhojiri, migraciia* respectively) of this concept are not used often among those affected by migration, let alone transnational migration. People speak rather about "working in Russia," "going to Russia," or "being in Russia."

2   While it is true that these rural women seemed unable to differentiate between this relatively novel term *migration* as an abstract noun and *migrant* as a subject, the conversation itself invoked thoughts about the semantics of *migration*. As argued by Faist, encyclopedic definitions of migration in the literature draw boundaries between the change of places and the actual agents who are in charge of this change (Everett, 1966:49; Petersen, 1968:286 as cited by Faist, 2000a:18). Everett in his definition explicitly excludes mobility induced by work (*Ibid.*). The statement "All of us here are *migraciia*" is of particular significance as it is said not by the movers themselves but by the stayers, the family members of migrants, who feel as affected by the process of migration as their relatives abroad.

family in the region that had no members working in Russia. While there is labor-induced seasonal migration within the region, notably from Tajikistan and Uzbekistan to the economically privileged Kazakhstan or from Uzbekistan and Tajikistan to Kyrgyzstan, the Russian Federation has, for the past decade, stood out as a major destination for migrants, in particular those from Kyrgyzstan, Tajikistan, and Uzbekistan.

This study explores labor migration processes in the former Soviet Union, from Central Asia to the Russian Federation. It seeks to understand multi-directional movements of labor migrants, adopting a transnational approach to international migration that brings to the foreground dense sustained ties not only of people, kinship, and communities, but also of networks and organizations across multiple nation-states. This research looks into the implications of migration to Russia on membership roles within migrant families, kin relations of migrants in the countries of origin and destination, and the perception of migrants as significant actors of social change in the Central Asian society.

The research question in this study is connected with the following puzzle: over the seventy years of the Soviet period, the state had strict control over the mobility and employment of the population. When the USSR collapsed, mobility increased rapidly. With the emergence of new state borders, internal administrative borders of the Soviet republics became international borders; consequently internal migration became international migration. During the Soviet period, the family as an institution enjoyed the full protection of the state, as social benefits were granted to families with a large number of children. Over time, together with other centralized state structures, the state's responsibility for the protection of the family weakened. Faced with economic crisis in the years immediately following the demise of the Soviet Union, the employable population acquired the independence to find employment abroad and to rely only on the provisions within kinship. Stressing the importance of kinship to understanding cross-border mobility, this research will be guided by the following questions:

- How are membership roles within kinship negotiated in the context of post-Soviet transnational mobility?
- What implications do family negotiations and practices have for the transnationalization process?

A description of what significant socio-economic and political factors are linked to the research topic will provide more clarity. Labor migration from Central Asia to Russia increased, especially at the end of the 1990s when the Russian economy started to recover. Because the economic transition process resulted in a deterioration of infrastructure, education, and the health system, the labor force from the agrarian and construction sectors as well as highly educated professionals began migrating to Russia in search of work. It is difficult to determine how many Central Asian labor migrants there really are in the Russian Federation. On the one hand, the number of migrants from the former Soviet republics in Russia is estimated to have reached 12 million in 2008.[3] On the other hand, because many migrants returned to their home countries due to the global financial crisis of 2009, the statistical information made available by various institutions is not very reliable. In addition, despite the government crackdown on illegal migration, most labor migrants in Russia are still undocumented.

Migrant earnings are crucial for the economies of sending states. In 2003, the remittances from Russia to Tajikistan made up ca. 20% of the GDP. While this is an official indicator based on the statistical data provided by the banks, the real amount of remittances could be as high as 40-50%, as it is still more advantageous for migrants to transfer their money privately in cash or through unofficial couriers. The monetary remittances to Tajikistan, which reached $280 million for the same year, exceeded the state budget of $250 million by 12%. In the neighboring country of Kyrgyzstan, which is equally impoverished, the remittances made up 55% of the state budget. In Uzbekistan around $500 million were received from migrants working in Russia which equaled ca. 5.7% of the GDP for 2003.[4] Five years later in 2008, indicators for these three countries looked different. According to the data published by the Central Bank of the Russian Federation, in 2008 approximately $1.2 billion was transferred to the Kyrgyz Republic, $2.5 billion to Tajikistan, and $3 billion to Uzbekistan.[5]

Notwithstanding these economic factors, each of the three sending states chose a different policy towards labor migration. In Kyrgyzstan and Tajikistan, the governments have been open about the mass out-flow of population in search of labor. The two countries have been working closely with international organizations such as the IOM, the UNDP, and the OSCE – not only at the state level in working out policies towards managing migration and legislation aimed at facilitating it, but also at the civil society level, within the framework of humanitarian and advocacy projects that include migrants and their families. With the assistance of the EU and the IOM, the Kyrgyz government has committed itself to the improvement of the legal framework on migration and employment, as well as to the protection of migrant rights. It has been conducting an open dialogue at the parliamentarian and federal levels with counterparts in Russia on the issues of legalization of migrants and setting up quotas and engaging Kyrgyz citizens in the Russian employ-

---

3 See, *Nezavisimaia Gazeta* at http://www.ng.ru/economics/2008-03-21/6_migranty.html
4 Olimova and Bosc, 2003.
5 Data taken from the homepage of the Central Bank of the Russian Federation. http://www.cbr.ru/eng/statistics/CrossBorder/print.asp?file=C-b_trans_countries_08_e.htm.
These statistics reflect the financial transfers made by individuals from Russia to these Central Asian countries. Not all of the numbers indicated in the statistics are labor migrant transfers, but a significant portion corresponds to monetary remittances. In addition, while it is true that the remittances have increased, so has the number of individuals opting for bank transfers.

ment market.⁶ Similar attitudes are observed in Tajikistan, although the path to mass labor migration from this sending state differs from that of Uzbekistan and Kyrgyzstan. After the outbreak of the Civil War in 1992 thousands fled to Russia, Kazakhstan, and other neighboring countries.⁷ In the last few years, the Tajik President Emomali Rahmon has visited Russia several times and conducted negotiations with his Russian counterpart on setting up migrant quotas. He also publicly showed concern about the rising death toll of Tajik citizens who had become victims of xenophobia.⁸ The government in Uzbekistan, by contrast, has, for the most part, ignored the phenomenon. While in Tajikistan and Kyrgyzstan conferences and roundtable discussions with politicians take place regularly and on a regional level, Uzbekistan seems, as yet, unable to acknowledge the socio-economic aspects of labor migration. During my fieldwork for this research, I was able to attend some conferences and workshops on migration in Kyrgyzstan and Tajikistan. I noticed that Uzbekistan was either underrepresented or that the participant(s) representing the country did not take part in the discussions.

In Russia, the country of destination for Central Asian labor migrants, the xenophobic attitude of the local population towards migrants from former Soviet republics is increasing. The local Slavic population has been urging the Russian government to bring an end to mass labor migration and implement stricter measures against undocumented migration. However, even those migrants from Central Asia who have been deported many times engage in labor migration to Russia repeatedly, since their economically weak countries of origin cannot provide them with employment. Nevertheless, the most recent global economic crisis has had an impact on the dimension of mass labor migration, as migrants have begun returning to their countries of origin. For a great number of them, there are no longer any prospects of employment at home and it remains to be seen if they will resume employment in Russia. A study conducted by the World Bank has estimated that, if in 2008 the region of Europe and Central Asia received $53 billion in financial transfers, this number may reach only $48 billion for 2009.⁹ Despite these factors, the Russian economy has taken advantage of cheap labor from Central Asia. Notwithstanding new migration and citizenship policies that were initiated to curb illegal migration during the final years of Putin's first presidency in the period of 2006-2008, there are still millions of undocumented migrants in Russia.

---

6   This information is based on interviews and discussions with IOM representatives in Bishkek in 2004 and 2008, but also on unpublished materials and reports by international organizations.
7   *cf.* Chapter 2, section 2.6.
8   http://www.cacianalyst.org/?q=node/4822/print. The visit of President Rahmon in February, 2008 took place in the midst of diplomatic frost between the two countries over the difficulties of reaching an agreement on Russian-backed hydroelectric power stations in Tajikistan on trans-boundary waters shared with Uzbekistan. Russia took the side of Uzbekistan and disapproved of the construction of the stations.
9   Ratha and Mohapatra, 2009.

While the short-term developments of labor movements remain somewhat unclear due to the current financial crisis worldwide, labor migration as a whole has remained of geopolitical significance for the countries involved. With the current extent of mass labor migration of Central Asian citizens to Russia, there is a growing interdependence between Central Asia and Russia in the spheres of the economy and security policy. Considering the strong dependence of the population on migrant remittances, mass deportation of Central Asian labor migrants would result in an escalation of social unrest in the southern region of the former USSR. The Russian government is, therefore, cautious about indirectly causing uproar in a region of such fragile stability.[10] Moreover, Kyrgyzstan, Tajikistan, and Uzbekistan are all Russia's strategic partners in security cooperation and they have economic agreements on raw materials, energy resources, and mobile technology.

My attention was drawn to the phenomenon of transnational migration between Central Asia and Russia at a time when studies conducted in Central Asia by Western and regional scholars were focusing mainly on topics such as security challenges, democratization, development of civil society, human rights, construction of national identities, nation and state building, clan structures, energy policies of Central Asian states, and Islam (including political Islam and religious extremism) in the region.[11] Increasing movements of people across the nation-state borders of the Central Asian states, which

---

10 For more on the relations between Central Asia and Russia in the context of labor migration, see Laruelle, 2007.
11 For a selected bibliography published after 2000, cf. Roy, Olivier (2000): The New Central Asia: The Creation of Nations. London: Tauris; Seifert, Arne (2002). *Risiken der Transformation in Zentralasien. Das Beispiel Tadschikistan.* Mitteilungen Band 64/2002. Hamburg: Deutsches Orient-Institut; Krämer, Annette (2002). *Geistliche Autorität und islamische Gesellschaft im Wandel. Studien über Frauenälteste (otin und xalfa) im unabhängigen Usbekistan.* Berlin: Klaus Schwarz Verlag; Balci, Bayram (2003). *Missionaires de l'Islam en Asie centrale. Les écoles turques de Fethullah Gülen.* Institut Français d'Etudes Anatoliennes. Paris: Masonneuve & Larose ; Kaiser, Markus (2003). "Forms of Transsociation as Counter-processes to Nation Building in Central Asia." *Central Asian Survey* 22 (2/2). S. 315-331. London: Taylor and Francis Group; Jones Luong, Pauline (ed) (2004). *The Transformation of Central Asia. States and Societies from Soviet Rule to Independence.* Ithaca/London; Finke, Peter (2004). *Nomaden im Transformationsprozeß. Kasachen in der post-sozialistischen Mongolei.* In: Johansen, Ulla/Rössler, Martin (Hrsg.) Kölner Ethnologische Studien. Band 29. Münster: Lit; Cornell University Press; Berg, Andrea (2004). *Globale Konzepte versus lokale Realität. Eine Studie zu Nicht-Regierungsorganisationen im unabhängigen Usbekistan.* Baden-Baden: Nomos; Fathi, Habiba (2004). *Femmes d'autorité dans l'Asie centrale contemporaine. Quête des ancêtres et recompositions identitaires dans l'islam postsoviétique.* Paris: Masonneuve & Larose; Gumppenberg, Marie-Carin von and Udo Steinbach (eds) (2005). *Zentralasien. Geschichte-Politik-Wirtschaft. Ein Lexikon.* München: Beck; Berg, Andrea und Anna Kreikemeyer (eds) (2006). Collins, Kathleen. (2006). *Clan Politics and Regime Change in Central Asia.* Cambridge and New York: Cambridge University Press. Berg, Andrea and Anna Kreikemeyer (2006). *Realities of Transformation: Democratization Policies in Central Asia Revisited.* Baden-Baden: Nomos; Machtmosaik Zentralasien. Traditionen, Restriktionen, Aspirationen. *Osteuropa* 8-9, 2007; Louw, Maria Elizabeth (2007). *Everyday Islam in Post-Soviet Central Asia.* London and New York: Routledge. Please note that in this footnote the full bibliographic information of the selected literature has been provided only to give the reader a general impression of the topics that have dominated the studies in this area since the early 2000s.

were shaping the society of the sending states, seemed as crucial to explore as the topics that attracted the majority of the scholars.[12] Disappointed by the failure of the processes of democratization and the development of civil society in the region, as were many political scientists, policy analysts, international donors, and advocacy groups, I sketched my research design determined to find out to what extent migrants contributed to the democratization process in their home countries. After all, within the scholarship on migration, a great deal of work has been devoted to the worldwide perception of transnational migrants as agents of development.[13]

At first I had not imagined that the migration of individuals was so deeply embedded in the development processes and socio-political events of their homelands. These aspects started unfolding as migrants and their loved ones in their homelands told me their own stories. For example, similar to many migration scholars, my point of departure had been from the assumption that labor migration had primarily economic reasons and that it was important to keep the analytical lens on financial remittances. After analyzing the data that were relevant for remittances, I began noticing the factors related to kinship ties, such as the roles that transnational migrants played as sons and daughters of their families. The seemingly dense ties of kin-members or spouses turned out, in fact, not to be devoid of social conflicts. Gradually, as the everyday lives of migrants and their families shifted to the center of my analysis, the scrutiny of monetary remittances became ancillary to other factors. I therefore opted to leave out the section on remitting practices and move on to drawing a broader picture. Part of this broader context became the approach to post-Soviet transnationalization. While, on the one hand, attempting to make visible how transnationalism has been shaped by the Soviet past of the countries concerned (from above), and how transnationalism is expressed through the kinship relations of Central Asian migrants (from below), I try, in this work, to understand the changes in kinship relations in the context of the transnational mobility of family members. Based on biographic interviews with labor migrants who arrived in the late 1990s and leaders of migrant organizations in Russia who settled there during the Soviet period, I argue that migrant transnationalism in the post-Soviet geographic zone differs from the contexts of US-Latin America or Great Britain-Southeast Asia. Migrations of these patterns derive either from colonial powers and their immigration policies in the 20th century or through state-supported programs that attracted cheap labor forces from other countries. Post-Soviet transnationalization, however, is not post-*colonial* by character, but rather post-*imperialist* and is based on the Sovietization policies of the USSR. Compulsory military service, Soviet education policies (e.g., promo-

---

12 More on migration scholarship on and in Central Asia since the end of 1990s is described in the section on the state of the art. Ancillary sources on migrations from Central Asia to Russia during the Soviet period are dealt with in the next chapter, which provides historical background of migrations.
13 For more on the migration-development nexus, see section 1.2.3.

tion of the Russian language at secondary schools), and careers in the Communist Party of the so-called titular nations of Central Asia have shaped the cultural and education background of an entire generation of Central Asian migrants in Russia.

1.2. State of the Art

1.2.1. Migrations in Central Asia

Sources such as publications, unpublished research, and reports on migrations in Central Asia since the 1990s have been classified as follows: first, there is a body of research either published through international development organizations or carried out by Central Asian scholars with their support. Proceedings and the results of conferences and seminars held by these organizations have often been published as a collection of articles.[14] Secondly, there is research carried out by Central Asian and Russian scholars working for higher education institutions in Russia and Central Asia. In this category I would include surveys by state institutions, such as demographers working for state statistic services (the so-called *goskomstat*s). The third group of research treating the issue of migrations in Central Asia consists of publications supported by Western publishers and scientific journals that also include publications written in cooperation between Russian/Central Asian and Western scholars.

With respect to the first category, analyses conducted by the International Organization for Migration (IOM), the World Bank, the United Nations Population Fund (UNFPA), and other international organizations mostly apply a quantitative approach and focus on social and economic problems, to which the increase in population mobility is attributed. Almost all the reports by international donor organizations warn their readers that the statistical indicators are far from reliable. The IOM regularly publishes migration reports and statistical materials.[15] A report published by the IOM in 2001 entitled "Migration Trends in Eastern Europe and Central Asia" covers the trends and the patterns of migration that predominated through 2001 and 2002 in Eastern Europe and Central Asia (EECA), a region defined by the IOM as including Armenia, Azerbaijan, Belarus, Georgia, Kazakhstan, Kyrgyzstan, Moldova, the Russian Federation, Tajikistan, Turkmenistan, Ukraine, and Uzbekistan. Two short essays are included in the report; the first takes a closer look at the structural challenges of migration management

---

14 The issue of research produced with the support of international organizations in Central Asia is also discussed by Krämer (2002:22) . Thus, the IOM funded an entire series of quantitative surveys on remittances following the Millennium Goals campaign of the United Nations.
15 e.g., Olimova and Bosc, 2003.

in the region, emphasizing the lack of effective cooperation between the countries and at technical facilities related to border management. The second essay focuses on new trends, especially female shuttle migration and female migrants' engagement in the "sex industry."

A further study conducted with the support of the IOM was a quantitative survey of Tajik migrant workers in 2003. This study adhered to the classic research on migration and concentrated on push and pull factors of labor migration. In addition, one of the recent publications related to migration is on counter-trafficking in Eastern Europe and Central Asia (EECA). Also published in 2003, this volume consists of short country reports and concludes with the mechanisms necessary for combating human trafficking in EECA. Indeed trafficking, fraud, and forced labor, all under the pretence of well-paid employment abroad, remain a serious issue in the region. The IOM has been cooperating closely with the EECA governments to tackle this problem; it has also been conducting various projects to improve cooperation between Central Asian governments in terms of migration management, promoting skills of potential labor migrants in Tajikistan, raising public awareness on human trafficking, etc. While organizations such as the OSCE, the UNDP, the IOM, the World Bank, and the Aga Khan Foundation regularly publish reports on labor migration or touch upon this issue in relation to topics such as security, poverty, and gender, until recently they mostly covered only two of the three sending states considered for this research – Kyrgyzstan and Tajikistan. Until recently, migrants from Uzbekistan or migration from Uzbekistan did not get much attention from scholars. International organizations have treated the phenomenon of migration as a by-product of other issues such as gender or human trafficking. The government of Uzbekistan has yet to acknowledge labor migration as a crucial social and economic phenomenon, which explains why the IOM has not yet been given permission to establish an office in that country. There are some signs, however, that this attitude might change in the future. In 2008, for example, the Swiss Agency for Development and Cooperation (SDC,) together with the UNDP, published a collection of articles written by Uzbek and Russian scholars on internal and external labor migration.[16]

With the increase of migration inflow to Russia, Russian scholars' interest in labor migration grew as well and gradually they came to include the mass inflow of population from the Central Asian countries. This can be observed in the selected publications that have appeared since the mid-1990s. Russian scholarship at the outset focused more on forced migrations in the aftermath of the conflicts in the Caucasus and Central Asia (the Civil War in Tajikistan). The focus then turned to the so-called "new diasporas" in newly independent countries, in which primarily Slavic minorities were considered. This trend in research was followed by research interests in the flow of eco-

---

16   Trudovaia Migraciia, 2008.

nomically-motivated undocumented migrants in Russia.[17] In 2002, Moscow State Social University launched a project on migrant workers limiting the research to the capital city and its suburbs (Moskovskaia Oblast'). The results of this quantitative research were published by the head of the project, Tatyana Yudina, in a monograph entitled "Sociology of Migration"[18] and in an article "Labor Migration into Russia: The Response of State and Society."[19]

A body of solid research covering Russian migration policy, the demographic crisis, and the dimension of foreign labor has been published by Vladimir Mukomel at the Russian Academy of Sciences.[20] The Center for German and European Studies based in St. Petersburg in Russia, through publication of articles, has been covering important topics related to Russia such as migration and nation-state, ethnicity, migration politics, emigration of ethnic Germans from Russia, and repatriation of ethnic Russians to the Russian Federation.[21] The journal *Vestnik Evrazii* (Rus. 'The Eurasia Bulletin') has also been publishing articles on Central Asian migrants in Russia.[22]

As far as the third category of research is concerned, the collection of articles edited by Komatsu *et al.* (2000) are among the earliest post-independence scholarship devoted to migrations in Central Asia. Taking an historical perspective on migration movements in Central Asia, this volume provides articles on migration movements during and after the Soviet period in chronological order, focusing also on the migrations induced by the economic difficulties of the mid-1990s. The volume views these population movements as the most recent trend and presents an overview of the transition process to the market economy and its impact on the mobility of the population in the Central Asian republics. With the vast out-migration population growth to Russia, Kazakhstan, South Korea, Canada, European countries, and (to a relatively lesser extent) the USA, scholars from Western institutions started showing interest in the phenomenon. Liebert focuses mainly on Kyrgyzstan-USA and analyzes immigration policies in the USA from an institutionalist perspective.[23] French scholar Peyrouse focuses on migration trends in the region over the last few years, highlighting the advantages of financial remittances for impoverished households, the need in Russia for low-paid employment from Central Asia, and the disdain of the Slavic population of Russia for Central Asian migrants, while his colleague Thorez concentrates on labor migration to Russia from the perspective of human geography.[24] Laruelle's interests lie in state and nation building processes in Central Asia and Russia and in view of the large out-flow labor force from Cen-

---

17 Tishkov, 1996; Modenov and Nosov, 2002, Tishkov 2005.
18 Yudina, 2004.
19 Yudina, 2005.
20 Mukomel, 2005 and 2006.
21 Baraulina and Karpenko, 2004.
22 Brusina 2008, Kalandarov, 2008.
23 Liebert, 2008.
24 Peyrouse, 2007; Thorez, 2007.

tral Asia, she highlights the new role that Russia might be playing through hosting millions of migrants.[25] Anderson and Hancilova published a working paper in 2009 that deals with labor migration into Kazakhstan, a migrant-receiving country of Central Asia. Their timely study focuses on the violation of migrant rights, trafficking in human beings, and exploitation of laborers in Kazakhstan that have worsened in the face of the most recent economic crisis.[26]

Finally, among the most recent relevant publications was the edited volume by Buckley and Ruble entitled "Migration, Homeland and Belonging in Eurasia."[27] Significant contributions in this publication are the introductory chapter by Buckley and the initial two chapters by Heleniak and Korobkov, respectively. The latter two authors provide an overview of migration trends in both the Soviet period and the post-Soviet space. Buckley does not specify the newness of the approaches in her contribution, although the title of her introductory chapter is about new approaches to migration. The reader is left to discover the part on transnationalism, which is comprised of articles on Crimean Tatars, returning ethnic Kazaks, and post-Soviet transnationalism of Germans, Jews, and Russians. It seems that Buckley perceives the transnationalist paradigm as new. We will see in the next section of this chapter, however, that the scholarship on migration has raised doubts about the novelty of the transnational approach.

Scholarship in area studies has not yet dealt with the phenomenon of transboundary migration in the framework of systematic research, in particular that originating from the three major senders of labor migrants to Russia. So far, it seems that this study is the only one of its kind, in that it includes systematic scrutiny of migrant families through fieldwork in the three major countries of origin in Central Asia and the country of arrival in Russia.

1.2.2. Theories of International Migration and the Transnational Paradigm

Migration scholars often explain the theories of international migration in terms of three generations. The first generation of international migration theories includes *neoclassical economics* and the *new economics of migration*.[28] The *macro-level* approach of *neoclassical economics* conceives international migration in terms of global supply and demand of labor and wage disparities. In geographic areas where wages are lower and labor supply is abundant, people are likely to move to areas where both wages and the demand for labor are higher.[29] The *micro-level* counterpart of this approach views migration as a decision taken by movers wanting to maximize their

---

25 Laruelle even talks about "diasporization of Central Asian states" (see title, 2007).
26 Anderson and Hancilova, 2009.
27 Buckley and Ruble, 2008.
28 I shall consider a review of international migration theories among others by Faist, 2000a (Ch 2) and Pries, 2001.
29 Faist, 2000a, 35-46.

individual profit. Its important assumption is the logic of cost-benefit relations, according to which an individual would migrate only as long as the profit made from moving would exceed the expenditures of moving.[30]

Positioned in contrast to the aforementioned neoclassical economics is the *new economics of migration*. Often associated with Stark and his colleagues, it extends the decision making processes linked to migration from individuals to families and households. As collective actors, they maximize profits and minimize transaction costs and risks. The new economics of migration also holds that individuals have a stronger penchant for migrating when they feel less privileged in relation to others within their social group (*relative deprivation*). Ultimately, this approach departs from an asymmetric distribution of information on the productivity of certain wage groups among labor migrants and their employers. Its proponents contend that employers pay their workers based not on their qualifications or workload but on what they had been paying on average for the type of labor in question.[31]

Macro-structural and *systems-centered* theories on international migration mark the second generation of theorizing that emerged in the 1970s. As far as the former is concerned, the *dual market* theory, associated with Piore and colleagues, deals with labor-capital dualism. Not necessarily opposed to neoclassical economics, it is different from it in that it shifts the focus to the pull factors in countries of destination, notably the high demand for labor and the economic structures of the industrialized countries. According to Piore, low-paying jobs in these countries open opportunities for the labor force coming from abroad.[32] *System theorists* approach international migration in relation to a complex system of division of labor and power structures. They build on the assumption that global expansion of the capitalist economy draws the labor force from the economically less privileged countries of the southern region; international migration is hence regarded as part of the economic growth of the capitalist world system. As Massey *et al.* argued in their theory overview, if in the past colonial powers entered into uncolonized territories in search of land, raw materials, and labor, in the contemporary period neo-colonizing powers and profit-maximizing corporations enter poor countries on the periphery of the world economy with the same purpose.[33]

The overview of these first two generations of theorizing is certainly very broad and it could be expanded to delve more into micro/macro dichotomies or multi-level analyses in migration research. Although such a

---

30 Pries, 2001:13-21.
31 A good example is how teachers, physicians, doctoral students, engineers, and often university faculty members from Central Asia are engaged in low-paying jobs such as road maintenance, agriculture, and construction in Russia. However, as Pries rightly points out, this approach does not fully explain the process of migration between the countries involved (Pries, 2001).
32 Piore, 1973.
33 Parsons, 1968; Wallerstein 1974; Bommes, 1990. On overviews of theories of international migration see also Zollberg, 1989; Massey *et al.*, 1993; Faist, 2000a; Pries, 2001; Wimmer and Glick-Schiller, 2003:577.

description would be important, it would leave relatively less space for the third generation of international migration theory which undergirds the present study. Complementary to these first two generations of theories, the *transnational approach* considers the linkages that go beyond the borders of nation-states which are involved in multi-directional migratory movements. This approach was developed at the beginning of 1990s, in the period of the last decade in which the flow of labor migrants from less developed countries into more developed countries accrued, and the number of refugees from conflict zones seeking asylum in other states grew tremendously.

Scholars of *transnationalism* Peter Kivisto and Thomas Faist have provided critical reviews of the theoretical development of this generation of migration research.[34] They underline the existence of three trends of conceptualization, of which I give a short summary: the first trend is associated with the earliest articulation of transnationalism by cultural anthropologists Nina Glick-Schiller, Linda Basch, and Cristina Szanton Blanc. Glick-Schiller and her colleagues presented transnational migration as something new emerging after WWII. As a unit of analysis the nation-state was too limited to do justice to the field action of immigrants that span multiple nation-state borders.[35] Based on Filipino, Haitian, and Grenadian expatriate communities, they argued further that social science must become "unbound." With the novel concept of migrant transnationalism, assimilation and cultural pluralism became inadequate concepts.[36]

The second form of conceptualization was developed by sociologists Alejandro Portes and his colleagues. Portes and his colleagues built their perspective of immigrant transnationalism on Latin American and Chinese migrants in the United States. They argued that not all migrants are transnationals and suggested that the term *transmigrants* used by Glick-Schiller be replaced by *immigrants*. They maintained that one should differentiate between those immigrants who have no ties or weak ties (e.g. sending occasional gifts home) to their families in their countries of origin and those who have maintained regular and strong relations to their sending countries. The transnational phenomenon as it occurs among individual immigrants and their support networks was termed by the adherents of this trend as 'transnationalism from below' and represented an adequate unit of analysis. The states, governments, and global economic forces responsible for shifting migrants across borders were perceived as 'transnationalism from above.'[37]

The third trend in theorizing migrant transnationalism is associated with political scientist Thomas Faist. Central to this more comprehensive theoriz-

---

[34] Kivisto, 2001; Kivisto and Faist, 2009.
[35] Glick Schiller *et al.* 1992 a and b, Basch *et al.* 1994; Glick-Schiller *et al.* 1995; Glick-Schiller, 1999, 2007.
[36] They put forward arguments on deterritorialized states which were debated by Bommes, 2004:91. For more on the container approach to national societies, see also Pries, 2005:174.
[37] Portes, 1997; 1999; Portes, Guarnizo, and Landolt 1999, also cited by Kivisto, 2001; Kivisto and Faist, 2009.

ing is the analytical tool of transnational social spaces, which includes "combinations of social and symbolic ties, positions in networks and organizations, and networks of organizations that can be found in at least two geographically and internationally distinct places." These spaces constitute pentagonal ties between the immigrant group and their sending and receiving states as well as civil societies.[38] In his work, Faist has focused on immigrant communities that included, but were by no means limited to, kinship. Transnational communities, according to him, "characterize situations in which international movers and stayers are connected by dense and strong social and symbolic ties over time and across space to patterns of networks and circuits in two countries." For long term sustainment of transnational communities it is necessary to keep ties with governmental and civil institutions in the countries involved in migration.[39]

On a broader note, scholarship adhering to the transnational approach of international migration argues that the previous two generations of migration theories focused primarily on the container model of nation-states, limiting it to nation-state boundaries of emigration and immigration countries. While nation-states are of crucial value for linkages between the multiple ends of migration, as transnationalist theorists hold, classic theories are silent about the participation of international migrants in the spaces that span the nation-states in question. Faist, Kivisto, and a number of other migration scholars have meanwhile called into question the novelty of the transnational phenomenon. [40]

Furthermore, there have been debates in international migration, which have evolved around the proponents of assimilation and ethnic pluralism theories, on the one hand, and migrant transnationalism on the other. Theories of assimilation start from the assumption that, as migrants integrate into host societies, their ties to their countries of origin would eventually disappear.[41] Transnational approaches have argued rather, that strong social and symbolic ties keep international migrants and stayers bound over time and across space, as well as nation-state borders which are involved in migration.[42] On the basis of studies focusing on Latin-American migrants in the United States, scholars such as Guarnizo contend that assimilation views take an exclusivist stance, concentrating only on the host countries. He and his associates demonstrate that migrant transnational political activism serves as

---

38 Faist views transnational social spaces as similar to social fields that can be found in the works of Glick-Schiller, Portes, and their associates (Faist, 2000a, Chapter 7).
39 Faist, 1999; 2000a; 2000b; 2006; 2007; 2008, also as cited in Kivisto and Faist, 2009.
40 Faist, 2000a:211; Kivisto, 2001:556, Waldinger and Fitzgerald, 2004; Bommes and Morawka, 2005:1; Kivisto and Faist 2009:191. Portes first argued that the phenomenon was new (1999). Later he contended that improved means of communication and transportation have contributed to the sustainment of transnational ties (Faist and Kivisto 2009:192).
41 Alba and Nee, 1997.
42 Faist, 2000a:207-208; Guarnizo, 2003; Vertovec 2004.

strong evidence for changing political processes in home countries.[43] There have also been attempts to reconcile assimilation models and transnationalism by suggesting that transnationalism could be conceived as a variation of assimilation, since migrant efforts to sustain transnational ties could occur simultaneously with acculturating into the host society.[44] Waldinger and Fitzgerald argue that transnationalism and assimilation should be seen as intricate social processes and not theories. Suggesting an interstate approach in which they analyze migrant relations with actors in state and civil societies in both home and host countries, the two authors urge the scholars of international migration to heed the processes that form a container-society, which in turn help overcome transnationalism vs. assimilation dichotomies.[45] Faist, in turn, views transnational ties as complementary to assimilation and ethnic pluralism, as they should be perceived as a possible result of the adaptation process in the host country.[46]

1.2.3. Transnational Migration and Development

Academic and public discourse has, since the 1960s, linked migratory movements and development processes in the sending countries. We also know that social scientists had already been considering the political, economic, and social effects of migration for a much longer period. Studies in these directions range from Thomas and Znanicki's *The Polish Peasant,* a work published in 1927 in which parishes of Polish émigrés in the US are reported to have sent financial aid to Poland at the beginning of the 20th century, to extensive research carried out on financial transfers from overseas-Chinese to mainland China in the 1950s-1960s, where the Communist regime attempted to control and channel these transfers into construction of houses and factories.[47] Research similar to the latter, one could argue, had already emerged in the greater context of the 1960s in which migration was expected to bring the necessary labor-capital balance: the outflow of surplus labor from underdeveloped countries into the industrialized developed countries with labor force deficits would improve development in the sending countries due to migrant remittances and capital investment. Behind this logic was the expectation that labor migrants would return to their home countries after having worked abroad for several years.

This changed in the 1970s as migration scholars influenced by world system theorists concluded that migration led to the outflow of skilled-workers and professionals from sending countries. The *brain drain* that resulted from this out-migration was detrimental to the development of under-

---

43 Guarnizo, 2003.
44 Kivisto, 2001:568.
45 Waldinger, 2004.
46 Faist and Kivisto, 2009.
47 Thomas and Znaniecki, 1927: 143-156 (v.5). On financial transfers to mainland China, *cf.* Wu, 1967.

developed sending countries. In the 1990s this stance changed as international migrants came to be viewed as potential agents who would contribute to the development of their homelands with the assistance of the states, international donor organizations, and NGOs.[48] International organizations functioning with the support of the World Bank started perceiving monetary remittances of migrants as a way out of development problems. In 2000, the United Nations launched the Millennium Development Goals campaign which included international migrants as contributors to the economic development of their home countries and to the global struggle against poverty through remittances, which have been referred to as "the third pillar of development."[49] This came about in view of quantitative evidence suggesting that the amount of remittances exceeded that of the financial aid given to the developing countries; migrants with their earnings and not just governments and organizations had become active providers of "foreign aid."[50] In addition, if migrants were to stay abroad permanently, their hometown connections or professional networks could be used by development organizations and nation-state institutions for the benefit of development projects at the community level or in the spheres of education and infrastructure in the migrants' places of origin.[51]

Of equal importance in the migration-development nexus has been the circulation of knowledge, resources, and practices known as "social remittances." Transfer of ideas such as human rights and democracy by migrants to their homelands generated a substantial body of research.[52] At the same time, scholars and analysts have shown caution about the great enthusiasm around remittances, be they monetary or social. They argue that, not only did the poorest households in developing countries not benefit from financial transfers since they had no relatives working abroad in the first place, but also, on a more critical note, remittances are of significance only during transient poverty.[53] As far as transfer of knowledge and skills through permanent

---

48 Known as co-development, the link between immigration policies and development was seen to be more efficient, as was highlighted during the EU Summit in Tampere in 1999 (Weil, 2002).
49 www.endpoverty2015.org, www.migration4development.org, Alfieri *et al*, 2005
50 Stahl and Habib, 1991:175, Kapur, 2004:7.
51 There are many more examples than the capacity of this chapter can allow. The most famous is the Mexican Three-for-One Citizen Initiative Program, which was launched in 2002. For each transferred US dollar, a government supported development project would receive one US dollar in matching grants from the state (Hernández-Coss, 2005; Burgess, 2005). Other examples include livelihood studies on Zimbabweans working in South Africa (Maphosa, 2005), the economic impact of migrant remittance in Moldova (Ghencea and Igor, 2005), and, in a similar vein, the Philippines (one of the latest studies being contributed by Martínez and Yang, 2007).
52 Levitt and Nyberg-Sørensen, 2004. For a critical analysis of migration-development discourse, see selected articles by Weil, 2002; Nyberg-Sørensen et al, 2002; Eckstein, 2003; Skeldon, 2003; Lacroix, 2005; Kapur, 2004; de Haas 2006a and b; Bakewell, 2007; Faist 2008.
53 Kapur, 2004, de Haan 2006. During my fieldwork, I witnessed that the campaign had also reached Central Asia. Employees of the UNDP, the IOM, and the World Bank spoke fondly about channeling remittances into development projects. However, not all migrant-

return to the countries of origin are concerned, critical analyses also point to the possibility of professional migrants changing their minds and deciding to stay in the host countries.[54]

Finally, scholarship in the migration-development nexus has also highlighted the so-called transfer of political ideas. Through transnational ties, ethno-national and diasporic communities can challenge the country of origin or the state that occupies the territory of an imagined homeland. Members of these communities, which consist of refugees, émigrés, and stateless diaspora members, engage themselves in a panoply of activities such as lobbying for human rights in the homeland, political action as exile opposition parties, and support of liberation movements.[55]

1.2.4. Migrations and Kinship

The literature on kinship in the context of migration is so vast that a detailed review would merit a chapter of its own. I shall therefore sketch the most relevant trends in this section and refer to the necessary sources in the course of the present research. One of the most significant and most cited contributions to the research on migration and kinship is the classic work by Thomas and Znaniecki, *The Polish Peasant to Europe and America*, which appeared in 1927. In a compilation of several series of letters which Polish migrants in Europe and the United States exchanged with their family members back home, the authors study the causes and consequences of migration and underline the effect of family ties on migrant social reorganization in the place of arrival.[56]

Since the 1950s and 1960s kinship, and in particular kin-based networks, have achieved more significance in the study of the dynamics of migration. Kinship networks have been found to be of utmost importance prior to departure, during migration, and in the process of settlement and adjustment in the place of arrival.[57] Migrant long-distance ties to extended families served as conduits of information on employment opportunities, accommodations and the social and cultural environment of the place of settlement. These ties, in turn, were essential for the kin members who had remained behind as they themselves followed their relatives. The kin members who preceded them would help them find accommodations and jobs, a process that MacDonald and MacDonald termed "chain migration."[58]

A number of studies conducted by Stark and his colleagues concentrate on migrant-supported households in explaining the dynamics of migration.

---

dependent families were attracted to ideas such as microfinance projects that specifically involved migrant spouses. (Field observations in Tajikistan 2007.)
54 Khadria, 2004.
55 Faist, 2008:35.
56 Thomas and Znaniecki, 1927. Volumes IV and V.
57 Litwak, 1960; Tilly and Brown, 1968; Choldin, 1973.
58 MacDonald and MacDonald, 1964.

Migrant kinship and friendship ties are perceived to be catalysts of migration, since the costs and risks of movements involved within these networks are low and the expected benefits are high. Along these network concepts, it is argued that each movement produces social capital, as kin members help each other migrate.[59] We can see that the 1980s issues of the journal *International Migration Review* have a great number of articles written by scholars on migrations into the United States and the role of kinship networks in the dynamics of migration.[60] Tilly's chapter on the history of immigration to the United States and his arguments that "networks migrate" and "the effective units of migration were (and are) neither individuals nor households but sets of people linked by acquaintance, kinship and work experience" have been cited in the literature.[61] A monograph by Joshi, *Sociology of Migration and Kinship,* is worthwhile mentioning as well. Even though the author focuses on internal migrations in India, she takes a close look at kinship patterns using the network theories.[62] Palloni and associates apply the theoretical concept of social capital and network analysis to demonstrate that people are far more likely to migrate when they have a close family member, such as a sibling, as a migrant. Based on Mexico/US migration statistics, the complex model they create relates social capital to the migration behavior of family members, or, more precisely, the way the migration experience of one sibling influences the other(s).[63]

With the development of the transnational paradigm in international migration research, scholars have shown increasing interest in the role of kinship. Kinship networks are viewed as an inherent part of the transnational ethnic community. Long-term family ties between multiple nation-states account for the social construction of transnational social spaces. It has been argued that, whereas remittances are considered crucial for reciprocity between kin members, transnational family ties are often emotionally laden, as members wish to keep close contact, suffer from long-distance relationships, and long to be reunified.[64]

In this context, aspects such as a sense of place and belonging in transnational families become significant in transnational studies. A number of scholarly works consider an oral history approach to analyze the long-distance ties and dynamics of migration in extended families. Thus, in a special issue of the journal *Global Networks*, six articles were published that addressed topics such as memory, nostalgia, and belonging in transnational families.[65] The articles show how family becomes a site of belonging in

---

59 Massey *et al.*, 1987, Stark, 1991.
60 For instance, DeJong, Root, and Abad, 1986; Boyd, 1989; Of particular interest would be a review by John Salt on international migration patterns and research trends (1989).
61 Tilly, 1990:84.
62 Joshi, 1999.
63 Palloni *et al.*, 2001.
64 Kivisto and Faist, 2009.
65 *Global Networks*, Volume 4, Issue 3, 2004. See Chamberlain and Leydesdorff, 2004 for the review of this issue.

which transnational family members have to negotiate their gender roles and redefine their membership positions. One of the articles in this issue is of particular interest to the present study. Pribilsky focuses on transnational conjugal relations between Ecuadorian men working in New York and their spouses back home and highlights the influence of migration on traditional gender roles in rural Ecuador. Migrant spouses in Ecuador gain a certain independence by managing their husbands' earnings and taking care of their children back home while their husbands are away. The author finds that migrant husbands in New York perceive themselves as having been "feminized" while living abroad since they have to do their household chores on their own.[66] One of the findings of the present study is, however, that by contrast to the Latin American context, Central Asian married migrant women find independence while being away from their husbands and parents-in-law.

The research on kinship and migration covering the Caribbean, Latin American, and Southeast Asian (notably Filipino) transnational families forms a considerable portion of literature. These regions and their migration patterns have attracted the attention of scholars, especially since the earliest elaborations on the transnational approach of maintaining dense ties across nation-states became a crucial focal point.[67] Furthermore, family-related migration in itself has crystallized as a broad topic in migration research, as the so-called traditional immigration states such as the United States, Australia, Great Britain, Canada, France, and the Netherlands allowed family members of migrants back home to join them. This pattern along with marriage migration generated a body of research of its own, analyzing the phenomenon itself rather than the places of arrival.[68] Finally, scholars have elaborated on transnational trends and kinship structures from predominantly Muslim societies, along with a variety of topics such as trans-boundary labor mobility, remittances, family values, changing gender roles, social organization, and rivalry and negotiations within kinship. The sending countries that have most frequently been addressed include, among others: Turkey, Morocco, Tunisia, Algeria, Pakistan, Bangladesh, Afghanistan, and Indonesia, contributing substantially to the overall research on transnationalism and kinship.[69]

---

66   Pribilsky, 2004.
67   On Caribbean migrant families see Olwig, 1993; Basch *et al.* 1994; Chamberlain 1997; Glick-Schiller and Fouron, 2001; Bryceton and Vuorela, 2002. On Latin American families, see Orozco, 2002; Levitt, 2001; Sana and Massey 2005. On Filipino migrations, see Tacoli, 1999, Parreñas, 2001 and 2005a and b.
68   Ballard, 1982 and 1990; Zlotnik, 1995; Lahav, 1997; Yeoh, Graham and Boyle, 2002; Kofman, 2004.
69   Böcker, 1994; Parekh, 1996; Monsutti, 2004, Charsley, 2005; Dannecker, 2005; Charsley and Shaw, 2006; Silvey. 2006; Sargent and Larchanché-Kim, 2006; de Haas 2006 a and b, Lachenmann and Dannecker, 2008; Rahman, 2009.

1.3. The Present Research

At this point, it is important to position the present research within the broader scholarly context and pinpoint its goals. As can be seen from this broad overview, with research burgeoning in transnational studies (in general and in the migration-development nexus in particular), little has been done to address the transnational ties between Central Asia and Russia. While the transnational approach to migration started developing initially in countries with a long history of immigration (namely the United States and Canada), and then reached other states with immigrant communities, migration(s) into Russia have gradually taken different forms. At the dawn of the transnational paradigm that emerged in the USA in the 1990s, Russia had just started establishing itself as an independent state after the fall of the Soviet Union.[70] The Russian Federation, which encompassed the largest territory among the fifteen socialist republics of the USSR, was known primarily for large outflows of populations.[71] During the Soviet Union, emigrants were primarily political refugees and ethnic and religious minorities. Shortly after the fall of the USSR, Russia experienced a great volume of emigration, in particular of professionals as well as immigration of ethnic Russians from other former Soviet countries. While net immigration to Russia was 1.5 million during the period of 1981-1990, between 1992 and 2006 this number increased to 4.8 million.[72] Parallel to the patterns mentioned above, the influx of shuttle migrants (petty traders) increased, as they took advantage of the automobile routes, railroads, and flights as well as the infrastructure which had been made available by the centralized Soviet system. Over time, sporadic short trade journeys of individuals reconfigured themselves into different patterns of labor migration. For example, shuttle migrants started engaging themselves in small trade at Russian markets, or switched from shuttle trading to preliminary employment as porters, which then helped them find more stable jobs. Industries such as construction and consumer markets that demanded more cheap labor from other successor states of the USSR have gradually boomed. The number of migrants grew exponentially and the linkages between migrant homelands and Russia became more and more solid. Towards the end of the 1990s and the beginning of the new millennium, as the transnational approach to international migration was being extended to other continents, scholars continued to complement and refine its theoretical basis and gain more insight through a variety of empirical evidence. With the exception of a small number of studies, the geographic zone of the former post-Soviet

---

70   This sentence should by no means be understood to mean that Russia had not dealt with population mobility in earlier periods in history. Chapter 3 will give more attention to the history of controlled movement of population in pre-Soviet Russia and the USSR.
71   This is seen from the perspective of international migration. For internal migration during the Soviet Union, see the next chapter. By and large, not only Russia, but the entire Soviet Union, used to be more of an emigration than an immigration country.
72   Korobkov, 2008:69.

states has not yet attracted sufficient attention.[73] I shall refer to this gap below while setting the research goals.

The goals of this study are two-fold. First, taking into account the ongoing migration-development debate in research, it aims to examine empirically and understand the developmental consequences of migration in Central Asia at the kinship level. Through a systematic analysis of migrant kinship at both ends of migration, it focuses on transnational labor migrants in Russia and their dependent families in Central Asia. It will argue that the transfer of resources in migration go beyond monetary means. Transnational practices of migrants can challenge existing notions of nuclear family, gender relations, customs, and traditions and may cause conflicts of a social and symbolic nature between movers and stayers.

The secondary goal of this research is to address the process of transnationalization in a post-Soviet context through transnational approaches to international migration. It aims to determine qualitative specificities of post-Soviet transnationalism and its theoretical implications in transnational migration. In this respect, it intends to fill a lacuna in transnational studies.

1.4. Outline

In Chapter 2 I describe the theories and methods applied in this research to analyze labor migrant kinship in Russia and Central Asia. This chapter will argue that kinship stands in a complex relationship between other types of informal organizations and state institutions and plays a key role in the durability of transnational ties. After Chapter 2, this book will take up the USSR's migration history and will end with perspectives for its successor migrant-sending countries in the region of Central Asia. Chapter 3, which provides an historical background, will focus primarily on the period from the earliest years of the foundation of the USSR until its disintegration in 1991. For a clear understanding of the state controlled movement of population during the Soviet Union and the traces the USSR's migration policies left on its successor states, notably the Russian Federation and the Central Asian countries, it is essential to come to terms with the situation of population control in pre-Soviet Russia. Institutionalized restriction on movement during the Stalinist period as well as the period of the Cold War will be elaborated on. While pointing out opportunities for and restrictions on mobility that influenced migration patterns during the Soviet period and immediately after its demise, this chapter will search for the pioneer migrants from Soviet Central Asia who settled on the territory of the RSFSR (Soviet Russia).

73　For instance, there is an entire chapter in "Global Transformations" (Held et al, 1999) which is dedicated to globalization and migration that does not mention the geographic territory in question. The exceptions specifically concerning transnational studies are Darieva, 2005; Izmirli, 2008, Mandel, 2008.

The settlement of these pioneer migrants along with the Sovietization and modernization policies of the USSR pave the way to what I will conceptualize as post-Soviet transnationalization in Chapter 4. Chapter 4 sets a conceptual framework for this study. Suggesting an approach to understanding post-Soviet transnationalization, it will argue that the post-Soviet transnational space of migratory movements is qualitatively different from other migration patterns that have thus far attracted most of the scholarly attention, such as: Latin America – the United States, South Asia – the United Kingdom, Sub-Saharan Africa – France, Latin America – Spain, North Africa – the Mediterranean countries, Turkey – Germany, France, and the Netherlands. These migrations occurred either due to the colonial powers' reconfiguration of the immigration policies of their empires following decolonization in the 20th century, or through state-fostered hiring of manpower from countries with underprivileged economies and a surplus labor force. Complementary to these patterns, the example of the former Soviet Union represents a post-imperialist pattern of transnationalization. Post-Soviet transnationalization, as this chapter elaborates, is anchored in the residuals of the Sovietization policies. Compulsory military service, promotion of the Russian language at secondary schools, careers in the Communist party, and Russification of the so-called titular nations of Central Asia will be looked upon as typical aspects of this approach that will be integrated into the transnational paradigm.

Chapter 5 is devoted to the remitting practices of migrants. It highlights the importance of monetary transactions to the countries of origin for the support of family members. It concludes that even if transactions through banks are increasingly replacing transportation of cash by persons, in order for transactions to be completed and to reach the final recipients, additional help from close friends and relatives is necessary. This chapter also reveals that the common dichotomy of *formal* and *informal* remittances often found in research are not appropriate terms to operate with when one closely observes the social practices of the transactions in the countries of origin and destination.

Having outlined remitting practices, I describe in Chapter 6 the critical role of labor migration for lifecycle practices in the countries of origin. Weddings are being celebrated more and more lavishly from labor migrants' earnings that are remitted from Russia. Leaving remitting practices aside, this chapter takes a closer look at two types of migrants: a) those who first celebrate an extravagant wedding and leave for Russia in order to pay back their debts and b) migrants who leave for Russia with a clear plan of earning enough money to be able to afford a wedding. Interestingly, in both patterns, what starts as a one-time project turns into a long-term commute, turning a single employment trip to Russia into transnational migration. For most migrants it turns out that weddings alone are not the only events that need to be financed. With the obligation of supporting their families in the celebration of lifecycle rituals, transnational migrants become *victims* and at the same time *galvanizers* of traditions (or reinvention thereof) in post-Soviet Central Asia.

Chapter 7 looks more closely into family relations in the context of transnational migration. It takes the perspectives of migrants as they see themselves in their families and presents them as migrant sons and daughters. Through empirical examples it will illustrate that the eldest son of a family carries most of the responsibility for solving the family's economic problems. Youngest and only sons of families do not find themselves in a more favorable position, however, as they must provide for their parents economically in countries that do not offer them adequate salaries, and fulfill the expectation of their societies not to leave their families. Examples will be given of daughters and their struggles as female migrants. It is also in this chapter that the more recent trend of labor migrants obtaining Russian citizenship and the impact of change of citizenship on family relations will be discussed.

Chapter 8 dwells further on kin relations and probes into transnationalism from the angle of gender relations, looking on the one hand at conjugal relations of migrant couples in Russia, and on the other at migrant spouses in the homelands. It gives examples of married women for whom migration served as a path to liberating themselves from their authoritarian husbands. It also touches upon emerging conflicts between migrant wives and their parents-in-law. It will be shown how the latter feel responsible for protecting the chastity of their daughters-in-law in the absence of their sons.

The situation of oppressed migrant wives who are left behind is placed in stark contrast to male migrants who engage in extramarital relations, often taking a second wife during their stays in Russia, as Chapter 9 on transnational polygamous relations will show. The discovery of polygamous relations was serendipitous during the research process. This chapter reflects emerging gender trends and the weakness of post-Soviet states in dealing with both polygamous marriages and the state-society gap in the context of transnational migration.

Finally, Chapter 10 shifts the focus of the research back to the post-Soviet transnational discourse and draws the reader's attention to the country of destination. It illustrates how migrant families and patronages with a Soviet background form migrant organizations. Using vignettes based on biographies of migrant organization leaders, this chapter discusses the type of migrant organizations that evolve as post-Soviet versions of student networks and associations (German *Landsmannschaft,* Russian *zemliachestvo, obshevstennaia,* and *organizaciia*) of former Soviet republics at higher education institutions in Russia. Often including family members in their structure, these organizations aid adaptation to the new situation and start assisting migrants to find jobs and adjust to their status as legal foreign workers. Central to this chapter is also the role of fictive kinship and patronages that either exist informally and are resistant to being discovered by an outsider, or function under the aegis of a migrant association. This chapter concludes that transnational patronages often consisting of close kin members represent the intermediate stage of the development of transnational kinship into transnational communities. Concluding remarks with findings and perspectives for future research will be outlined in Chapter 11.

1.5. Technical Comments

The interviews for this research were carried out in the Tajik, Uzbek, and Russian languages. Feeling more comfortable in their native language, some migrants even spoke Kyrgyz, especially in the South of Kyrgyzstan. Considering the proximity of this language to Uzbek of which I am a native speaker, this posed no problem. Excerpts of the interviews in the book will be given in English while some terms and sentences will be transliterated in the original language. The Latin transliteration of words, short sentences from interviews, and technical terms in Kyrgyz, Russian, Tajik, and Uzbek languages have been carried out according to the transliteration table provided by the Central Eurasian Studies Society hosted by Miami University in Ohio, USA.[74] Thus, Russian letters 'ж' and 'ц' are transliterated as 'zh' and 'ts' as in *grazhdanstvo* (citizenship) and *tsentr* (center); the Russian letter x is transliterated as 'x' instead of 'kh.' In the plural forms of the words used in the languages mentioned above I apply, for reasons of simplicity, the English plural ending 's', e.g. *orgnabor*s (Soviet labor recruitment service) and not *orgnabory* as the correct plural form of the Russian term would require, or *kelin*s (daughters-in-law) instead of *kelinlar*. Further, I have tried to maintain the spelling of the geographic names of provinces and towns in Central Asia as they are spelled or transliterated in the official language of the states. Abbreviations such as (RUS) or (KYR) are added to the name of the geographic places to indicate the name of the country and to avoid confusion.

To guarantee the anonymity and security of my informants, all of their names were changed as were names of some of the geographic places I visited. On several occasions, at the beginning of the interview I asked some of my female informants who were about the same age as me or younger to give me a name under which they wished to be anonymized. It seemed that they had fun selecting a name they had either saved for their daughters or wished their parents had given them at birth. This method helped me maintain the regional distinction of personal names. At the same time, the name-giving part of the interview functioned well as an ice-breaker. Some villages where I conducted fieldwork are so small that it would be easy to track down the real identity of the informants. For the sake of the safety of migrant organization leaders, their personal names had to be changed as well, especially since some of them have political ambitions in their countries of origin. This is a topic that will not be discussed in this book since it merits a study of its own.

---

74   http://www.cesr-cess.org/CESR_trans_cyr.html

2. Theories and Methods

This chapter explains the theories and methods which will guide this empirical research. The theoretical section of this chapter combines the transnational approach to international migration research with political transformation studies in Central Asia. This, in turn, will explain the importance of kinship as a unit of analysis in order to better understand the role of kin members in making possible migrants' journeys across post-Soviet nation-states. In addition, this chapter will comprise a separate section on the methodological basis of the present research.

2.1. Theoretical Arguments

My vantage point in this section is that transnational migration should be seen as part of the post-Soviet transformation. I lay out my theoretical arguments in the following order: in the first step, I will roughly review how the concept of kinship is treated in the research on political and economic transformation. In doing so, I will draw specifically on the studies which have so far addressed informal power structures in post-Soviet Central Asia and Russia. In the second step, bearing in mind the significance of kinship in the dynamics of mobility, I will provide further contextual background and disentangle three components: the concepts of (1) kinship, (2) non-kin informal institutions, and (3) formal organizations. I will propose post-Soviet transnational social spaces as a complementary analytical tool, which consists of complex triadic relationships among these three components and functions between the sending and receiving countries.

I will argue in this section that kinship alone does not contribute to the density of transnational ties. However, I will contend that the conceptual angle of kinship can serve as a significant analytical conduit to understanding the process of transnationalization. In the last step, I will project onto the post-Soviet transformation studies, the analytical tool of transnational social spaces, which has been elaborated in the transnational approach to migration. I shall briefly summarize how my arguments fit into a broader picture within social theories in general and into the transnational paradigm of migration research in particular.

2.1.1. Kinship as a Unit of Analysis: Institutional Approaches to Kinship in Transformation Studies

Informal practices, such as the use of kinship and friendship ties as well as corruption and clientelism, have existed in all the former Soviet republics. They were important in the distribution of political power and resources in the years after the demise of the USSR. Personal networks, tribalism, clientelism, clan structures, mafia, and *blat* networks have, according to transformation scholars, shaped the politics and societies of the post-Communist world.[75] When it comes to the analytical unit of kinship in social studies, many scholars working on the transition processes, especially in successor states of the USSR, operate with broad concepts such as *informal organizations* and *informal institutions* to explain the impediments to processes such as democratic consolidation, regime change, regime stability, and state- and nation- building. Among informal institutions, clan structures have attracted considerable attention. Referring to the Soviet period, Kosals, for instance, assesses hidden clan-based practices as the most crucial characteristic in the Soviet society. He contends that they were present in every state institution and eventually influenced the transformation processes. Explaining the system of clan capitalism in the current Russian economy, he emphasizes the strong links which informal actors use in social, economic, and political spheres. "Secretive and closed social groups" as they currently are in Russia, according to Kosals, may [...] consist of family members.[76] Ledeneva carried out an interesting study on *blat* networks in Russia. These networks are used to obtain goods and services in Russia and successor states of the Soviet Union. Ledeneva explains that one can distinguish between "svoi liudi" (one's own people), a narrow circle of actors who share the same social stratum, and "nujnye liudi" (useful people), those who may represent different social strata and can be part of the same kinship network or connected to each other through personal contacts.[77] Further, analysts such as Gibson have been critical about the development of civil society in Russia. He and his colleagues conducted a survey on trust and its relation to the establishment of civil society. The respondents of their survey gave negative answers with respect to trust of people with whom they are not well acquainted.[78]

As far as the region of Central Asia is concerned, political scientists studying regionalism, clientelism, and factionalism sometimes have difficulty identifying kin ties of political actors to be able to explain the distribution of power and resources.[79] The sources on transformation studies mention the influence of kinship in distribution of power and resources, but they do not elaborate on them further.[80] This is surprising, since most scholarship on the post-Communist states has begun paying more attention to the role of informal organizations in analyzing their ramifications in the transformation processes.

---

75   Bönker *et al.* 2002; Jones-Luong, 2004, Collins, 2006; Ledeneva, 2006; Kosals, 2006.
76   Kosals, 2006:72-73.
77   Ledeneva, 1998, cited in Ledeneva, 2008. Comparing Russian informal practices to *guanxi* in China, Ledeneva observes that Chinese practices are more rooted in the kinship networks than in Russia.
78   Gibson, 2000.
79   This point has also been raised by Schatz, 2005:237.
80   With the exception of anthropological analyses by Kandiyoti.

Some attempts, however, have been made to address the importance of kinship specifically during the Soviet period. In his comparative study on Central Asia and the Middle East, Lindholm accentuates the political and social implications of kinship structures.[81] Another scholar, Walder, was of the opinion that through Sovietization such informal practices had been aggravated, whereas the Communist Party was firmly determined to fight them.[82]

Perhaps one of the most relevant and recent contributions specifically in the area of this study is Collins' systematic research on clan politics in Central Asia. Analyzing regime transition and democratization in Central Asia, she places clans at the core of her research. She concludes that the dynamic interaction between clans can explain the entire political development starting from the years preceding the fall of the Soviet Union until the most recent political struggles, including regime stability, regime type, distribution of power among political actors, and informal governing negotiations.[83] Of particular interest for the theoretical arguments of the current study on transnational migration is the usage of the conceptual unit of *clan*. Defining the term *clan*, Collins states that it is

> ...an informal organization comprising a network of individuals linked by kin-based bonds. Affective ties of kinship are its essence, constituting the identity and bonds of its organization. These bonds are both vertical and horizontal, linking elites and non-elites and they reflect both actual blood ties and fictive kinship that is constructed or metaphorical kinship based on close friendships or marriage bonds that redefine the boundaries of the genealogical unit.[84]...Clan identities are rooted in kinship, and kinship bonds have significant staying power because they carry meaning and cultural content for the members of the kin organization.[85]

As illustrated by this quotation, Collins underlines the importance of kinship, yet she applies the term *clan* to kin-based informal networks. Collins concludes that these networks shape the politics of the Central Asian successor states even though she admits that *clan* is a complex concept to work with.

Observations of kinship networks by Edward Schatz are particularly interesting for the present research and will be used as a point of departure. In his study of kinship networks and statehood in Kazakhstan, Schatz perceives clans as kinship-based social units. He makes bolder arguments than Collins and illustrates the prevalence of blood and fictive kinship in the politics of Central Asia and Northern Caucasus.[86] Schatz refrains from asserting that state power and economic resources can be entirely explained in terms of

---

81   Lindholm, 1986, *cf.* Collins, 2006:39.
82   Walder, 1986 as cited by Collins, 2006:39.
83   Collins, 2006:7.
84   Collins, 2004:231.
85   Collins, 2006:44.
86   Schatz, 2005.

clan structures. Rather, he advances a view that clans represent "one of several political roles."[87] He contends that the Soviet policy of eradicating clan ties contributed to the expansion of such informal practices as political actors continued them in a covert manner.[88] As a significant contribution to the formation of clan and ethnic identity, Schatz elaborates on genealogical information since members of kinship networks view themselves as having a blood relationship to each other. The view on genealogical information is advanced further by Gullette, who adopts the term "genealogical imagination" in his article on factionalism in the context of Kyrgyzstan.[89] Illustrating relatedness through patrilineal ancestry, "genealogical imagination" is explained by Gullette as being constructed through personal and collective memory, which contributes not only to the Kyrgyz people's perception of relatedness, but also to the Kyrgyz government's nation-building projects.[90]

Similar to Schatz, who argues that kin-based structures cannot be made entirely responsible for the way power and economic resources are distributed in the political context of Central Asia, I argue in this research that kinship structures, which are known to be pivotal for maintaining dense ties across nation-states, should be seen in the context of a complex combination of other institutions. For the study of transnational migration between Central Asia and Russia, it is crucial to see how kinship ties provide the framework for a single individual voyage to develop into large-scale labor mobility and transnationalization. We shall see in the next section that kinship is a significant component of transnational social spaces in addition to other social units and practices with which they stand in interdependent relations.

2.1.2. Distinction of Kinship from other Formal/Informal Institutions and Organizations

Studying kinship structures of transnational migrants is facilitated by the mere fact that they are less difficult than other structures to identify. For the conceptual framework of this study, however, it is first necessary to distinguish between (non-kinship) informal institutions and formal organizations. Critical eyes, especially proponents of transformation studies, may immediately object and argue that kinship is generally categorized under informal institutions along with personal networks, clans, mafia networks, or *blat* in the former Soviet countries.[91] The main argument here is that kinship should be referred to as representing a category of its own and be disentangled from other informal institutions. When perceived in terms of separate dimensions, it easier to approach kinship analytically and to highlight its interactions with other informal institutions and formal organizations. My intention is to show

---

87 Schatz, 2005:234.
88 Schatz, 2004 as cited by Gullette, 2007:378.
89 Gullette, 2007.
90 Gullette, 2007:384.
91 Helmke and Levitsky, 2003:18.

the triadic relationship among (1) kinship, (2) (non-kinship) informal institutions, and (3) formal organizations. This triadic relationship is essential for the durability of transnational ties. Having stated this, I would first like to give a brief explanation of the concepts of informal institutions and formal organizations, and hope to tackle the terminological problems which might lead to confusion.

For this purpose, I refer once again to the scholarship on transformation. Helmke and Levitsky (2003) and Ledeneva (2006) operate with the term "informal institutions." Analyzing the interactions between formal and informal institutions in Latin American countries and in Russia, respectively, these scholars rely on an institutional framework developed by institutional economist North, who perceived institutions as "rules of the game of a society (that) consist of formal and informal constraints constructed to order interpersonal relationships."[92] The two studies emphasize that players must be separated from the rules of the game, meaning that informal institutions (rules) should not be confused with informal organizations (players or actors). [93] Further, distinguishing the importance of the focus on informal institutional analysis in comparative politics, Helmke and Levitsky point out

> A key challenge for informal institutional analysis thus lies in avoiding accounts that either take informal institutions as historical givens or explain them in functionalist terms. To do this, we must move beyond the *what* and the w*hy* of informal institutions to identify the *who* and the *how*. An important step in explaining the emergence of any informal institution is to identify the relevant actors, coalitions and interests behind it. *Like formal institutions, informal institutions are generally created in a context in which power and resources are unevenly distributed,* and like their formal counterparts, they tend to produce winners and losers.[94] (The emphasis in the last sentence is mine.)

The decisive point in this argument is that situating the analysis in the cultural and social context in which it takes place is significant. This point has guided my view on separating kinship and its social practices from other forms of informal practices.[95] Further, it is important to distinguish organiza-

---

92 North, 1990:31, Denzau and North, 1994:4.
93 Helmke and Levitsky, 2003:10.
94 *Ibid.*, p.18
95 This significance of contextualization can be found in the research on migration. In his analysis of the meso link between macro and micro levels of migration, Faist comments that the level and the type of social reorganization depend on the context. He draws on the social reorganization processes based on the study by Thomas and Znaniecki on Polish peasants' migrations between Russian (Congress) Poland and the USA at the turn of the 19th and the beginning of the 20th century, and emphasizes that in times of traditional social organizations, we are confronted with disorganization of larger structures such as nation-states and their economies. The series of occurrences at the macro level take place concomitantly at the lower levels such as the household or kinship level. Faist goes further in his arguments and states, "The lesson is that no analysis can sufficiently describe and explain migration process without taking into account the ties within the social, economic, cultural and political units (in which) potential migrants and their significant others are enmeshed." (Faist, 2000a:99-100)

tions from institutions, which would be consistent with the usage by transformation scholars. They argue that "just as formal organizations (political parties, trade unions) may be distinguished from formal institutions, informal organizations such as clans, mafias and kinship networks should be distinguished from informal institutions." [96] In line with Helmke and Levitsky, I use the term "informal institutions" to mean *socially shared unwritten rules that are created, communicated, and enforced outside of officially sanctioned channels*.[97] Here, it should be stated that the term *formal organizations* in the present research will be used to refer to *state and non-state actors such as non-profit and non-government organizations, advocacy groups, and diasporas*. The table below will be used to better illustrate my arguments.

Figure 1: Triadic Relations for Post-Soviet Transnational Spaces

Migrant kinship	**Non-kinship informal institutions**	**Formal organizations** (state organizations, international organizations and NGOs, national NGOs registered with the Ministry of Justice)
Blood and fictive kinship, patronage ties	Friendship networks, neighborhoods ties, *blat*, mafia, corruption, protection racketeering, semi-legal arrangements	Ministries of Internal Affairs, passport offices, consulates, government offices for migration, law enforcement agencies, Federal Migration Service (Russia), IOM, OSCE, advocacy groups, diasporas, labor agencies

It should be added that formality is strongly linked to the judicial framework of the states involved in migration, within which organizations are required to function and by which individuals must abide. Formal organizations are basically all state and non-state organizations that are registered in the countries involved in migration. Given the strict control of the states over non-governmental and international organizations, formality in terms of legality can be seen as a viable category.

I argue that the three columns in Figure 1 with their seemingly disparate aspects represent the fulcrum for the durability of transnational migration in that they are in constant dynamic and mutual interplay with each other. They function in interdependence on each other, in both the countries of origin and

---

96   Helmke and Levitsky, 2003:10.
97   *Ibid.*

destination. The aim of the present research is to take the kinship angle and carry out a systematic analysis on the forms of interaction that are changing membership roles in kinship networks, which are taking place in the context of migration in the post-Soviet period. It will be revealed in later stages of the research that in both the countries of origin and destination, migrants and their family members deal on a daily basis with opportunities and constraints that range from formal to informal, across institutions and organizations.

The three columns may be illustrated by the example of a 17-year-old young man from Central Asia. In a phone call from his elder sister in Russia, he learns that a job opening at a construction site has been reserved for him. However, he cannot leave immediately since a representative from the recruitment department of the military service in his town has visited him twice, demanding that he come to enlist in the army. He knows from other friends that he can ask his second cousin, who is a physician, to arrange a certificate about his poor health and be medically disqualified for military service. Alternatively, he could consider waiting until he is recruited into the army, where he would try to bribe his commander who, in turn, would pretend that he is among the enlisted soldiers and let the young man make his living in Russia. In the latter case, the young potential migrant would risk losing the job reserved for him in Russia.[98] Thus, the first column in Figure 1 stands for the migrant and his kin who help him not only to find a job in the country of destination, but also to overcome constraints imposed by, in this example, his sending state. Without overcoming these constraints, it is almost impossible to migrate. The second column stands for the entire institution in which informal negotiations, which are essential for transnational ties, are made. The third column in this particular example is the sending state with its formal organization that is responsible for the obstacle of mandatory military service.

Having made these arguments, we should note that the three components are often intertwined in a complex relationship in the country of origin, which is transferred to the country of destination in a similar pattern, even though they are sketched in three columns in the table above. Hence, if we were to broadly examine the informal institutions involved in different aspects of migration, the dimension of kinship would not receive the attention it merits not only in migration research, but also in the scholarship devoted to transformation studies in the post-Soviet states.

2.1.3. Structuration and Post-Soviet Transnationalization

Having explained my arguments on the significance of kinship as a unit of analysis in transnational migration and having established a linkage to transformation studies, in this section I shall briefly position this research in the

---

98   Interview with Sobir.

broader picture within social theories. I will then link the arguments described above to the general transnational discourse.

In its theoretical underpinnings, this study has been partially influenced by Giddens' structuration theory. Explaining the concept of duality of structure, Giddens argues that "the properties of social systems are both medium and outcome of the practices they recursively organize."[99] One of the advantages of the structuration theory is that it helps to overcome the structure-agency dichotomies, especially since this work treats migration processes that have emerged in post-Soviet social systems and focuses on transnational kinship as agents.

The feasibility of the structuration theory had already been discussed in the scholarship on migration before it attracted the attention of the proponents of transnationalism. Acknowledging the theoretical impasse created by functionalist and structuralist schools in the study of cross-border movements, Goss and Lindquist try, in the case of Filipino migrants, to demonstrate that international migration can be conceptualized in terms of knowledgeable individuals' strategic action.[100] Tackling agency-structure that is problematic in migration research, the authors advance the concept of "migration institution" that captures the rules and resources responsible for the constraints and opportunities of individuals in an adequate framework. Goss and Lindquist suggest that migrant networks be conceptualized as migrant institutions, since they bring together the potential migrants and their employers abroad by spanning across time and space through social relations. They remind us that the functionalists perceive the increasing diversity and dimension of international migration as simply borne by supply and demand factors in international labor migration. Contrary to this trend, the structuralists are mentioned to relate international migration to the global capitalist economy and differences in the distribution of capital among countries which, in turn, is linked to demand and supply of labor. Complementing these two views, Goss and Lindquist adhere to the structuration theory. They draw our attention to the increase of international migration as resulting from the extension of social systems across time and space, which is *time-space distanciation* of social activity.[101]

Theorists of transnationalism have been influenced by, among others, Giddens, and in particular by his concept of "time-space distanciation." For example, Pries emphasizes that the relationship between geographic space and social space is being redefined. Two or three centuries ago the *social space* that constituted everyday life and social institutions that were shaping human life were interwoven with the *geographic space*. Each social space, accordingly, "occupied" one and only one geographically specific space (or

---

99   Giddens, 1984:26.
100 Goss and Lindquist, 1995.
101 Goss and Lindquist, 1995: 335, Kaspersen, 2000:53, Giddens, 1984:181.

locale).¹⁰² This congruence of geographic and social space, Pries contends, has changed over time. In this respect, Pries notes that the social space in the course of such developments can loosen or "uncouple" from its geographic space and develop elsewhere.¹⁰³ The concept of space in the theories of transnational migration has been used by Faist even more elaborately as he argues that it

> [...] does not only refer to physical features, but also to larger opportunity structures, the social life and the subjective images, values, and meanings that the specific and limited place represents to migrants. Space is thus different from place in that it encompasses or spans various territorial locations. It includes two or more places. Space has a social meaning that extends beyond simple territoriality; only with concrete social or symbolic ties does it gain meaning for potential migrants.¹⁰⁴

According to Thomas Faist, *transnational social spaces* consist of pentagonic relationships between transnational groups, the government and civil society of the receiving country, those of the emigration country, organizations in the country of immigration, and the rulers of the country of emigration.¹⁰⁵ It is at this point that I project the arguments I made in the last section to the analytical tool of *social spaces* applied in the transnational approach to international migration. I perceive post-Soviet transnational space as an analytical tool to examine everyday practices of transnational kinship. Figure 1 in the last section shows that if we reflect the triadic relations in the transnational post-Soviet social spaces, we can see that the same pentagonic relationship applied in Faist's elaboration exists in the post-Soviet transnational spaces. The difference is that the civil society which has its own position in Faist's pentagonic pattern is replaced in the post-Soviet context by informal institutions.¹⁰⁶ I will elaborate more on post-Soviet transnationalism in Chapter 4 after having described the historical trajectory of migrations during the Soviet Union in Chapter 3.

2.2. Methodology

This research has chosen 'multi-sited ethnography' as elaborated by George Marcus.¹⁰⁷ As an ethnographic project, it has involved thorough attention to everyday practices and intimate knowledge of the individuals studied. I was inspired by David Fitzgerald's methodological strategies for ethnographic

---

102 Pries, 1997:19.
103 Pries, 1997:19-20.
104 Faist, 2000a, 45-46, Kivisto and Faist, 2009:193.
105 Faist 2000a:200.
106 *Ibid.*
107 For multi-sited ethnography, see Marcus, George (1998). *Ethnography Through Thick and Thin*. Princeton: Princeton University Press.

research on transnational migration. The techniques of multi-sited fieldwork include tracing the objects of study within broader complex cultural contexts, be they people or things.[108] In migration studies it is common to follow the interviewees during their journeys between the places of origin and destination. As mentioned elsewhere, this was possible in my research only to a marginal extent. I have explained safety and gender-related limitations in the introduction and therefore do not claim that I was able to geographically connect the migrants to their families in the places of origin. However, during fieldwork in Russia, I was able to follow the migrants to their places of work and participate in their daily undertakings. I applied a similar practice in the countries of origin, which helped me to get deeper insight into the daily life and cultural settings of migrants and their families.

By including sites of both sending and receiving countries, I believe I have been able to remove the so-called "national blinders" and have been cautious about "methodological nationalism." As Wimmer and Glick-Schiller hold in their explanation of this term, excessively limiting the research to the frontiers of the nation-states and taking these as natural givens would lead us to neglect the inherent societies which both migrants and non-migrants of the research represent.[109] As an additional strategy, Fitzgerald rightly argues that researchers should historicize their field. I have done so first by providing a chapter on the historical background of migration patterns in the years during the Soviet period and immediately after the dissolution of the USSR.[110] Second, I have concentrated on the Soviet background of the subjects who were involved in this research, which helped me understand post-Soviet transnationalization and develop a framework which I have illustrated in this chapter.

2.2.1. Data Collection and Data Analysis

The data collected for this study consists primarily of recorded interviews and mnemonic transcription of unrecorded interviews, but also field notes taken during the fieldwork, observation protocols, occasional encounters and conversations, and spontaneous visits which migrants or their family members back home paid to their relatives.[111] I carried out interviews with migrants irrespective of their legal status, age, gender, or length of stay in Russia. The reason for selecting this rather wide cohort of subjects was that the research domain of migration in the post-Soviet context has not yet been sufficiently explored. Moreover, this research strategy allowed me to take an

---

108 Marcus, 1995:106.
109 *Ibid.*
110 For this chapter it was also necessary to consult archival records of the Soviet press of the 1970s and 1980s. This small portion of study revealed that labor migration from the Central Asian region to Russia is not an entirely new phenomenon. (cf. Chapter 2.)
111 Werner, 1999.

unbiased stance and discover multiple aspects of post-Soviet transnational migration while focusing on the kinship level.

I was not able to record all the interviews. About one third of the people with whom I spoke were not willing to speak into a recorder because they were anxious that the authorities would somehow track them down. Migrants feared that they would lose their jobs if their employers or brokers found out that they had spoken to me. In such cases I had to take notes during the interview and reconstruct the content of the interview from memory.[112] During the transcription process of the recorded interviews, instead of transcribing first in the original language, I directly translated the conversations into English. Due to the linguistic and ethnic constellation of the population in the former USSR, the subjects interviewed for this study often spoke a mixture of at least two languages: Kyrgyz and Russian; Tajik, Uzbek, and Russian; Uzbek and Kyrgyz; etc., not to mention a host of dialects. I had no difficulty understanding my interviewees, however it would have been difficult to transcribe the mixture of languages and loanwords they used to express their opinions. Occasionally, an interview with a return migrant in rural Central Asia in the presence of his or her family contained narrations in Russian. In spite of their limited vocabulary, some returning migrants wanted to demonstrate their command of Russian in the presence of their family and friends, even though it would have been easier for them to converse in their native language. The result was often the expression of opinions in broken Russian with added concepts in Tajik, Uzbek, and Kyrgyz which would not have been easy to transcribe. Having noted this, if I had taken into account the linguistic aspect of the interviews, I would have had to address an entirely different dimension in this research.[113] This would have made it more difficult to streamline the contours of the overall research.

Participant observation was of no less value for this research than the interviews.[114] Hammersley and Atkinson emphasize the impossibility of exploring the world without being part of it. In this respect their view is that "participant observation is not a technique but a mode of being-in-the-world, characteristic of researchers."[115] During the fieldwork I was confronted with situations in which participation was the only way to gain access to migrants. For instance, seasonal female migrants at a large food storage compound in St. Petersburg worked hard all day long and were given only a 20 minute

---

112 There were also situations in which I could not even take notes and had to rely completely on my memory. Once in Moscow, during the interview with the leader of a migrant organization, my interlocutor started telling about the history of his organization's establishment. He became impatient when I started taking notes and made the following remark: "Now put down your pen. I am telling about the history of this place. So, first listen to me, you will write things down later." (Field notes, Moscow, September 2005).
113 My objective was not to carry out research in the field of linguistic anthropology, although language as a cultural resource of post-Soviet migrant practices would have deserved such attention. (For more on linguistic anthropology, see e.g. Duranti, 1997)
114 For an overview of participant observation, cf. Atkinson and Hammersley, 1994:248-261. See also Schnell *et al.*, 2005, Chapter 7 and Flick, 2006.
115 Atkinson and Hammersley, 1994:249.

lunch break during the day. The only way to interact with them was to get permission from their employers to help them, so our conversations had to take place while sorting out rotten tomatoes from fresh ones. In Central Asia, besides simple observation, it was important to participate in various household chores such as weeding and driving cattle. Participant observation was as important at the micro-level as it was at the meso-level. Analysis of migrant organizations in Russia often required precisely this method, which enabled me to better gauge their activities as I spent several hours observing them.

The accumulated data was analyzed according to the grounded theory method proposed first by Glaser and Strauss and developed further by others.[116] In grounded theory, a theory is induced from the data through the process of constant and systematic comparison. It requires that the researcher code the material (search for categories) in a multi-step procedure in order to develop theories from them at a later stage. Conforming to the coding procedures, in the first step I *coded* the data *openly* which entailed segmentation of the data.[117] For instance, since the interviews were semi-structured, most migrants or their families first told me their age, named family members, and gave information about their close kin members working in Russia. The individuals then explained the circumstances in which they left their country to earn money in Russia. The data was accordingly segmented into general parts, for instance *introduction*, *migration decision-making*, and the *roles* that migrants play as family members. Some parts of the interviews were coded sentence-by-sentence and some paragraph-by-paragraph. This step resulted in a group of categories or codes that were of utmost relevance for the elaboration of the theory. In a second step, these striking categories were selected for *axial coding*. This step tried to connect the categories that emerged from the data and compare them to one another. The categories and subcategories of one group were compared to and connected with the next groups of categories. Most importantly, it is in this step that a phenomenon from categories was elaborated and its causes and consequences were related to one another. The third step, known as *selective coding*, required a higher level abstraction of the axial coding. Strauss and Corbin emphasize that at this level the *story line* must be formulated. This means that "a concept attached to the central phenomenon of the story" should be elaborated and stand in connection to other categories.[118] Selective coding processes should result in *one* core category and *one* core phenomenon. Therefore, as a core category *transnational migrants with kinship ties in Central Asia* was determined. The core phenomenon which resulted from the coding process was *post-Soviet transna-*

---

116 Glaser and Strauss, 2009 (1st edition was published in 1967), Chapter 1. This method was later developed by Glaser (1978), and Strauss and Corbin (1998). See also Flick, 2006 and Dey, 1999: Chapter 1.
117 Glaser and Strauss, 2009.
118 Dey, 1999:302.

tionalism. These have crystallized into a framework for understanding post-Soviet transnationalism which will be explained in Chapter 4.

2.2.2. Fieldwork

For this research I conducted six months of fieldwork in the countries of origin of migrants from Kyrgyzstan, Tajikistan and Uzbekistan as well as in Russia, the country of destination. I spent the month of September in 2005 in Moscow. From late July 2006 until October 2006 I traveled to St. Petersburg (Russia), Bukhara (Uzbekistan), and the Leninabad Province (northern Tajikistan). April and May of 2007 I spent in Tajikistan, carrying out interviews in the Province of Khatlon. I then traveled to the city of Astrakhan (Russia) in July 2007. I completed my fieldwork after having spent a month in Kyrgyzstan in February/March 2008.[119] Uzbekistan is the country of origin in which I spent the least time for this research. Researchers specializing in social studies in Central Asia have experienced increased difficulty in carrying out qualitative analysis in the region. This is due, on the one hand, to administrative barriers, which are not always possible to overcome. On the other hand, it is also due to the caution (which is determined by the level of authoritarianism in the three states of origin) with which the intelligence institutions work and the wariness with which people are inclined to greet curious researchers and answer questions no one has ever asked them before. Nevertheless, I hope that the number of Uzbek citizens with whom I have been able to speak in Russia will contribute to the credibility of the part of the analysis on Uzbekistan. In addition, it is worth noting that it seems to me that these Uzbek migrants would have never spoken to me with such openness in their homeland as they did while away from it.

Interviews with 56 people constitute the bulk of my data. Moreover, I talked with many more individuals during my journeys whose narrations I jotted down to include in my field notes. Among the individuals I spoke with were labor migrants, their family members, neighbors, and relatives as well as representatives of NGOs, state institutions, international organizations running specifically migration-related projects, and international development organizations. I met some of my informants via the snowball system. Sometimes I was introduced to relatives or friends of local employees of international organizations and NGOs whose families depended on labor migrant remittances. Oftentimes I engaged in conversations with people on the street or at the market. I took public buses to travel to remote places and simply talked to people. I spoke with both women and men. Indeed, in retrospect, I am positively surprised by the number of interviews I conducted with male migrants and often by the openness with which they talked to me.

---

119 Since I conducted my research in the period 2005-2009, I do not address the inter-ethnic violence which broke out in Kyrgyzstan in June 2010, nor do I discuss the implications of inter-ethnic tensions for migration patterns within and from Kyrgyzstan.

I tried to avoid staying in hotels and renting apartments during the fieldwork and instead preferred being accommodated by host families, partly because hotels and apartments were unaffordable in Russia, but also because living with host families was a valuable opportunity to participate in the everyday lives of migrants and their families. In Central Asia, notably in the provinces, living alone would have raised doubts among my informants about the decency of my behavior.

The fieldwork for this study was not devoid of hurdles. As a holder of a German passport, I was required to apply for a visa for every country I visited and obtain registration at the place of my residence. Had I still held my Uzbek citizenship, I would not have needed a visa for Uzbekistan, Russia, and Kyrgyzstan, but I would most probably have been viewed negatively by the Russian authorities, the subjects of my research. In spite of the fact that I was born and raised in Uzbekistan and speak the languages of my informants fluently (except Kyrgyz), my informants sometimes treated me with a certain distrust at the beginning of our encounters.[120] This distrust then disappeared over time, and they would feel that they could trust me even more than their own neighbors, as I would soon leave and take all the information I had received from them with me.[121]

The fact that I was travelling alone as a married woman in Central Asia and Russia, sometimes did not make a good impression on my informants. I had been warned that I would be entering a dangerous terrain, especially in Russia. I used caution and tried not to go too far into the spaces where I would be least welcome. In remote villages I was dressed in traditional clothes like other women in order blend in and not be too noticeable, even though my appearance and my accent often betrayed me.[122]

---

120 I was aware of the methodological issues related to conducting qualitative research in the region of which I am considered native. At the same time, some problems that other migration scholars faced did not quite apply in my research. For instance, there are methodological discussions concerning researchers' *positionality*, and doing ethnography as cultural "insiders." Scholars with a migration background involved in qualitative social research in migrant communities of similar background in France and Great Britain have admitted that representatives of different generations within migrant communities treated them with different social proximity (Ganga and Scott, 2006). Although I was a researcher with a migration background, my migration background differs greatly from that of my informants, and moreover, I do not have the same country of destination as my informants. I am a different cultural "insider" and therefore my advantages and disadvantages vary from those of other scholars.

121 In Astrakhan, it once took me four calls to try to set up an appointment with a female migrant from Nukus, Uzbekistan. After having delayed our interview repeatedly she finally said, "My whole life is so ruined, so please let us not meet, our conversation will make me feel worse."

122 My traditional clothes were not always welcomed by the younger generation, however. In southern Tajikistan, my 14-year-old host sister Gulshoda and her friend said, "Please take off that awful Tajik dress and put on your pants when we go walk to the next neighbor's house. You have those modern skirts and pants yet you walk around in these clothes. They really don't look great on you." As far as my accent is concerned, in southern Kyrgyzstan, ethnic Uzbeks often did not believe that I was from Uzbekistan, although there were no language barriers between us at all. My Bukharan accent was unfamiliar to most ethnic Uzbeks in Osh and Jalalabad. Comments such as "O'zbeklarga o'xshamaysiz lekin,

At this point I should mention some of the weaknesses of this research. I am aware that some scholars are critical of multi-sited ethnography where researchers change sites too often, spreading the data too thin, instead of focusing on a single site and carrying out an in-depth analysis.[123] While it may be true that I have jumped from site to site, I believe I have also been able to accumulate a variety of data and have had the opportunity to look at transnationalism from different angles. To this weakness I would like to add that for reasons of time and space, I have not been able to conduct a proper content analysis of publications and reports released by international donor organizations. This would have enabled me to look at labor migration through the lens of development actors in the region. I had originally planned to meet labor migrants in Russia and either follow them to their home countries or track their families in Central Asia.[124] I succeeded in doing this with one family in Uzbekistan and one in Tajikistan. The data from these observations have been included in this book. For health and personal safety reasons, I had to distance myself from this part of my research design and cope with the idea that labor migrants whom I interviewed in Russia and migrants families whom I interviewed in Central Asia were not related to each other. As much as I admired David Fitzgerald's article in which he argued precisely for conducting fieldwork in migration sites that are connected to each other, I had planned my fieldwork accordingly without realizing one small cultural detail: it became obvious after my first encounter with a male migrant (which my informants in Russia often were) that it would have sounded extremely odd for a female researcher with Central Asian background to ask a male married informant from the same region for his address in order to introduce herself to his wife as 'having met with your husband in Russia,' let alone follow the migrant during his visit. As I mentioned, I managed to follow two informants, but I also had to be cautious about creating awkward situations.

---

mehmon." (Uzb. "But you don't look like Uzbeks, guest.") or "Haqiqatdan ham o'zbekistonlikmisiz?" (Uzb. "Are you really from Uzbekistan?") were often made. To my question "Well, have you ever travelled to Uzbekistan?" some of my interlocutors would either say, "Why sure, I have been to Tashkent, for example!" or they would shake their heads and click their tongues to mean, "No, never."

123   Gowan and Riain, 2000:xii; Burawoy, 2000:4; Fitzgerald, 2006.
124   I had initially planned to follow Fitzgerald and explore the sites that are connected to each other (2006).

Part One

From a History of Migrations and Mobility Control in the Soviet Union towards a Conceptual Framework for Post-Soviet Transnationalism

3. Historical Overview of Migrations during the Soviet Period and in the Early Years after the USSR's Dissolution[125]

This chapter provides a general outline of the history of migration in the Soviet Union. Transnational migration between Central Asia and Russia is rooted in policies and trends of migrations that evolved during the Soviet era. The dynamics of Soviet migration reflect opportunities offered and constraints imposed by the party state. The analysis of the socio-political contexts of post-Soviet transnational migration requires drawing upon the historical trajectories of these Soviet policies and dynamics in the places of origin as well as in the places of destination.

Central Asia is home to people who represent various ethnic groups and languages. In this study we will encounter interviewees and their families who are introduced as Kyrgyz, Tajik, or Uzbek. Their nationalities, as they were defined in the Soviet system of citizenship (*grazhdanstvo*) and nationality (*natsionalnost'*), may not, however, correspond to the title of the republic they originate from. The former union republics of Kyrgyzstan, Tajikistan, and Uzbekistan and their titular nations, the Kyrgyz, Tajiks, and Uzbeks, emerged as a result of complex policies during the Soviet era. The ethnic and linguistic composition of the population in these sending states and their transnational migrants in Russia arose from the Soviet border demarcation and nationality policies of the 1920s and 1930s. Research on Central Asian labor migrants must bear in mind the complexities that result from, for instance, the presence of ethnic Uzbeks in Kyrgyzstan or Tajikistan or a Tajik-speaking population in some parts of Uzbekistan. This ethnic complexity is also represented among labor migrants in Russia. Although this study is not about the inter-ethnic relations of transnational migrants in Russia since the fall of the Soviet Union, it is necessary to take into account the social settings in which the qualitative data for this research was compiled. Scholars of transnational migration argue that neglecting the background of the subjects of our studies and representing them as if they strictly belonged to individual countries (in this case e.g., Uzbeks to Uzbekistan, Tajiks to Tajikistan) would make the analysis susceptible to 'methodological nationalism.'[126] Overcoming methodological nationalism therefore requires paying close attention to the work of historians, sociologists, and demographers who elaborate on the influence of the purposeful state-sponsored construction of nations during the Soviet period upon the newly emerged

---

125 A version of this chapter was published under the title "Migrations during the Soviet Period and in the Early Years of USSR's Dissolution: A Focus on Central Asia" in *Revue Européenne des Migrations Internationales* 2010 (26) 3, pp. 9-30.
126 Wimmer and Glick-Schiller, 2002.

sending and receiving countries, which adopted their own nationalist agendas at the dawn of independence.[127]

Research on transnational migration has further emphasized that "while transnational practices extend beyond two or more national territories, they are built within the confines of specific social, economic and political relations which are bound together by perceived shared interests and meanings."[128] In the chapter on post-Soviet transnationalization, I will elaborate more upon the Soviet state's impact on the emergence of transnational ties between Central Asian sending states and Russia. In the present chapter my objective is to describe the opportunities for and restrictions on mobility that influenced the migration patterns during the Soviet period as well as the dynamics of mass migration from Central Asia to Russia since the 1990s.

3.1. The Genesis: The Early Years of Mobility Control in Pre-Soviet Russia

Any person who travels to Russia or to some countries in the Central Asian region nowadays has, without a doubt, been confronted (in one form or another) with a mandatory registration of residence, known in Russian as *propiska* or *registraciia*. While some historians hold Tsar Peter the Great responsible for the initial concept of registering the population[129] in order to engage more recruits for his reformed army, collect taxes, and rule with more law and order than his predecessors had, others argue that as early as the end of the 16th century the tsars kept a systematic registration of peasants who were bound to work for the feudal lords.[130]

According to the regulation of 1714, it was mandatory for every owner of a household in the cities of the Russian Empire to register with the police any arrivals, short or long term visits, and the residence and departures of the subjects. Their names, professions, ethnic backgrounds, and places of origin had to be entered as well. It was not until 1857 that the Russian Empire finally published a "Collection of Statutes on Passports and Runaways" which was a concise text of rules and regulations that included those issued under Peter the Great's predecessors.[131] This collection contained a regulation dating back to 1719 according to which no subject was allowed to move without his (internal) passport. Every subject had to be registered in the place of residence and needed official permission to leave. In rural areas, the serf-owner had to issue permits for peasants; in urban areas this permission was in the form of a certificate of residence, which was called *vid na zhitel'stvo*.[132] It is

---

127 On historicization of the field, see Fitzgerald, 2006:2.
128 Smith and Guarnizo, 1998:13.
129 Garcelon, 2001:90.
130 Matthews 1993:1.
131 Matthews, 1993.
132 Matthews, 1993:4.

precisely this term that has outlived the tsarist and Soviet periods. It is still applied in the newly independent countries of the former Soviet Union and denotes – at least in the Russian version of the legislation texts – "permanent residence permit."

Under the regulations of the Russian tsars, individual choice for mobility, particularly among the peasants, was limited. Movements of people took place for commercial or professional reasons whereas personal travels were greatly restricted. However, subjects of higher ranks such as nobles and higher military personnel were issued permanent passports and enjoyed freedom of movement. The lower the rank, the more constrained the subjects were in their mobility. In cities, especially in St. Petersburg and Moscow, the subjects who were registered temporarily received address tickets that they were required to retain until their departure.[133]

By the mid-19th century, strict control over population mobility became a hindrance as the demand for blue collar manpower increased alongside the industrialization of the urban areas. Issuance of passports became expensive for the impoverished and consequently residents became increasingly reluctant to abide by the rules. In 1894, when the Statute on Residence Certificates was adopted under Alexander III, it was no longer required that urban residents obtain a permanent permit. When Central Asia was annexed to the Russian Empire in the 1860s, the statute loosened control over travels of subjects even more.

3.2. *Control of Movement through Labor in the Period before the 1917 Revolution*

After the toppling of the tsarist regime and the establishment of the Bolshevik power, management of migration, settlement, and employment acquired importance in the newly founded socialist state's policies of forming a large multiethnic state – one in which every member would work to contribute to the benefit of the socialist society. Following the October revolution, Bolsheviks who had vigorously criticized and intended to abolish the tsars' oppressive policies towards the exploited class, soon established full control over the entire population with the same firmness. What is remarkable is that, with an attitude similar to that which the tsars had had towards peasants whose movement they restricted, the Bolsheviks demanded that all former members of bourgeoisie and upper classes obtain residence registrations. In doing so, the Bolsheviks compelled the former "exploiters" to participate in military service and socially beneficial labor such as construction and maintenance. Holders of registration cards, who were adult men aged 18 to 45, were obliged to have their employment information entered into their documents

---

133   Matthews, 1993:10-12.

by their employers and trade unions. This procedure was carried out through a policy of "labor books" implemented in October 1918.[134] The regulation initially applied to all people who had previously belonged to the upper classes. Labor books were to substitute for identity documents and passports. They contained personal data and all information on jobs assumed by the holder, who had to update it on a monthly basis at the local administrative or police offices. Most importantly, labor books had a special entry on the holder's place of residence.[135] *Propiska,* the term for 'residence registration' that emerged initially as an entry in these labor books, was a tit-for-tat instrument of control at the onset of Bolshevik power. This practice would survive decades of state migration policies during and after the Soviet period and would be widely used in the ex-Soviet countries.

In December 1918, shortly after the introduction of "labor books" for members of the former upper classes, RSFSR employment legislation stipulated that every employable individual acquire a "worker's book" (*rabochaia knizhka*), a document which would include information on the place of employment, hours of service, salaries, vacations, sicknesses, maternity leaves, rewards, promotions, and penalties. As of February 22, 1922, any employment and/or leave of a worker involved getting permission from the local labor officials. Until recently, a similar document called "trudovaia knizhka" (work book) served as evidence for *inter alia,* determining the years of work to calculate pension rates. Between 1924 and 1925, after a one-year period of liberalization of regulations on population movements, new legislation was adopted which stated that any person assuming residence for three days or more must register with the landlords, administrator of the residence, or a hotel. Individuals receiving visitors had to register them with a law enforcement office within 48 hours after their arrival.[136] Details about the person were to be entered into the "house book" (*domovaia kniga*).[137] This book was to be kept at every abode with a detailed record of its residents; it too retained its significance until the 21st century in each of the four countries involved in labor migration.

---

134 Matthews, 1993:16-19.
135 *Ibid.*
136 According to the Federal Law on Migration Registration of Foreign Citizens and Stateless Persons of the Russian Federation adopted in January 2007, the host party is required to notify the Federal Migration Service about the arrival of a foreign visitor.
137 Matthews, 1993:20, Buckley, 1995:902.

3.3. Institutionalized Restriction on Movement of People under Stalin with a Focus on the Soviet Central Asia

When considering the institutional constraints imposed on the movements of people, it is important to keep in mind the Soviet state's construction of nationalities in the 1920s and 1930s. It was during this period that the allocation of geographical territories of the Soviet republics took place. In describing this period, I will draw upon the studies conducted by historians of the Soviet Union such as Roy (1997), Edgar (2004), Hirsch (2005), and others. One of the most important historical milestones is the year 1922, which marked the establishment of Soviet power in Turkestan – the region which later became known as Central Asia – as well as the founding of the Union of the Soviet Socialist Republics (USSR). Two years later, in 1924, when the delimitation of administrative borders in Central Asia resulted in the creation of the Turkmen SSR and the Uzbek SSR, the latter first included the Tajik ASSR in its territory. The Tajik ASSR then became the Tajik SSR in 1929. Kazakhstan was known as the Kazakh Autonomous Soviet Socialist Republic of the RSFSR. Also belonging to the RSFSR was the Kara-Kyrgyz Autonomous Oblast' (Province). In 1936, these administrative units were renamed the Kazakh SSR and the Kyrgyz SSR, respectively.

In the mid 1920s, the Soviets launched their first population census. For this purpose, they engaged ethnographers who had been working for the Commission for the Study of the Tribal Composition of the Population of Russia.[138] Prior to this period, the ethnographers' primary task had been to acquire ethnographic data for the Russian Empire during the First World War. Following the October revolution, when they became consultants to the Bolsheviks, they were committed to all-Union censuses and participated in the activities that involved defining the internal frontiers of the Soviet Union. The Russian ethnographers carried out field research in remote areas and conducted in-depth studies of different peoples of the USSR. However, as Hirsch argues, they did far more than merely accumulate data in the remotest places of the USSR; they contributed to a change in population composition by applying an approach that Hirsch terms as "state-sponsored evolutionism." According to her, the state, which was marked by a strong Leninist school of thought, envisioned the evolution of the population of the USSR. The Soviets, adhering to the Marxist ideology of development, held that it was feasible to expedite the evolutionary process by forming nationalities through clustering clans and tribes, which in turn, were deemed to be residuals of the feudal period.[139] Nationalities would be formed into Socialist-era nations, which

---

138 Hirsch, 2005.
139 Edgar, 2004; Hirsch, 2005. Hirsch's elaborate work leaves the impression that the creation of ethnicities/nationalities in Central Asia began mainly with the formation of the USSR, particularly under Stalin. However, earlier scholarship on Central Asia points out that even in the 19th century, the tsars had the tendency to perceive a "people" by the language spoken (*Volk*). This German romanticism was then passed onto Marxists who advanced

some day in the era of Communism would all be united. In Lubin's words, "a 'flourishing of nations' was to lead to their eventual 'coming together,' or 'rapprochement,' which was ultimately to lead to their 'merging' or assimilation."[140] Thus, in compliance with the government's official list of nationalities, citizens had to choose or declare themselves as belonging to an official nationality during individual encounters with census-takers.[141]

A further relevant aspect for the study of post-Soviet migration is the principle of "double assimilation" applied by the Soviet regime. The characteristic of this kind of assimilation is the co-occurrence of top-down and bottom-up processes, which meant that not only did the Soviet government implement measures from above such as delineating national borders and publishing an official list of nationalities, but also that local elites were involved in the decision making and had to fight for resources, land, and power. Archival materials bear witness to the fact that even smaller population groups, such as peasants, protested and complained to higher authorities about inappropriate distribution of their territories to the national territorial units they did not want to be part of.[142]

Prior to the formation of the Soviet Union and the enhancement of the state nationality policies, the sense of identification with which Central Asian people associated themselves was based on their language, clan, tribe, geographic place, religion, and religious and/or noble ancestry.[143] The border delimitation and the first all-Union census of 1926 gradually altered people's sense of self-identification, as the Soviet republics in Central Asia included national majorities and minorities. Roy points out that the delimitation of these borders did not have any geographic, economic, or ethnic rationality. This resulted, as he rightly points out, in the emergence of such complex constellations of peoples as the large Uzbek population for which the Province of Osh in the south of Kyrgyzstan is known, or the ethnic Uzbeks living in Tashauz and Charjau (now Türkmenabad) in Turkmenistan as well as Shymkent and Jambul in Kazakhstan. In Tajikistan, the Uzbek speaking population is distributed primarily in the north in Sughd Province and the region of Hissor as well as some villages in the Province of Khatlon in the south. Similarly, in Uzbekistan, there is a large Tajik-speaking population in Buxoro, Samarqand, Surxondaryo, and even in the Ferghana Valley and the north of Toshkent. There are ethnic Kyrgyz in the north and south of Tajiki-

---

their own vision of constructing nations following the revolution in 1917 (Roy, 1997:98, 109).
140 Lubin, 1984:6. More on 'merging' (*sliianie*) and 'coming together' (*sblizhenie*) of nations, see also Smith, 1996:8-9.
141 Hirsch, 2005:9.
142 Hirsch, 2005 and Edgar (2004:53, 60-61). Edgar points out interesting examples from the 1920s in which Soviet ethnographers were unable to determine the nationality of certain nomadic tribes based on their languages. There were cases in which the Soviet authorities found it extremely difficult to distribute certain territories during the border delimitation process.
143 Roy, 1993:48-60, Edgar, 2004:18, Hirsch, 2005:110-114.

stan.[144] Precisely this mixture of languages and cultures is represented by the population of Central Asians at both ends of migratory movements between Central Asia and Russia, making the study equally fascinating and challenging.

In the midst of the border demarcation process and creation of nations, the party-state was responsible especially for controlling rural out-migration and managing the mobility of the population. The establishment of Soviet power resulted in the emigration of thousands of people who opposed the Communists. In the Central Asian republics, the former upper class people were marginalized and driven from urban to rural areas. The formation of Socialist collective farms led thousands of better-off peasants to flee from the Soviet regime into exile. Particularly in the 1930s, the so-called *kulak*s, or rich peasants/entrepreneurs, were placed under state scrutiny. Repression and execution of the *kulak*s forced a great number of people to seek refuge in Afghanistan, Iran, China, Turkey, Saudi Arabia, and in Western European countries.[145] In nomadic regions of Turkmenistan, Uzbekistan, Kyrgyzstan, and Kazakhstan, collectivization was used as a tool to bring about a sedentary lifestyle. As Edgar argues, nomads were perceived by the Soviet administration as people difficult to control, who were opposed to Soviet power and prone to cross the Soviet border to flee. According to Soviet understanding, only those who possessed a great deal of wealth were able to afford to lead a nomadic life, as any change of place of residence with family and household would require considerable means.[146]

The first Five-year Plan which was launched in 1928 marked a head start towards the 'modernization of culturally backward people,' sedentarization, and enhancement of development through industrialization and collectivization of agriculture.[147] At the same time, the Soviets implemented a policy of distribution of labor that they coupled with strict migration control. It is in this context that the Central Asia region started receiving labor migrants from Russia through *orgnabor*s, an organized system of labor force recruitment for the mining industry, railway and motorway construction and technical personnel for construction of factories and plants, etc.[148]

---

144 Roy, 1993:116-118. I refrain from referring to the Tajik-speaking population as Tajiks and the Uzbek-speaking population as Uzbeks. The Soviet citizenship passport had a special nationality entry. Following the demise of the USSR, when citizenship passports in each Central Asian country were introduced, the citizens in Central Asian countries were once again confused. Either the citizenship passports did not have such an entry (Uzbekistan) or representatives of ethnic/linguistic minorities were categorized according to their place of birth, as in the case of Tajiks who were registered as Uzbeks since they had been born in Buxoro in the 1940s and moved to Tajikistan during the Soviet era. They do not necessarily speak Uzbek.
145 On political immigration from Central Asia in the 1930s see Kocaoglu, 2000; on immigration of Kazakhs in particular, see Mendikulova, 2006:132-133.
146 Edgar, 2004:195.
147 Edgar, 2004:88, Collins, 2006:85. Specifically on internal migration control and collectivization, see, Garcelon, 2001.
148 Shigabdinov and Nikitenko, 2000:104.

In 1932, Stalin issued a decree according to which internal passports were to be issued – allegedly not only in order to acquire more precise statistical information from urban areas, but also in order to secure the deportation from these places of persons who are not connected with industry or with work in offices and schools, and who are not engaged in socially useful labor (with the exception of infirm persons and pensioners), and also in order to cleanse these places of kulak, criminal and other anti-social elements finding refuge there...[149]

The decree applied to any individual older than 16 years residing in border zones, urban areas, or towns (or within 100 km around them).[150] Four months after this legislation was issued, it was complemented by a further decree determining a list of 25 towns and 100 km radiuses to which the decree would apply. All other individuals living beyond the officially designated "regime zones" were deprived of passports and were required to be registered with the rural district authorities. This meant that minority populations who had been allocated to reside in designated territories (army members and, particularly, peasants, i.e. collective farmers who constituted a majority of the population) were also Soviet citizens, but they had difficulty traveling and seeking residence and employment as they wished in the areas which were under strict control through internal passports.[151] Without a passport it was impossible to travel to distant locations since boarding trains and buses required showing a valid internal passport. Only on a seasonal basis and with the permission of their supervisors were members of kolkhozes allowed to work in the spheres of industry and construction.[152] In addition, under the oppressive regime of Stalin, defiance of passport and registration rules was punished. Penalties varied from fines to a prison sentence of up to two years; forgery of documents was prosecuted severely.[153]

In light of the Soviet efforts to develop industry and cotton monoculture in Central Asia, arid oases in the south were to be cultivated. Due to a great deficit in manpower in these parts of the region, population groups were involuntarily relocated from the Ferghana Valley to these areas. During the period from 1929 until the mid-1950s, in accordance with Stalin's oppressive approach to kulaks and other 'undesirable' minority populations in Central Russia and Siberia, "special settlements" (*spetsposelenie*) were established in the region where these forced settlers had to reside.[154] A typical example is

---

149 Matthews, 1993:28.
150 Hirsch mentions that the internal passport system of the USSR distinguished among three territorial categories: (1) "regime zones," which encompassed territories of geopolitical or economic importance that later would include surrounding regions within 100 km designated as such, as well as frontier regions that were located 100 km within the Soviet territories bordering the European and Far Eastern states, (2) "non-regime zones," the term applied to rural regions and provinces, and (3) "extra-administrative zones" that included the Gulag (2005:275).
151 For more on Soviet citizenship, see next chapter.
152 Lewis and Rowland, 1979:22.
153 Lewis and Rowland, 1979:22, Matthews, 1993:28, Garcelon, 2001:91.
154 Shigabdinov and Nikitenko, 2000:103.

the deportation of 171,781 Koreans to Kazak and Uzbek SSR in the late 1930s, which occurred because of increased Soviet suspicion of ethnic Koreans residing in the frontier territories of the Far East. The Soviets feared that ethnic Koreans might establish close ties to Korean nationals and Japanese intelligence agents with Korean nationality.[155]

Despite the strict control on movement, the period during World War II and the years immediately afterwards witnessed different migration flows including rural-to-urban movements as a result of the increase of industrialization and expansion of urban areas. Migration of the Slavic population to Central Asia increased during and after World War II, partly related to the evacuation of the population from Russian territories under the German occupation, but also as a result of the transfer of plants, construction of military infrastructure, provision of clothing and food supplies, and redistribution of resources during the war.[156] Among the Central Asian republics, the Kyrgyz SSR and the Kazakh SSR had the largest inflow of Russian-speaking migrants in the decades after World War II.[157]

The onset of World War II and the invasion by Nazi troops was marked by the deportation of Germans from the Volga Region to Central Asia, their overall number in 1941-1942 amounting to 1,209,430. Forced relocation of minorities in the USSR was not confined only to Germans, however. The number of "special settlements" grew as Chechens, Ingushes, Crimean Tatars, Kurds and Greek political migrants were forcefully resettled in the various regions of Central Asia.[158] For instance, a relatively large group of around 60,000 Meskhetian Turks was resettled from Georgia to the Ferghana Valley in Central Asia in 1944.[159] Almost 40,000 Greeks were relocated from the Black Sea region, mainly to Kazakhstan and Uzbekistan during the same period.[160]

Notwithstanding the adoption of strict policies such as the introduction of mandatory registration at the place of residence and the internal passport system, there seems to have been some difference between policy and practice. Lewis & Rowland and Buckley state that in reality, those wishing to change their place of residence succeeded in doing so by using informal channels. Lewis and Rowland argue that despite the common understanding in the West that Stalinist policies severely restricted mobility, one should place the migration regulations of that time in context. The decline of the economy, extreme poverty, starvation and the collectivization of the 1920s and 1930s led the population to move to urban areas. Between 1926 and 1939, as Soviet statistics show, 18.7 million people migrated from rural areas

---

155 *Ibid.* p.104.
156 *Ibid.*
157 Islamov, 2000:181-182.
158 For more sources on forced relocation of minorities during the Stalinist period, see Polyan, 2001 and Berdinskikh, 2005 among others.
159 Rubin and Lubin, 2000:177, Ref.9
160 Bugai and Kotsonis, 1999:55,117.

to urban areas.[161] Despite the limitations imposed on the cities that were officially "closed" to migrants from outside through the notorious *propiska* (residence permit) regulation, many potential migrants sought different alternatives such as informal practices to attain their goals and eventually succeeded in settling. An elaborate study conducted by Buckley shows that, in reality, the restrictive measures employed by the Soviets to control the vast growth of the cities were quite unsuccessful.[162]

3.4. Migration Patterns in the 1960s and 1980s

3.4.1. The Presence of the Slavic Population in Central Asia

During this period the Central Asian republics experienced a steep increase of demographic growth. The population of the RSFSR declined slightly, with the exception of some industrial regions.[163] The statistical data on the changes of residence of individuals within the USSR show that the population of the Central Asian republics remained relatively stationary, whereas in RSFSR people were more mobile and moved between different regions.[164] For the period of 1959-1979, the Central Asian republics reported the following data on the increase of the population among the titular nationalities: Uzbekistan – 6.7%, Kyrgyzstan – 7.5%, and Tajikistan – 5.8%.[165]

With Khrushchev's accession to power in 1956 and his policy of de-Stalinization, control over workers' mobility was loosened. Through the *orgnabor*s (the aforementioned organized labor recruiting service), the government continued to administer the distribution of labor force, relocating 28 million people in the period between 1930 and 1970. This organized recruitment was not mandatory, however. From 1951 until 1970, the number of resettled workers declined, totaling merely 573,100 in the period of 1966-1970.[166]

By the mid-1970s, collective farmers who had reached the age of 15 were permitted to obtain internal passports with which they were able to travel longer distances. The sources provided by Islamov suggest that in the time period of 1959-1979, Kyrgyzstan, Tajikistan, and Turkmenistan saw increases in ethnic Russians of 13.1%, 8.5%, and 10.9% respectively.[167] By 1970, around 30 million Russians were residing in areas primarily inhabited by non-Russians that were located beyond the administrative borders of the RSFSR. This number constituted 23 percent of the overall Russian popula-

---

161 Lewis and Rowland, 1979:25.
162 Buckley, 1995.
163 Gibson, 1991:152.
164 Lubin, 1984:41 and Gibson, 1991; see also Moskvin.
165 Islamov, p.182.
166 Lewis and Rowland, 1979:19; this decline is also mentioned by Lubin, 1984:42-43.
167 *Ibid.*.

tion. Between 1979 and 1989, however, more Russians were reported to have left Central Asia than to have arrived.[168] Gibson notes that the number of migrants from the RSFSR to Central Asia dropped by 50% during the period of 1971-1980.[169] The post-Stalinist period was marked by the redistribution of power and education and employment opportunities among Russian-speaking professionals and representatives of the so-called titular nationality. As argued by Korobkov, with regional governing bodies in Central Asia promoting more employment and education opportunities for the titular nationality, Russian speakers were pushed to take lower-level jobs which in turn led them to leave the region.[170]

3.4.2. Emigration of the Jewish Population

The period between the late 1960s and 1980s was characterized by a large-scale emigration of Jews from the entire Soviet Union (including Central Asia). Prior to this period, the USSR had never before witnessed a mass permanent outflow of its citizens. In September 1968, the Embassy of the Netherlands in Moscow launched the issuance of exit permits that would allow Jews to immigrate to Israel.[171] What is more, it occurred at the time when very few citizens were given permission to travel to foreign countries. By 1971, the outflow of the Jewish minority strongly increased. Within this year, at least 13,000 people were allowed to leave. A year later, almost three times as many Jews left the USSR for Israel. Buwalda distinguishes between two waves within this exodus of the Soviet Jews. The first wave was in the 1970s when 220,000 people emigrated.[172] During this period the majority of Jewish emigrants left for Israel. Between 1975 and 1987, two thirds of the emigrants preferred to settle in countries other than Israel.[173] The second wave started in 1987 and continued through 1991, with the number of Jewish emigrants amounting to 300,000.[174]

The shift from strict controls on travel abroad to sweeping permission for such a great number of people to emigrate in the midst of the Cold War seems remarkable. In this context, too, we should address the opportunities and constraints that shaped this pattern of migration. Zaslavsky and Brym, in their joint work, discuss the *extrinsic* and *intrinsic* modes in the scholarship on Jewish out-migration from the Soviet Union.[175] The first of the two ap-

---

168 Here I am relying on the 1989 census data provided by Shigabdinov and Nikitenko, 2000:104.
169 Gibson, 1991:153.
170 Korobkov, 2008:71.
171 Buwalda, 1997:9-11. The period of the late 1960s and early 1970s is considered by scholars such as Buwalda to be the second exodus of Jews. Buwalda points out that the first exodus of Jews took place in the period of 1881-1914 in which roughly two million Jews left the Russian Empire.
172 Buwalda, 1997, Chapter 1.
173 Gitelman, 1997:29, as cited in Dietz, 2000: 639.
174 Buwalda, 1997:9-11.
175 Zaslavsky and Brym, 1983: 2-3, 64-76.

proaches links the outflow of the Jewish population to external factors occurring in the late 1960s and 1970s. The revival of the Jewish national consciousness and the strong desire of the Soviet Jews to immigrate to Israel are explained as an outcome of the Six Day War in 1967, in which Israel claimed victory. In this context, it should not go unmentioned that the Kremlin was against Israel during the Six Day War and this position had a major impact on the Jewish community all over the USSR. A further factor in this approach was the pressure which the West exerted on the USSR due to its desire that Jews be able to leave the country.[176]

The second approach is related to social changes occurring within the confines of the USSR and shifts external factors into the background. The extent to which the Jewish out-migration took place is explained in terms of the Soviet policy of preventing a sudden deficit in labor force, particularly in the technical and scientific spheres. [I think this needs a bit more explanation because the prior text suggests a significant "brain drain". Do you mean that the Soviets controlled the pace of emigration?] A further reason is argued to have been individual decision making: some merely had no desire to abandon the society in which they had been brought up, whereas others were induced to emigrate by having heard the stories of their friends and relatives.

There are indeed a number of other push and pull factors which cannot be analyzed here.[177] One of the most important and detrimental implications of the Jewish emigration from the Soviet Union has been brain-drain. It is worthwhile pointing out this aspect, since the onset of the brain-drain out of the Soviet Union became discernible in the republics of the Central Asian region that had been home to thousands of Jews throughout many centuries.[178] It is difficult to determine precisely how many Jewish scientists, professionals, and skilled workers in all emigrated from Central Asia between 1970 and 1991. On the one hand, statistical data accumulation in the Soviet Union is a controversial topic in the sense that, in the context of anti-Semitism, some individuals had chosen to identify themselves as belonging to different nationalities. On the other hand, in their quantitative data and discussions on the issue, some Western scholars (notably in the US) seem to

---

176 Zaslavsky and Brym provide some details about how Soviet-American trade agreements correlated with the Kremlin's number of exit permits for Jews. Thus, in 1972-1973 when the wheat agreement was signed, between 32,000 and 35,000 emigrants were recorded. The Jackson-Vanik amendment, which warned that trade would be blocked if Jews were not permitted to leave, caused a decline in exits. Further wheat accords resulted in an increase of emigration permissions, which then declined with the start of the Soviet military actions in Afghanistan in 1980 and the wheat embargo.
177 There is an entire body of research in and outside of the former Soviet Union that deals specifically with Jewish emigration from the Soviet Union, including topics such as the Stalinist attitude towards nationality policy (Hirsch, 2005; Zaslavsky and Brym, 1983), the rise of anti-Semitism in Russia (Zaslavsky and Brym, 1983), persecution and discrimination against Jews in the USSR (Buwalda, 1997), Soviet Jewish immigrants in Israel (Berthomière, 2003), and the Jewish minority population that chose not to emigrate (Ryvkina, 1996).
178 According to the sources provided by Zaslavsky and Brym, the total number Jews in 1970 in Uzbekistan was 102,855; Tajikistan, 14,615; and in the Kyrgyz Republic, 7,680 (p.13).

have an anti-Soviet bias. What becomes clear is that Soviet authorities must have sensed the danger of brain-drain as a serious consequence of emigration when they imposed a so-called 'education tax' in August 1972.[179] According to this regulation, every emigrant had to compensate the Soviet state for the free education that they had obtained before their departure. The cost of emigration was in some cases as high as five to ten years of wages of a professional employee.[180] Other sources state that the fee was 4,500 rubles for a graduate in the humanities and 19,400 rubles for a doctor of sciences. Towards the end of that same year, the education fee had to be abolished, as the Western countries and President Johnson of the US threatened the USSR with sanctions.[181]

Although Western scholars working on this subject claim that, due to the anti-Semitism that was present during the Soviet Union, the overall percentage of Jews who obtained higher education was only 1% in the entire USSR, having lived in the vicinity of a Jewish district, I cannot confirm the accuracy of such a low percentage in Central Asia. What became easily noticeable throughout the last two decades of the Soviet era was the absence of Jewish academicians, university professors, teachers, medical doctors, and scientists. In addition to brain-drain, the emigration of Jews meant the ultimate loss of a culture which was unique in itself, that had been developed and passed on through generations. Inherent to it were architecture, artisanship, music, and art of which almost no traces are left, and to which scholars focusing on emigration generally tend to pay too little attention.

3.4.3 'Friendship of Nations' and Construction of a Multiethnic Soviet Society: Education Migration, Internationalization of the Division of Labor and Solidarity among Nations

In 1966, an earthquake of 7.5 on the Richter scale devastated the city of Toshkent, the capital of Uzbek SSR. Immediately, it became a major incentive for the Soviet authorities to reconstruct a new modern city that would embody the Soviet rhetoric of the 'friendship of nations.' The Soviet urban planners took necessary advantage of the damage caused by this natural disaster. They wiped out the majority of the residential buildings in the old town of Toshkent. The reconstruction efforts involved construction of multi-storied concrete residential buildings, schools, and hospitals, as well as creation of new industries and measures to develop infrastructure. This resulted in the inflow of thousands of migrants, particularly from the Slavic regions of the USSR. Around 30,000 people are estimated to have settled yearly during the

---

179 This is not to deny that there was certainly more than mere fear of brain-drain when the authorities in the USSR established education fees. The historical passage of movement control in the USSR that covers the period prior to the Jewish emigration shows that the authorities most probably intended to prevent emigration.
180 Zaslavsky and Brym, 1983:64.
181 Buwalda, 1997, Ch. 6 (p.91).

early 1970s, all of them set to design Toshkent as a multicultural city epitomizing the 'friendship of nations.'[182]

What is interesting and has been neglected in the research is that immediately after the earthquake, some higher education institutions in Toshkent evacuated their students and transferred them to the RSFSR. Despite the scarce research which has been done particularly on the issue of outmigration after the earthquake, empirical data for the present study has indicated that some students among this generation settled in their new locations in Russia permanently. During my field research, I encountered a case in which one of the former students had meanwhile become an important person in a patronage network of Central Asian migrants.[183]

Along with the Russification policies and the efforts to raise the level of education in the less-developed peripheries of the USSR such as the Caucasus and Central Asia, the period from the late 1960s through early 1980s was a time during which the educated youth, often the children of the party cadres and education elites, went to Russia to study at higher education institutions. Many of them came back to their region of origin as expected and pursued promising careers; some, however, chose to settle in Russia. From 2004 – 2007, Sahadeo conducted a survey of this precise category of migrants who had lived in the cities of Leningrad and Moscow during the Soviet era, who serve as evidence for the existence of an entire generation of education migrants in Russia and who recount different attitudes they were confronted with in their Slavic host societies.[184] During my own field research, I came across a number of such migrants as well. Their role in migrant organizations of Central Asia will be described in various chapters of this research.

Research conducted by Lubin in late 1970s, which focuses mainly on Soviet Uzbekistan, brings into the foreground two further aspects, which are of great significance for the present study: first, according to Lubin, the Central Asian (specifically Uzbek SSR) employable population migrated to the RSFSR for vocational, professional, and educational purposes. Second, she mentions that the Soviet Army served as a channel through which male migrants from Central Asia were allocated to different Russian cities. Lubin states that no data had been published on those migrants who had chosen not to return to Uzbekistan and that the individuals she had interviewed showed strong willingness to return to Uzbekistan.[185] However, in the meantime, we do know that some migrants did opt to stay permanently in Russia. Indeed, census data indicates that in 1959, 42,000 Uzbeks were residing outside the territory of the Central Asian region. In 1979 the number of such migrants doubled, but considering that the number of the Uzbeks in the entire USSR

---

182 Lubin, 1984:42. More on 'friendship of nations,' see Roman 2002 and Sahadeo 2007.
183 See the story of Madamin Ota in Chapter 9.
184 Sahadeo, 2007.
185 Lubin, 1984:43.

was 12.5 million, 91,000 residing outside of the Uzbek SSR seems miniscule.[186]

According to sources provided by Sahadeo, in 1970, 140,000 Kyrgyz, Tajiks, Uzbeks, and Turkmens were registered as residents in Russia. This number increased to 248,000 in 1989.[187] The present study will show that precisely these types of pioneer migrants – originating from all Central Asian republics, arriving in the 1960s and 1970s and staying in Russia, meanwhile maintaining ties to their regions of origin – played a crucial role in forming labor migrant networks in the 1990s. As we shall see in the course of this study, these actors became significant propellers of the inflow of cheap labor force. Those whose ties to their homelands had been rather weak benefited from their resources in Russia, and established migrant organizations and recruitment offices or have acted as informal job brokers and supervisors.[188]

Russia's First Central Asian Labor Migrants?

Military service and education were not the sole purposes for Central Asians to migrate to Russia for longer periods. Contrary to the common impression that the current mass labor migration from the Central Asian republics of the former Soviet Union to the Russian Federation commenced in the 1990s, sufficient data has been found that indicates that the phenomenon of labor force movement from Central Asia to Russia is not just characteristic of the post-Soviet period. While I argue that the dynamics of labor migration has represented a new challenge to the newly independent states, there was a period not too long before 1991 when the Soviet state encouraged the able-bodied population of Central Asia to settle in the regions of Russia that had labor deficits for the sake of resource allocation and production.

During the 1970s, together with urbanization and industrialization in the RSFSR, the party-state staged efforts to cultivate virgin land to increase food supplies, which of course required a labor force. Soviet demographers criticized and complained about the great reluctance of Central Asia's employable population to migrate to different regions of the USSR to work. They stated that it was due first to a lack of education of Central Asians and secondly because the regions in Russia with severe labor deficits were not appealing to Central Asians in cultural, social, and material terms. The third argument was that the potential migrants were fairly satisfied with the environment in which they were living, regardless of the economic challenges of the period.[189]

---

186 Lubin, 1984:43.
187 Sahadeo, 2007:563.
188 Here, we should be cautious about developing the two abovementioned aspects into categories such as education/vocation and military migrants as one might be tempted to do. Among Lubin's interviewees there were also those who stayed to study in Russian after the military service, which can make clear distinctions difficult. Similar cases emerged during my own fieldwork in Russia from 2005-2008.
189 Wimbush and Ponomareff, 1979:11, Ref. 21.

It goes without saying that the vast mobility of labor from Central Asian countries to Russia since the 1990s, on which the present research focuses, has refuted these statements. What should be made clear is that there is significant historical data about the movements of people from Central Asia to RSFSR during the Soviet period. In the second half of the 1970s, the Soviets expanded their agricultural development projects in the grey and brown earth zones of Moscow and Novgorod (known as the non-black earth zone, Rus. *nechernozem*) that extend to the north and the east of Russia, the territory covering Murmansk and the Urals.[190] It was planned that by 1980, the non-black earth zones would produce one–sixth of the overall agriculture of the whole USSR.[191] Development of agriculture in the non-black earth zone, the lower Volga, and Siberia, as well the establishment of Baikal-Amur Railroad, entailed engaging manpower from the regions with a larger labor force.[192] In 1978 the first group consisting of 1,200 Uzbeks was sent and a year later as many as 3,900 were sent to the non-black earth zone to contribute to the development of agriculture.[193] While both Lubin and Gibson provide us with marginal information on this topic and treat it within a broad macro-level study, I was able to explore some details of this phenomenon from newspaper articles published in the early 1980s.

In an article on Uzbek workers who opted to stay in the non-black earth zone, the Toshkent newspaper *Yosh Leninchi* (Uzb. 'Young Leninist') published an interview with Uzbek workers of both Slavic and Uzbek origin who expressed their strong desire to stay in Novgorod, Russia, and work there "not temporarily, but permanently."[194] Uzbek workers are quoted as promising that they will not go anywhere "until we turn the non-black earth lands into a productive area...." According to another report, Uzbek workers, judging from their names, had meanwhile married local Russian women, founded families, and were provided with apartments.[195] They did not return to Uzbekistan, even though their training had finished long ago. Uzbek migrants and their families were described as living a normal life. More weddings were planned to be celebrated the year after the report and concert ensembles from Uzbekistan were reported to be on tour in the Russian region.

Newspapers from other Central Asian republics attest that these projects were not limited to the Uzbek SSR. The newspaper *Kommunist Tadzhikistana* reported on May 15, 1983 that an entire train had left Dushanbe, the

---

190 Wimbush and Ponomareff, 1979.
191 Wimbush and Ponomareff, 1979:18-19.
192 Lubin, 1984:43, 256, Ref. 27; Gibson, 1991:149.
193 Lubin, 1986:43.
194 Notes from the Nonchernozem Zone. Article by Gh. Shermuhamedov in *Yosh Leninchi*, 25th of March, 1983. United States. (1983). *USSR, post report*. Washington, D.C.: U.S. Dept. of State. The articles which I have been able to consult in the archives were in the form of short reviews translated from the original language. The reviews reflected relevant press articles published in the Kyrgyz, Tajik. and Uzbek SSRs during the 1980s. The name Nonchernozem was translated as such from Uzbek into English.
195 On intermarriage as the ultimate evidence of the 'merger of nations,' see Sahadeo, 2007: 562.

capital of Tajik SSR, for Khabarovsk, carrying 70 families or more than 300 people, whose average age was 30. This train was the second, following the first one that had left two months previously with 100 families. The report quoted the train supervisor as saying that all the migrants [*sic*] were bound to the Far East to live and were skilled people. Experienced drivers, crane truck operators, technicians, construction specialists, and engineers with previous professional experience specifically in land cultivation projects in Kazakhstan were being sponsored by the Soviet government to work and live in the Far East. G.D. Dzhavov, deputy chairman of the Tajik SSR State Committee on Labor, stated that within that five-year period, Tajikistan intended to send 6,000 workers to the Far East. The deputy chairman contended with pride that Tajikistan would do its own share in the projects of the Far East.[196]

Lubin's findings on Central Asian workers' definite plans to return to their native regions resulted from her fieldwork which she carried out in the late 1970s, i.e. shortly after these projects started. We can see from sources dated several years later however, that a considerable number of these migrants did opt to stay. The scarcity of data on Kyrgyzstan does not mean that its population was not affected by organized interregional labor. As far as this country is concerned, only one source mentions that in the 1980s approximately 30,000-40,000 workers were engaged from Kyrgyzstan in other Soviet republics, among whom 6,000-9,000 were reported to be students from the Kyrgyz SSR. They were involved mostly in construction sites, in groups known as *stroiotriad*s.[197]

A further aspect, which is particularly relevant in the context of migration and labor, is again the rhetoric of the "friendship of nations" with which these migrant workers were mobilized. Among the workers from Central Asia there were both ethnic Slavic and Central Asian nations, as the names of the persons suggest. What is really remarkable is the way the interviewees stress that they had been working in a multiethnic environment. As one engineer states, his group consisted of "representatives of 14 nationalities working selflessly."[198] Attention should be drawn also to the "group approach" with which the Soviet leadership mobilized the out-migration of Central Asians. By sending entire groups or *collective*s, as they were called, the leadership intended to facilitate the adjustment of these workers in the region of arrival. In 1976, according to the decree of the Central Committee of the CPSU, the Uzbek SSR was commissioned to assign construction trusts or groups to carry out land reclamation work in the Novgorodskaia and Ivanovskaia oblasts within the framework of the aforementioned non-black

---

196 Bon Voyage! Tadzhikistan to the Aid of the Country. Article by Serebrennikov L., in *Kommunist Tadzhikistana*, 15th of May, 1983. United States. (1983). *USSR, post report*. Washington, D.C.: U.S. Dept. of State.
197 Abazov, 2000:231.
198 Notes from the Nonchernozem Zone. Article by Gh. Shermuhamedov in *Yosh Leninchi*, 25th of March, 1983. United States. (1983). *USSR, post report*. Washington, D.C.: U.S. Dept. of State.

earth cultivation project.[199] In Novgorod, for instance, the trust was called Uznovgorodstroi and had 2,500 members in 1979. In addition to irrigating and draining land and constructing houses, schools, and hospitals, the trusts had to found state farms and give them as gifts to their oblasts before their departure, as the plan was to make the region a major supplier of vegetable, meat, and dairy products. The two state farms in Novgorod were proudly named "Toshkent" and "Druzhba" (Russian 'friendship').

These examples illustrate first that the Soviet state made efforts to design a multicultural society and promoted cooperation among different republics. Second, by creating facilities for Central Asian youth to study outside of their region of origin, especially in the RSFSR, and by sending young recruits from the region to serve in the Soviet Army, the 'merger of nations' was further promoted. Third, through shifting different skilled human resources among the regions within the USSR, the Soviet state supported its own development through a migration strategy that should be addressed as characteristic in its own way. Ultimately, studies conducted by Sahadeo, Roman, and Hirsch contend that the Soviet ideology of internationalization privileged Russians over non-Russians and thus engendered more ethnic discrimination towards the non-Slavic population in Russia.

An Excursus on Patterns of Movement in the Soviet Union between 1926 and the Final Years of the Soviet Era

According to Gibson, there were three main phases of migration flows between 1926, the year in which the first all-Union census took place, and the final years of Soviet power, based on the concise statistical summary published in the USSR in 1987. These phases are important to summarize as they once again point to the overall landscape of population movements and demographic patterns when the USSR fell apart. The first trend, Gibson argues, can be identified as the migration of the population mainly from Central European Russia to the east and the north, where the development of the industrial sector and availability of more space for settlement than in crowded cities of the West served as push factors. World War II should be noted here as well, as it caused the evacuation of 25 million people towards the East. In the 1950s and 1960s, with Khrushchev's effort to give more freedom of

---

199 Construction "trusts" (in Russian *trust*) consist of a group of industrial or commercial enterprises with centralized direction (cf. Oxford Russian-English Dictionary 1973). The official name of the resolution was "Ob obiazatel'stvax kollektivov vodoxoziaistvennykh i stroititel'nykh organizatsii Uzbekskoi SSR po okazaniiu pomoshchi Ivanovskoi i Novgorodskoi oblastiam v vypolnenii postanovleniia CK KPSS i Soveta Ministrov SSSR po dal'neishemu razvitiiu sel'skogo xoziaistva nechernozemnoi zony RSFSR." [On the obligations of groups belonging to organizations in charge of water management and construction of the Uzbek SSR in its assistance in Ivanovsk and Novgorod Provinces within the framework of the decree of the Central Committee of the CPSU on further development of agriculture in the non-black zone of the RSFSR] (Wimbush and Ponomareff, 1979:14, also Ref. 35).

movement to workers and to liberate political prisoners, people moved back to their original places of residence. As a result of this, Siberia experienced a loss of population. Then in the 1970s with the development of an oil and gas sector in Western Siberia, the tendency towards moving eastward increased.[200]

The second pattern is observed as rural-to-urban migration which took place due to the collectivization of policies and industrial development efforts that led populations to leave rural settlements, partly in order to escape famine but also to seek labor in urban areas where the demand for manpower was increasing. This trend occurred in spite of the restrictions imposed by the Soviet state particularly between the 1920s and 1930s. The peak of rural out-migration is considered to be the years during and after World War II with a decline only in the 1970s. According to Gibson, approximately 82-84 million Soviet citizens left rural areas to take up residence in urban regions during the time between 1926 and 1986. In 1986, they constituted 45% of the USSR's urban population. According to quantitative data mentioned by Gibson, around 40.4% of Soviet citizens were not residing in the same place as they had been born. From the 1950s, the RSFSR witnessed increased mobility by and a sharp decline of the rural population. By contrast, in Central Asia, mobility declined and the population grew. Where movement did occur, it was marked by patterns such as urban-to-urban in Uzbekistan and rural-to-rural in Kyrgyzstan and Tajikistan.[201]

The third pattern pointed out by Gibson was characterized by movements to large metropolises, urban centers of provinces (oblasts), and republics, due to the deterioration of the quality of life in rural areas. Whereas in 1926, 36% of the Soviet population was living in cities that had 100,000 inhabitants, this percentage grew to more than 60% in 1987. That same year, more than 23 cities in which the population exceeded 1,000,000 could be counted.[202] We can see from the table below that during the Soviet period, by comparison to other regions, Central Asia had the highest rate of natural increase in population. During the Brezhnev period, within the first five years of the 1980s, the population increased from 10 to 29.4%. Hence, in our quest to explain the mass labor migration especially since the end of 1990s, it is essential to keep in mind the demographic increment that the region was facing when the USSR fell apart.

---

[200] Gibson, 1991:144. These patterns are relevant to this study, particularly in the discussions referring to Russia's current demographic crisis and the change of migration regulation to solve this problem. In this view, the demand for foreign labor from Russia's near abroad such as Central Asia gains in importance.
[201] Gibson, 1991:144.
[202] Gibson, 1991: 144-145.

Table 1: Regional Population Growth in the USSR, 1981-1985. Source: Goskomstat SSSR 1988, 16-33, 160-69 (Gibson, 1991:146)

	Population (1000s)		Rate of natural increase (per 1000s) 1985	
	Jan. 1, 1981 number	percentage	Jan. 1, 1986 number	
USSR	266 599 [97.3]	100	278 784	8.8
RSFSR				
North	5 699	2.1	6 003	7.7
Northwest	7 800	2.9	8 134	1.6
Centre	29 188	10.9	29 275	0.9
Volga-Vyatka	8 357	3.1	8 362	3.5
Central Black Earth	7 743	2.9	7 652	0.4
Volga	15 665	5.9	16 081	5.3
North Caucasus	15 748	5.9	16 340	7.3
Urals	19 560	7.3	19 980	6.8
Western Siberia	13 225	5.0	14 358	8.3
Eastern Siberia	8 337	3.1	8 875	10.4
Far East	7 026	2.6	7 651	10.0
Ukraine				
Donetsk-Prednepr	21 204	8.0	21 568	1.7
Southwest	21 700	8.1	21 938	3.5
South	7 231	2.7	7 488	4.0
Prebaltic[1]	8 286	3.1	8 616	4.0
Belorussia	9 675	3.6	10 008	5.9
Moldavia	3 995	1.5	4 147	10.7
Transcaucasus[2]	14 392	5.4	15 304	16.1
Kazakhstan	15 053	5.6	16 028	16.9
Central Asia[3]	26 715	10.0	30 456	29.4

NOTES: 1 The Baltic republics of Estonia, Latvia and Lithuania plus Kaliningrad Oblast of the RSFSR.
2 The Transcaucasian republics of Georgia, Armenia, and Azerbaidzhan.
3 The Central Asian Republics of Turkmenistan, Tadzhikistan, Uzbekistan and Kirgizia.

3.5. Migration in the Late 1980s and the Demise of the USSR: Wither the "Friendship of Nations" and the "Brotherhood of Peoples"?

In June 1989, when the USSR was facing a major economic crisis, interethnic clashes took place in the Ferghana Valley of the Uzbek SSR between Uzbeks and the Meskhetian Turks who had been resettled during the Stalinist period.[203] A fight that started at a small market kindled major violence against Meskhetian Turks in the cities of Farg'ona, Qo'qon, Marg'ilon, and Namangan. According to official reports, 171 people died as a result of the violent clashes and the vast majority of them were Meskhetian Turks.[204] As a reaction to these clashes, the Soviet government relocated almost all of the 15,000 Meskhetians out of Uzbekistan.[205]

In the next month, July 1989, ethnic clashes broke out between Tajiks and Kyrgyz in the Isfara Raion in the north of Tajikistan that borders on Kyrgyzstan. Around 5,000 ethnic Kyrgyz refugees from Tajikistan settled in the south of Kyrgyzstan.[206] A series of other inter-ethnic violent acts followed. In mid-February in Dushanbe, the capital of Tajikistan, there was a failed attempt at a *coup d'état*. Opponents of Mahkamov, the First Secretary of the Supreme Soviet of the Tajik SSR, plotted it by spreading rumors that thousands of Armenians fleeing from the clashes in Nagorno-Karabakh would be provided with housing and employment. The riot which was triggered by these rumors cost the lives of 22 people. As a result, representatives of ethnic minorities such as Russians, Germans, Armenians, and Buxoron Jews, a total of about 100,000 people, left Tajikistan.[207] The same false rumors about Armenian refugees settling in Bishkek, Kyrgyzstan resulted in mass protests. Although the skirmishes in Bishkek did not have any consequences related to migration, the ideology of 'friendship of nations' and 'fraternity of peoples' which had been meant to construct a multiethnic society in the USSR was shattered.

In 1989, approximately 25.3 million Russians were residing beyond the borders of the RSFSR, which corresponded to 18.5% of all Russians living in the USSR.[208] The late 1980s marked the period during which Gorbachev's liberal policies and reforms had corollaries such as the rise of national self-consciousness, the declaration by Central Asian republics of their respective titular language as the official language, and the replacement of Russian party cadres by representatives of the titular nations. The latest waves of Jewish emigration became concatenated with the permanent move of the Russian

---

203 See p. 10 of this chapter on resettlement of minorities into the territory of Central Asia.
204 Rubin and Lubin, 2000: 45-46, Megoran, 2002: 243, Ref. 305.
205 Rubin and Lubin, 2000: 45-45, also *Ibid.* p.177 Ref. 9.
206 Smith, 1996:397.
207 Smith, 1996:380.
208 Zaionchkovskaya, p.11.

speaking population toward the RSFSR or the regions where Russian was still an official language, such as Kazakhstan. Towards the final years of *perestroika* and the beginning of independence, emigration of ethnic Russians to Russia increased rapidly. Additional incentives for Russian out-migration were the economic crisis in the USSR that resulted in wage differences between Russia and Central Asia as well as ethnic clashes that broke out in the region, which, in turn, were characterized by discriminatory attitudes towards Russians, who had, until then, been given privileged treatment.

Towards the final years of the *perestroika* period, the USSR's emigration procedures became less strict, its relations with the Western countries improved, and a reunified Germany started welcoming ethnic Germans from the former Soviet Union. Ethnic Germans who had been resettled during the Stalinist period in the Central Asian region and had already started emigrating in fairly small numbers during the 1970s began leaving in droves in 1990. The remaining Jews emigrated as well, switching their destination from Israel to the USA, then in addition Western Europe, making Germany their primary destination in the 1990s.

3.6. Migration patterns in Central Asia and Russia in the 1990s: The Demise of the Soviet Union and Further Increase of the Rates of Emigration and Mobility

Between 1990 and 1999, Germany received 1.63 million ethnic Germans from the former Soviet Union within the framework of the German repatriation program (*Spätaussiedler*). Approximately 120,000 Jews emigrated from the ex-Soviet countries to Germany as well.[209] The majority of these emigrants belonged to families who had been forcefully resettled during the Stalinist period to the Central Asian region, mainly to Kazakhstan. According to the data provided by the Statistical Committee of the Commonwealth of Independent States, 49,505 ethnic Germans left Kazakhstan in 1997.[210] From Kyrgyzstan, 2,183 ethnic Germans emigrated to their historic homeland in the same year.[211] The statistical information indicates that the number of ethnic Germans tended to be much smaller for other Central Asian countries for 1997. Uzbekistan, for instance, recorded the emigration of 917 ethnic Germans, Turkmenistan recorded 345, and Tajikistan, only 247.[212] The reason for this stark difference is not only the large proportion of forced resettlement of ethnic Germans primarily in Kazakhstan, but also the fact that many ethnic Germans had already emigrated in the earliest years of the independence of their countries of residence and at a time when Germany did not

---

209 Dietz, 2000:1.
210 IOM 1999:76.
211 IOM 1999:91.
212 Data taken from the 1999 IOM Report "Migration in the CIS 1997-1998."

yet require language proficiency for entry into Germany, i.e. prior to 1996. This is particularly true for Tajikistan where the outbreak of ethnic clashes and the Civil War in 1992 resulted in massive emigration and a sharp decline in the number of ethnic Germans. Whilst in 1989 33,000 ethnic Germans were registered as residing in Tajikistan,[213] the number of ethnic Germans and Jews who left Tajikistan between 1990 and 1992 amounted altogether to 230,000. [214]

The emigration of ethnic Germans was not the only migratory consequence of the Civil War in Tajikistan. The violent clashes of 1992-1997 led to other ethnic minorities as well thousands of Tajikistanis leaving the country. During this period, 697,653 Tajikistanis were registered as internally displaced, however the majority returned to their place of origin in 1997. Thousands fled to Afghanistan, Uzbekistan, Kazakhstan, Turkmenistan, and Russia. The Russian Federal Migration Service reported in 1998 that 50,192 refugees and 126,625 forced migrants were residing in the Russian Federation. The majority of those who had fled to countries other than Russia had repatriated to Tajikistan when the conflicting parties signed a peace treaty in 1997. Those Tajiks who had been granted refugee status in Russia stayed permanently and have, meanwhile, obtained Russian citizenship. In 1997-1998, together with half of the 60,000 Tajiks who had fled to Afghanistan from the Civil War, Tajikistan received approximately 2,500 Afghans who had fled from the armed conflicts in Afghanistan. These people have, meanwhile, obtained refugee status in Tajikistan.[215]

The Russian-speaking population continued emigrating from all the Central Asian republics. Kazakhstan, while experiencing a major outflow of population, allowed all persons with Kazakh ancestry residing outside the borders of the republic to return to their historic homeland. By the mid-1990s, notwithstanding the repatriation of approximately 160,000 ethnic Kazakhs from neighboring countries and due to large-scale emigration of ethnic minorities, the population of this country dropped from 17 million to 15 million. In 1998, the government of Kazakhstan implemented a state-sponsored repatriation program in order to alleviate the demographic crisis. The program was conceptualized to facilitate the settlement of repatriates (*oralman*) by offering assistance with employment, access to a number of social benefits, and support of repatriates through integration programs.[216]

Similar to Kazakhstan, albeit on a much smaller scale, Kyrgyzstan and Turkmenistan also allowed ethnic Kyrgyz and Turkmen migrants to return to their respective historic homelands from neighboring countries, although the governments have not yet opted to provide the returnees with financial support. The International Organization for Migration is currently working

---

213   IOM, 1999:139.
214   Bushkov, 2000:155.
215   IOM, 1999:139-140.
216   Darieva, 2005.

together with NGOs and the Kyrgyz government to promote the development of a legal framework for a return project of ethnic Kyrgyz called *kairylman* (returnee).

Poor ecological conditions around the evaporating Aral Sea (the Karakalpak Autonomous Province and the Xorazm Region in Uzbekistan) forced thousands to move to different areas. By 1997, the number of ecological migrants was reported to have reached 16,000. Besides the economic crisis affecting all of the republics of the former Soviet Union with the transition to a market economy, the governments of the Central Asian republics were confronted with domestic and foreign policy challenges. Managing the migration of the population was, hence, not at the top of their agenda. Although the newly independent countries adopted their own citizenship policies and introduced citizenship passports that enabled their residents to travel rather freely, challenges such as irregular migration, illegal border-crossing, and trafficking in human beings did not attract much attention. Only towards the end of the 1990s and the beginning of the 21st century did the governments start making efforts to solve these problems.[217] Apart from Kazakhstan and Turkmenistan, three countries of the region, *viz.* Kyrgyzstan, Tajikistan, and Uzbekistan, have witnessed a large outflow of irregular labor migrants to Russia. Until the end of the 1990s, Uzbekistan did not report on the state of labor migration to Russia, but approximately 50,000-60,000 people from Kyrgyzstan and as many as 250,000 from Tajikistan are estimated to have migrated annually to the Russian Federation in search of employment.[218]

We have seen in this chapter that labor migration from Central Asia to Russia as it exists today has been structured by a complex array of political and social factors. Through the historical trajectory of migrations from the earliest days of the Soviet Union until its demise in 1991, it has been illustrated that the population of the Soviet Union not only had strict constraints on movement, but was also subject to forced relocations between different regions. Nonetheless, Soviet citizens increasingly engaged in rural-to-urban migration, which expanded the urban population to a considerable extent. As far as Central Asia is concerned, it has been shown that the region continuously experienced as much in-migration as out-migration of people.

It has been illustrated in this chapter that labor migrants from Central Asia to Russia had already started to arrive during the Soviet period. The current flow of the labor force is therefore not an entirely new phenomenon. The party-state managed labor migration of Central Asia's employable population to Russia in the late 1970s and early 1980s was designed to enhance production through the cultivation of virgin lands. Together with Central Asian recruits in the Soviet Army in Russia and Central Asian students at Russian higher education institutions, this generation of pioneer labor

---

217   IOM report 1999 and 2002.
218   IOM report 1999.

migrants may have played a significant role in the formation of migrant networks.

In studying the current patterns of migration and, in particular, increased labor migration, we should bear in mind the ethnic heterogeneity of the population in this region. The three countries of origin (Kyrgyzstan, Tajikistan, and Uzbekistan) share a common Soviet past: it started with the annexation of their historical territories to the Russian Empire, the process of administrative territorial border demarcation in the 1920s and 1930s and the creation of nationalities by the Soviet state, and it continued as the states underwent the Sovietization processes, including the ideological project of 'friendship and brotherhood of nations' that gradually molded the society in the region. It is in view of these policies of migration, patterns of mobility, and state ideologies which tied the receiving and sending states together that it is necessary to conceptualize transnationalization in Central Asia and Russia as post-Soviet. Chapter 4 will serve to elaborate on the conceptual framework of post-Soviet transnationalization which will guide the present research.

4. Conceptualizing Post-Soviet Transnationalization

We have seen in Chapter 3 that during the seventy years of the Soviet period, the three sending states, Kyrgyzstan, Tajikistan, and Uzbekistan, underwent more or less similar changes in terms of social, political, cultural, educational, and economic development.[219] As was mentioned at the beginning of this work, since the time these three countries obtained independence until now when labor migration movements have reached an unprecedented magnitude, each state has gone through a different path of transformation and developed different policies towards its migrants. The task of this chapter is to situate transnational kinship in the broader spectrum of the transformation processes that followed the demise of the USSR. This will be done in the following order:

a) Referring to the historical path of some of the major immigration countries represented by former colonial rulers, this chapter will demonstrate that the former USSR that encompassed the territory of its predecessor, the Russian Empire, adopted different attitudes towards its minority populations than, for instance, France and the United Kingdom.
b) Studies on post-Soviet transition point to the socio-political significance of kinship ties in political development after the fall of the USSR. Drawing on the literature that specifically addresses the issues of personal networks, kinship, clans, patronages, and other informal practices that have exerted influence on the political developments, regime structures, and decision-making processes in the states in question, this part of the study focuses on the crucial role of kinship ties and the way their dimension is conceptualized in the scholarship on post-Soviet transition processes. The Central Asian states will be shifted to the foreground, although considerable attention will be paid to Russia as well. By referring to sources on the importance of kinship ties that shape the political and social spheres in Russia and Central Asia, I wish to describe the terrain on which transnational ties between the two poles of the migration trajectories emerged.
c) Further, keeping in mind the body of research on post-Soviet transformation studies, the scholarship on informal institutions and organizations in other regions, which focuses on these informal institutions and their significant impact on the course of their social and political development, will also be taken into account. I will suggest that, in the context of the Central Asian states (Kyrgyzstan, Tajikistan, and Uzbekistan) from which the majority of Central Asian labor migrants in Russia originates, kinship as an analytical unit should be distinguished from

---

219   Collins, 2006:356.

other informal institutions. The argument in favor of this approach is that kinship represents an inherent part of social, economic, and political life. Categorizing kinship ties as informal institutions would blur their interactions with other informal institutions, thus not endowing them with sufficient importance.

4.1. A Framework for Understanding Post-Soviet Transnationalization

4.1.1. The Unusual Case of the Former Soviet Union

International migration studies have largely dealt with prototypical migration patterns such as between Latin America and the United States, South Asia and the United Kingdom, Sub-Saharan Africa and France, Latin America and Spain, North Africa and the Mediterranean countries, Turkey and Germany, etc. These patterns are usually associated with a colonial history and reconfigurations of immigration policies of the empires following decolonization in the twentieth century or with labor migration encouraged by receiving states such as the case of *braceros* – Mexican laborers in the United States or *Gastarbeiter* – Turkish workers in Germany.[220] Complementary to these patterns is a lesser-known model in which a labor force from economically underprivileged former Soviet countries is being engaged in low-paid jobs in Russia. I argue that transnational labor migration as it occurs specifically on the territory of the former USSR should be perceived in terms of post-Soviet transnationalization, emphasizing the Soviet past as a mark of distinction from the aforementioned trajectories. In a frequently cited paragraph, Glick-Schiller defines the phenomenon of transnationalism as follows:

> We have defined transnationalism as the processes by which immigrants build social fields that link together their country of origin and their country of settlement. Immigrants who build such social fields are designated "transmigrants." Transmigrants develop and maintain multiple relations – familial, economic, social, organizational, religious and political that span borders. Transmigrants take actions, make decisions, and feel concerns and develop identities within social networks that connect them to two or more societies simultaneously.[221]

---

220 Between 1942 and 1964, around 350,000 Mexican peasants crossed the US/Mexican border annually to engage themselves in seasonal agricultural labor. They contributed to a large extent to the agricultural industry of the USA. Similarly, in the 1960s and 1970s, up to 130,000 workers yearly were employed in the German industrial sector. For more on the historical perspectives of international labor migration to highly developed countries, see Castles and Miller, 1993; Pries, 2001.
221 Glick-Schiller *et al*, 1992: 1-2, also cited by Mahler, 1998:74 and Portes, 1997: PAGE. Glick-Schiller *et al*. later distanced themselves from the term "transmigrants." Here, "transmigrants" should be seen as coterminous with "transnational migrants." A separate section of this chapter will deal with migration theories and definitions of terms applied in this study.

Post-Soviet transnationalization comprises a number of complex processes such as the change from a socialist to a market economy, state building, attempts at democratization or the failure thereof, resulting in strengthening of authoritarian regimes, as well as the allocation or distribution of power among the former Soviet elites as a result of decentralization. Above all, rapid changes in the balance between demand and supply of low-paid labor should be mentioned, not only in the economically and industrially privileged republics ('centers') and less supported republics ('peripheries') of the former USSR, but also between the urban and rural center-peripheries, if we were to borrow terms from neo-Marxist dependency theorists.[222] The central argument about post-Soviet transnationalization is that it was geared, i.e. structured, if not programmed, by the very policies of the centralized state in the USSR from the time of its foundation until its dissolution. The multiple transnational relations spanning at least two nation-states, which we often encounter in the literature on transnationalism, are, in this case, taking place on the territory that formerly represented one multinational country.

Scholars of migrant transnationalism suggest that labor mobility between former colonial powers and independent ex-colonies should be perceived in terms of the global distribution of power, thus pointing towards capitalist modes of production and capital accumulation.[223] While I generally agree with this interpretation, there are elements concerning the citizenship policies of the receiving states and the geographic proximity between the receiving and sending states that distinguish the case of the former USSR. Despite the annexation of the geographical territory now known as the Central Asian states to the Russian Empire in the 19th century, the characteristics associated with colonial empires and independent states that emerged in the 20th century are not the same as those in the newly independent states which emerged after the demise of the USSR.

Looking at the history of how empires restructured their systems of citizenship in continental Europe in the period after WWI and in the years following WWII can perhaps shed more light on the case analyzed in this paper. In so doing, the exclusionist/inclusionist policies that post-imperial nations created for the subjects in their colonies to acquire citizenship should be examined more closely. For this purpose, France and Great Britain are perhaps the most feasible receiving states that could be discussed. Following the abolition of slavery in 1794, until decolonization in the twentieth century, the French Republican colonial regimes applied the principle that former slaves from the Caribbean, Africa, and/or Indochina should be given the possibility of becoming citizens of the Republic. At the same time, assimilation through citizenship with full rights was not to occur immediately but step by step through the processes of education and modernization. Their understanding was that colonial people were not capable of assimilating unless they became

---

222   Goss and Lindquist, 1995:7.
223   Glick-Schiller *et Al.*, 1992.

'civilized' and 'educated.' Citizenship was, hence, granted to few, usually to the elite and those who relinquished their indigenous civil status, whereas others who fell short of the assimilation requirements were considered unqualified to become citizens.[224] One could recall the historical example of the Senegalese soldiers whose recruitment in WWI was possible only under the condition that France made them citizens, a demand advanced by Blaise Diagne, the Senegalese deputy. A further indicator of biased citizenship regulations at the turn of the twentieth century in France is that of Algerian Muslims who had to renounce their Islamic civic status in order to obtain French citizenship.[225]

In Great Britain, we can see the conditions under which full citizenship was made possible to former colonial subjects only after WWII.[226] In the nineteenth and the twentieth centuries, *jus soli* in the territory of the United Kingdom and 'allegiance to the crown' were the predominant conditions for obtaining citizenship, and until 1948 Britain referred to holders of the British citizenship as 'British subjects.' Further, individuals born of a British father outside of the territory of the United Kingdom could not automatically claim citizenship rights, but the father had to prove a *jus soli* status as well 'allegiance to the crown.' Gosewinkel points out that when the citizenship law changed in 1948 and the term 'subjects' was to be used equally with 'Commonwealth citizens,' the Conservative Party opposed this suggestion that had been made by the Labour government.[227] They argued that the term 'citizen' had an unhistorical connotation and would not express the individual's loyal relationship to the monarch. 'Citizenship' was, according to them, a term associated with equality and was inappropriate to be used for people from different cultural backgrounds. In spite of these changes, the shared status of equality was at variance with individual discrimination on the basis of racial background that had existed during the colonial era. When citizens from the former colonies started migrating to the United Kingdom to exercise their right to freedom of movement and had ambitions to reside there permanently, Britain added restrictions to its immigration policy. (The new immigration act of 1981, by the way, stipulated birth in the territory of the United Kingdom *and* parentage by at least one British citizen for acquiring citizenship. This legislation highlighted the territorial supremacy of the United Kingdom and ethnic filtering of migration flows.[228])

The citizenship legislation of the French and British empires is in a way similar in that the colonial citizenship laws differentiated individuals on the basis of their ethnic backgrounds. By contrast, the establishment of the Soviet Union was influenced largely by the implementation of national self-determination, resulting in the construction of a multi-national and multi-

---

224 Cooper, 2005:175, Dubois, 2000:14.
225 Castles and Miller, 1993:131, Cooper, 2005:175.
226 Joppke, 1996.
227 Gosewinkel, 2008:104.
228 Gosewinkel, 2008:105.

ethnic state.²²⁹ By 1922 when the USSR was established, it inherited from the former Russian Empire a contiguous continental territory inhabited by heterogeneous ethnicities and languages. As far as the legislative framework is concerned, Article 3 of the 1924 Constitution stated: "Everybody who is in the Soviet Union will be recognized as a citizen of the Soviet Union until he proves that he possesses a foreign citizenship." Accordingly, based on the principle of *presumed citizenship*, an individual would be deemed a Soviet citizen as long as he personally did not claim otherwise.²³⁰ In addition, the Soviet Union granted citizenship to every individual, provided that he or she was allied with the working class and belonged to an oppressed people.²³¹ Article 2 stated that "persons who exercise their occupation in the territory of the Soviet Union and belong to the working class or to the class of peasants who are not employers, are possessed of all rights of Soviet citizens."²³²

What is relevant in the discussion of the post-Soviet approach to transnationalization is that for many actual and potential migrants from Central Asia to Russia, the ideology that prevailed through seventy years of multinational USSR of having equal citizens under the banner of 'friendship' and 'brotherhood of the nations' has not yet been forgotten. In view of the absence of national territorial borders *per se* during the Soviet era, unlike in postcolonial migration movements, terms such as 'home' and 'host' countries still sound strange to many ears.²³³ Hence, while post-colonial migration patterns indicate a colonial past, the post-Soviet type pattern is clearly rooted in Soviet history.

4.1.2. The Soviet Era and the Residuals of Sovietization Policies

Following the history of the emergence of the Soviet state and linking to the citizenship issues discussed in Chapter 3, we should mention aspects of Sovietization policies, as they lay at the core of the centralized system of the USSR. It is important to summarize them, as they became advantageous for many individuals in their migratory undertakings later on after the collapse of the USSR. Owing to the centralized system, the key factors that still shape the quality of the post-Soviet pattern are Russification, promotion of the

---

229 More on self-definition and new passport regulations, Hirsch, 2005:292-293.
230 See *Sobranie zakonov SSSR* 1924 (collection of legislation of the USSR), as cited in Ginsburgs, 1963:13.
231 Gosewinkel, 2008:103 and Soviet Union 1932, Article 20 of the RSFSR. This is not to deny the deportation of Germans, Poles, Estonians, Latvians, Finns, Bulgarians, and Greeks during Stalin's regime in the 1930s (Hirsch, 2005: 291). Here, historians such as Cooper draw our attention to the fact that by suppressing nationhood, the state was indeed institutionalizing it by dividing itself into fifty national homelands and marking each person's ethnic nationality in his/her citizenship passport according to his/her descent. (Cooper, 2005:81).
232 See *Sobranie zakonov SSSR* 1924 (collection of legislation of the USSR), as cited in Ginsburgs, 1963:13.
233 Interviews with naturalized Central Asian immigrants in Russia and labor migrants in Russia and Central Asia. For more on 'brotherhood of the nations,' see Sahadeo, 2007.

Russian language, compulsory military service, and a Communist Party career.

1. *Russification.* Western Sovietologists use the term Sovietization to explain the social policies of modernization and industrialization that were implemented in tandem with the spread of Russian language (Russianization) and culture within the former USSR. *Russification* is a term applied to the process in which non-Russians allegedly "lost their ethnic identity in favor of identification with Russia culture."[234] I am inclined to use Russification in a broader sense and argue that it is also applicable to the population with Central Asian origins in Russia holding Russian citizenship, as well as those who were born in Central Asia and use Russian as their primary language due to the fact that they graduated from a Russian secondary school, often encouraged by their parents or caretakers, who in turn favored the Russian language and had had a Russian/Soviet education or belonged to the Soviet intelligentsia. The Russification process in Central Asia was more successful in those areas that were more modernized, industrialized, and urbanized between the 1950s and 1970s. The proportion of Russians increased together with measures taken towards the improvement of the level of education. At the same time, as education was promoted (more in urban than in rural areas), young graduates (especially those from Russian secondary schools in Central Asia) were encouraged to study at higher education institutions in Russia.

2. *Promoting Russian Language Acquisition in Non-Russian Schools.* In the republics of the Soviet Union in which the proportion of the Slavic population was lower than the indigenous one, the language used in the education system was the native language of the titular nation, particularly in Central Asia and the Caucasus. Starting from the late 1950s, new Soviet education reforms were introduced that required the increase and intensification of the Russian language. By the end of the 1970s, according to the Russian Language Institute of the Academy of Science of the USSR, the last phase of the five-year plan of the Ministry of Education was the achievement of total bilingualism in the Soviet Union and making Russian everyone's second native language.[235] Following these requirements and considering the status of the Russian language as the language of interethnic communication among the peoples of the Soviet Union, the Soviet central government was determined to promote learn-

---

[234] Dostal and Knippenberg, 1979:197. By contrast to arguments about the lost ethnic identity of non-Russians, described as Russification, subjects interviewed for this researched admitted that they while they were "obrusevshie" (Russian for "Russified"), and probably some of them no longer used the language of their parents as a primary language, they did not deny originating from Central Asia.
[235] Solchanyk, 1982:1.

ing of the Russian language among the non-Russian population and extend Russian classes to all levels of the Soviet education system by the late 1970s.[236]

Notwithstanding these efforts, even during the early years of independence of the Central Asian states from 1991, the role of the Russian language started to diminish. The situation was aggravated particularly in the rural areas of Kyrgyzstan, Tajikistan, and Uzbekistan. Kyrgyzstan was recovering from both an inter-ethnic conflict that flared up in 1990 and an economic crisis, Tajikistan was struggling (to say the least) with a very serious armed conflict, and Uzbekistan had oriented itself towards modernization measures similar to those of Turkey. To make matters worse, after the fall of the Soviet Union, the elites in each newly independent state had their own priorities for the employment of professionals. The founding of the new nation-states and nationalism resulted in the ethnic Russian population no longer finding itself a privileged minority. Soon after 1991, these people started returning to Russia.[237] Hence, the current situation of labor migrants is such that the generation born after approximately the mid-1980s and coming from provincial and rural areas is no longer fluent in Russian and its members may often not speak Russian at all when they make the initial trip to Russia.

3. *Compulsory Military Service in the Soviet Union.* As also noted by Sovietological scholarship, it was mandatory for Central Asian young men to learn Russian in the Red Army.[238] Even though the level of Russian taught during secondary education in the rural areas of Central Asia was considerably lower than in urban centers, the average 24 months during which young recruits had to speak Russian, regardless of the military service location, was a sufficient time frame for them to return at least with an intermediate level of Russian. An entire generation of respondents interviewed for this study served in the Red Army and stayed in Russia. Their participation as job brokers for the younger generation of labor migrants or in taking leadership roles in diasporic organizations, often referred to as *obshchina* (community), has been crucial.[239]

4. *Political Careers in the Communist Party.* From early on, the Communist Party acknowledged the Soviet Union to be a multinational country which shared a similar ideology of liberating oppressed nations. Within the process of liberation, the socialists' goal was to blend them all into one Soviet nation. The Soviet nationality policy created nations that had not previously existed in these forms and assigned ethnic groups admin-

---

236 *Ibid.*
237 Brubaker, 2000.
238 see also Fleming, 1975:37.
239 Labor migrants representing the 1980s generation often mentioned having followed a close kinsman who had served in the Soviet military service.

istrative borders and territorial units. The policy of *korenizatsia* (nativization) was implemented with the aim of creating local indigenous elites, trained as party cadres to take party and state posts. Korenizatsia also entailed Russification of the titular *nomenklatura*.[240] While Collins comments on the communiqués on appointments and dismissal of cadres between Moscow and the republics, what seems to be forgotten in such observations is the frequency of party and state officials' trips to Russian cities where they attended training, conferences, and seminars. Among the informants for this study there are some who settled in Russia as they successfully pursued a party career.

An aspect which is not quite coherent with the structural dimensions, yet is of great relevance, is knowledge of the destination country. As mentioned in the preceding sections, by the time migrants leave for Russia for the first time, they are likely to have developed tacit knowledge about their country of destination, not only because information is transferred to them through the social ties that facilitate or arrange the initial trip, but simply because they are, to a certain degree, familiar with Russian culture, politics, literature, and media. Certainly, such knowledge about the country of destination varies according to the educational background of migrants, and what they learned at school about the Russian society might not correspond to what they experience as a labor migrant.[241] What indeed matters is that a uniform education system during the Soviet era provided them with certain knowledge about the country of destination. In this context, the role of the mass media should not go unnoticed. Russian channels have been broadcasting continuously in all parts of Central Asia since the development of television and pro-government newspapers and magazines, at least, have been accessible to the mainstream population. Again, the level at which some migrants are affected by the aforementioned factors varies.

We can now advance this approach and find linkages to the transnational paradigm of migration theories. Faist elaborates four fundamental reasons for the emergence of transnational social spaces.[242] It is important to mention these reasons in combination with the specificity of the case in point. The first reason for the evolution of transnational spaces is the increase of cumulation. Rooted in pre-migration ties and migrant and migration networks, transnational social spaces connect the space between the places of origin and destination. We have seen in the earlier part of this paper that, in the case of the former USSR, the places of origin and destination basically constituted the same country.

---

240   Ewing, 1977:4, Collins, 2006:90.
241   This being argued, many among the subjects interviewed complained that because of their illegal status, they do not have a chance to enjoy public life more, i.e. participate at cultural events or go sightseeing.
242   Faist, 2000a:314.

The second reason is the macro conditions such as international travel, communication, and liberal policies of immigration states that provide fertile ground for transnational social spaces to develop. As illustrated above, the USSR had prepared the conditions for migration movements to develop after its fall. Faist points out that immigration states that do not enforce assimilation or assimilation-return policies are likely to contribute to the strengthening of immigrant transnationalization.[243] The Russian policy makers are currently preoccupied with the development of policies that would manage migration, such as the introduction of citizenship laws and setting and resetting of labor migrant quotas for blue-collar jobs from the so-called 'near abroad' countries. So far, assimilation measures are taken only within the framework of citizenship laws where language proficiency is required. In addition, the means and the routes of travel to the majority of destination places have largely been inherited from the Soviet period.

The third reason is characterized by the different dynamics accompanying economic, political, and cultural transnationalization and can be linked with the second reason, in that it can include the expansion of travel and communication facilities that develop in tandem with the mobility of the labor force. One needs to take into account the speed with which new air and railway routes, as well as financial transfer agencies, are burgeoning between Central Asian and Russian cities. The emergence of labor agencies, as well as the expansion of mobile and IP communications, which offer special deals for long-distance calls between the places of origin and destination, complement this.

The fourth reason has to do with the future of transnational spaces. It is argued that as long as the relations between the countries at the two poles of migration are not endangered by armed conflicts, transnational social spaces are sustained.[244] Although I would use caution in making premature statements about the future of labor migration, the relations between Russia and sending states in Central Asia (particularly Kyrgyzstan and Tajikistan) in the last five years have shown that the countries are likely to combine efforts in adapting their migration policies to the conditions of the mass labor mobility.

Along with the description of the reasons for the evolution of transnational social spaces, it is necessary to analyze the developing stages of transnational social spaces.[245] The first stage is characterized by secondary consequences of international migration involving the first generation of migrants. It is at this stage that individuals form networks and institutions at both ends of their trajectories, thereby engendering chain migration. Faist reminds us that migration is not a mere movement between places of origin and destination with few social and material ties. Post-colonial and hegemonic linkages that were established during the period predating the mass migration move-

---

243   *Ibid.*
244   *Ibid.*
245   Faist, 2000a: 201-202.

ments contribute to their dynamic growth or, in the case of the former Soviet territory, this growth can be attributed partly to reactivation and extension of such ties. During a second stage, which is marked by a generational sequence of migrants, transnational social spaces develop from chain migration, comprising cultural practices of not only the two countries of migration but also elements from additional countries. Moreover, through the maintenance and densification of the ties between the places of origin and destination, first generation migrants contribute greatly to the cumulation of migration processes.[246] The scope of migratory movements in what Gunnar Myrdal refers to as the "Soviet orbit" might require overcoming challenges related to the above-mentioned phases if we were to elaborate more on cumulative causation. The reason is that the fall of the USSR and labor induced migratory movements occurring thereafter on its former territory involve complex stages. As illustrated earlier in this chapter, there is an entire generation of ethnic Central Asians who left their places of birth for Russian cities between the 1960s and 1980s. Some obtained their education at a Russian university and stayed; others served in the Soviet Army and, in addition, pursued a career in the Communist Party and were promoted by their employers. It is in this context that we can see such educational elites as forerunners for the establishment of transnational ties. Hence, unlike the labor migrants from Mexico to the USA or Turkey to Germany, the very first generation of migrants from Central Asia to Russia were not crossing national borders and therefore not involved in international migration. There is also an entire generation of individuals who, during the decades preceding the fall of the USSR, traveled between different places and engaged themselves in shuttle trade, for instance selling fruit and vegetables during the high season. These traders in turn continued their small businesses in the years following the collapse of the USSR, when new national territorial borders emerged in 1991.[247] Hence the self-feeding processes of transnational social spaces can, on the one hand, be seen as taking place in the mid-1990s, when the social spaces of the Central Asian "shuttle migrants" or small traders turned transnational, or more precisely trans-state, with the demarcation of state borders (which, in turn, were based on Soviet administrative borders) and each newly independent state introduced citizenship passports.[248] Hence, one could argue that in this case we are dealing with an 'invisible generation.' On the other hand, empirical data collected for the current project shows that by the early 21st century, the influx of low-skilled labor into Russia had increased dramatically. While there is a generation of children born among the so-called Soviet education migrants in the 1970s and 1980s, who grew up as residents in the RSFSR and later became Russian citizens, a different type of genera-

---

246 *Ibid.*
247 The problems with the demarcation of national state borders between Central Asian states are yet to be fully resolved.
248 Faist, 2006; Faist, 2007.

tional succession is observed among labor migrants of the late 1990s and early 21st century, occurring in the form of children joining their parents in Russia as early as at the age of 14. Therefore, unlike, for instance, Massey *et al.* who demonstrate various stages of out-migration patterns from 19 Mexican communities, it is a cumbersome task to determine and label precise stages of out-migration of pioneers from Central Asia to Russia. [249]

In this chapter I have underlined the need for conceptualizing post-Soviet transnationalization. In an historical perspective I have shown that the French and British empires, on one hand, and the Russian Empire and its Soviet successor, on the other, differ in many ways with respect to citizenship policies that were implemented towards their colonial subjects. A further point which should be addressed here is the development of transnationalization in the post-Soviet context in terms of top-down or bottom-up directions. The post-Soviet transnational space demonstrates a case in which processes of "transnationalism from above" and "transnationalism from below," often seen in such a dyadic relationship in the research related to other geographical places, converge. Sarah Mahler's view of "transnationalism from above" is that "multinational corporations, media, commodization ('mediascapes,' 'technoscapes,' and 'finanscapes' in Appadurai's terms [1990: 196-299]) and other macro-level structures and processes that transcend two or more states are not produced and projected equally in all areas, but are controlled by powerful elites who seek, although do not necessarily find, political, economic and social dominance in the world."[250] Taking Mahler's observation into account, we can note that the centralized system of the Soviet policies created the framework for processes that can be characterized as "from above." "Transnationalism from below" is seen in "the ways that everyday practices of ordinary people, their feelings and understandings of their conditions of existence, often modify those very conditions and thereby shape rather than merely reflect new modes of urban culture."[251]

Before proceeding to the next Part of the book, I will summarize the preceding chapters. Chapter 1 was devoted to the introduction to this book including the research topic and state of the art of migration research. In Chapter 2, in which I discussed the theories and methods applied in this study, I chose kinship as a unit of analysis and embedded it in a framework that includes formal organizations and informal institutions. I have made a proposition for a complex triadic relationship that bolsters the transnational ties between Central Asian sending states and Russia. Chapter 3 on the historical background of migrations during the Soviet period and immediately after the demise of the USSR illustrated the strict control the party-state had over the mobility of its population. Given not only the historical conditions pre-existing during the Soviet period and the events that turned internal

---

249 Massey *et al.*, 1994.
250 Mahler, 1998:67.
251 Smith, M.P. 1992: 493-494 as quoted by Mahler, 1998:67.

movements of population into international migrations in 1991, but also the circumstances under which labor migration from Central Asia to Russia took on a massive scale, there was a need to conceptualize post-Soviet transnationalization as an emerging pattern complementary to those that have, up to now, attracted the attention of migration scholars. In Chapter 4 we have seen that the scholarship on the transformation processes of former Soviet countries and Latin America underlines the essential role of kinship and informal institutions in state-policy relationships. It can be suggested therefore that labor migration be referred to as part of the transformation process of the Soviet successor states. We can now proceed to examine the roles that kin members play in the transnational life-world and in so doing, pay close attention to kinship ties as linchpins for maintaining transnational ties among multiple nation-states.

Part Two

Analyzing Transnational Migrant Practices and Filial and Conjugal Relationships in Kinship

5. Sending Cash Home: Monetary Remittance Practices of Central Asian Transnational Migrants in Russia

Monetary remittances are central for reciprocity between kin members and hence crucial for maintaining the dense ties which contribute to migrant transnationalism.The purpose of this chapter is to explore remittance practices of Central Asian transnational labor migrants in Russia to their countries of origin. As was discussed in the introduction, the importance of earning money to support kin members became very evident during observations of the day-to-day life of migrants and their families in both the countries of origin and of destination. Personal narratives of migrants on their experiences of cash transfers have provided additional insight into the significance of their day-to-day struggles and the social ties needed for every step from finding employment in Russia to the actual accomplishment of sending cash home, irrespective of official or unofficial channels.

Analyses of monetary remittance practices in the scholarship on migration and development tend to divide financial transactions of migrants into *formal* and *informal* types. *Formal* transactions are those carried out through banking systems and money transfer services. Conversely, any interactions or arrangements which circumvent the banks are usually deemed as *informal* transfers. This distinction is fairly common, and the working papers published by the World Bank and the International Monetary Fund in particular contain sections defining the difference between formal and informal monetary transfers. These contributions also underline the limits of precise statistics on migrant transfers due to practices that circumvent banking systems.[252]

Migrant social practices involving remittance transfers between receiving countries and sending regions such as South-East Asia, East Asia, Maghreb, and Latin America have been extensively analyzed. A general description of informal value transfer systems provided by scholars such as Kapur elaborates on *hawala* and *hundi* transfers as being practiced in South Asia, *fei chi'en* in China, *Phoe kuan* in Thailand, or *casa de cambio* among Latin American migrants.[253] The objective here is not to provide yet another contribution to the literature by discussing the problems related to formal or informal remittances, because substantial work and criticism have already addressed this issue. Pieke *et al.* for instance, in their critical discussions on formal and informal remittance systems, point out that there are conceptual problems with the definitions of these terms. Based on the data accumulated in African, Caribbean, and Pacific countries, they demonstrate that under strict state-imposed regulations, certain informal systems become "form-

---

252 Cf. Hernández-Coss, 2005.
253 Kapur, 2004:8.

alized" or, vice versa, there are certain situations in which formal remittance systems are marginalized and become informal following the implementation of new legislative measures.[254] Using empirical evidence, this chapter will explain that invisible as it may seem, each individual cash transfer to family members can involve complex social practices. The undocumented status of migrants in the host country often leads to informal social organization and the seeking of more creative ways to overcome obstacles that prevent them from carying out cash transactions. This chapter will, furthermore, describe practices involved with receiving of cash transfers. In so doing, it aims to give voice to the recipients, i.e. dependent family members who are as important in reciprocal relations as the remitters.

5.1. Informal and Formal Cash Transfer Mechanisms

Before analyzing remittance practices between Central Asia and Russia, the relevant arguments laid out in the theoretical chapter should be briefly summarized. This part of the study attempted to explain the dynamic interplay between formal organizations and informal institutions in the post-Soviet context. Following Helmke and Levitsky, informal institutions were perceived as "socially shared unwritten rules that are created, communicated and enforced outside of officially sanctioned channels." [255] It was also argued that in Central Asia and Russia, formality in terms of legality should be viewed as a viable category. It has been observed that migrants and their family members face opportunities and constraints in their everyday lives that range from formal to informal across institutions and organizations. It will be seen in this chapter that, similar to the formal organizations and informal institutions discussed previously, the boundary between formal and informal remitting practices often becomes fuzzy as the social practices related to cash transfers are scrutinized.

As El Qorchi *et al.* argue, informal cash transfers are stable in countries where formal banking systems have failed.[256] Interestingly, such practices also occur where formal banking systems once failed but have recovered as a result of economic growth. Since the economic crash of the mid-1990s and the devaluation of the Russian *ruble* in 1998, the steady growth of seasonal labor migration between Russia and the former Soviet Union republics has helped the banking systems start to regain trust among the population.[257]

---

254 Pieke *et al.* 2005:16.
255 Helmke and Levitsky, 2003:9.
256 El Qorchi *et al.*, 2003.
257 This changed again during the economic crisis of 2008-2009. Even if wiring cash through so-called official channels is currently being used on a regular basis, the population in Central Asia – especially migrant-dependent families – have distanced themselves from saving their money in the banks. In view of these changes, it remains important to observe migrant cash transfer practices closely, as they try to adapt to new economic situations.

In the context of Afghanistan and Pakistan, where informal *hawala* systems function as a reliable method of remitting cash, formal banking systems are challenged. Especially in the case of Afghanistan, where the financial sector has been utterly devastated in the course of armed clashes over three decades, reforms are yet to be implemented and the infrastructure yet to be developed. The situation in Central Asia is different. Following the criteria of the international donor organizations, Olimova in her study on Tajikistan notes that in 2003, 54.8 percent of the migrants transferred through banks, 33.2 percent through friends, 24.8 percent transported the currency personally, and only 5 percent through *hawala*.[258] Although the three sending countries (Kyrgyzstan, Tajikistan, and Uzbekistan) are geographically close to Afghanistan and Pakistan where the informal *hawala* transfer system is a common practice, in the countries where the current research has been carried out *hawala* is very rarely associated with monetary transactions. Olimova specifically mentions that in Central Asia the method of *hawala* is used by Tajik labor migrants in Russia,[259] however I, personally, have not been able to find anything similar to such methods. At the same time, it should be mentioned that a black market for foreign currency exchange exists in all three sending countries. Parallel to the black market, the personnel at official exchange offices are often engaged in unofficial business. Hence if the personnel at an official exchange office are engaged in practices similar to *hawala*, either I have not been able to gain access to such individuals or such practices are not called *hawala*. The use of the term *hawala* is a reminder of another small yet important detail: *remittances* in the families are not referred to as such. As Chapter 7 will show, receiving families call them 'Russian money.' In the Province of Khatlon (TAJ) I heard *sumi Rossiia*, among Uzbek speakers *Rossiiani puli* (as in "Rossiiani puliga kun ko'ramiz" or "We live on Russian money") or *Rossiia aqshasy* in Kyrgyz.

5.2. Monetary Transactions and Social Ties

The interviews with Central Asian labor migrants have indicated that migrants are likely to use both informal ties and banks to send cash to their families from Russia. If a close relative or a friend is leaving to go home, migrants send some money with him or her, partly because they feel they should take advantage of not paying any transaction costs and partly because they feel their families back home might anticipate that they would send cash. For instance, a family of migrants whom I observed at the wholesale market of Mytishinskiy in Moscow sends cash and gifts with shuttle migrants. The shuttle migrants, or petty traders as they are also called, commute between

---

258 Olimova, 2005:11.
259 Olimova, 2005:14.

Moscow and various cities of Uzbekistan in small buses. For a box of 20 kilos of gifts and some cash, a shuttle migrant earns roughly 50 US dollars.

Those migrants who said that they did not send money through banks or family ties at all said that they preferred to use the services of the so-called *posrednik*s. *Posrednik* is a word which means mediator or intermediary in Russian and is applied to a person, or oftentimes an organized network of persons (pl. *posrediniki*), who facilitate(s) monetary transfers through informal ties. While some migrants prefer to keep the mediator's identity as anonymous as possible, others admit that it is frequently the case that train conductors agree to deliver cash and packages. Since the Soviet period, train conductors have practiced transporting goods and money to earn extra cash. While in the case of remittances, the Russian word *posrednik* (mediator) is an overarching term also used also for people who smuggle cash across borders, it can also be applied to job brokers or mediators who "organize" the registrations or residence permits for migrants. Although, for safety reasons, no interview with such cash middlemen was possible during the fieldwork, migrants and their family members were willing to talk about their experiences when I asked them questions.

5.2.1. Legal Status and Brokerage Practices of Women

The migrants' choices and practices of sending cash to their families are closely linked to their legal status. During the fieldwork in Moscow in September 2005 and from August-September 2006 in St. Petersburg as well as in Astrakhan in June 2007, the majority of the migrants with whom I spoke had no legal status.[260] Considering that my informants were residing in Russia illegally and were often afraid to leave their place of residence, I was astonished that the transfers they were making were often through banks.[261] Frequently, their colleagues or friends who had legal status would go to the bank and wire cash on behalf of undocumented migrants. Faced with administrative constraints and difficulties with corrupt law enforcement agents in Russia, undocumented migrants come up with creative ways to organize the transfer of money. What goes unnoticed is the role of female brokerage services and their practices. During the interviews carried out with representatives of the NGOs in the city of Khujand (TAJ), one of my informants told an interesting anecdote about monetary transfer practices of Tajikistani labor migrants.

---

260 Due to the new migration law that came into force in January 2007, Russia has been introducing strict measures against illegal migration. While some migrants are voluntarily going through the legalization processes, others still hold false residency permits. During the last series of interviews from February-March 2008, far more migrants told me that they had a legal status or had even obtained Russian citizenship.

261 Undocumented migrants of Mexican origin in the US, according to the calculations of Amuedo-Dorantes and Pozo, prefer non-banking methods of transferring and thus do not have to go through procedures in which they are required to show identification documents (2005:16).

I know of undocumented migrants who go to someone called *jenshchina vestern yunion*.²⁶² These are women who have a legal status. They have a valid registration or even Russian citizenship. The migrants pay them a small amount for going to the bank and making a transfer through the Western Union. It is often the case that these women make one transfer for several people. They come back with a transfer number and the workers can call their families to notify them about remittances. (Komil, b. 1966)

The practice of having a female coordinator in a group of Tajikistani migrants in some large Russian cities occurs often indeed. In Moscow, in the wholesale market of Mytishinsky, migrants described a female coordinator who takes orders from migrants of various ethnic groups. The Russian employment market for cheap labor is a terrain of tight competition – especially during economic crises – among various ethnic, regional, and kinship groups which, in turn, are often supported by authoritative persons and patrons.²⁶³ Having a coordinator enables illegal migrants to have confidence in one person within their narrow circle. This person is also responsible for going to a commercial center and buying groceries for other co-workers. If the people fulfilling the functions of a coordinator are caught and/or detained by the police despite their legal registration, the 'fine' they pay to bribe the police is compensated collectively by the group that sent them from the working and living compound. This is notably the case in large cities such as Moscow and St.Petersburg where police are, according to my interlocutors, more notorious than elsewhere.

I had the impression that women find creative ways to overcome their daily obstacles. The female migrant who hosted me in Moscow during my fieldwork told me about her plans to get pregnant. One evening, as we were chatting in a circle of female migrants, her close friend who was, at the time, in her fourth month of pregnancy, told me that her belly often protects her from policemen. She said that pregnant women in small networks are often sent to run errands because it is often the case that when policemen control them, they 'leave them alone' out of pity instead of extorting bribes from them out of respect for these future mothers.²⁶⁴

5. 3. *The Somewhat Different Collective Remittances*

In migration scholarship the term *collective remittances* is used to signify the joint efforts of migrants to achieve a common goal in their homeland (actual

---

262   Russian for literally *Western Union Woman*.
263   See Chapter 10 on patron-client ties.
264   Field notes in Moscow, September 2005.

or imagined), be it political, religious, or related to development projects.[265] One of the findings during observations of Central Asian labor migrants has been the practice of a different type of collective remittance, namely transfer of collective earnings in order to reduce security risks and transaction costs. For example, Faridun, to whom I was introduced in Russia during my fieldwork in 2006, was a Tajik man in his mid-40s. He hires a group of male construction workers to build villas. Faridun was introduced to me as a job broker. After having analyzed his behavior and attitude to his workers more thoroughly, I have categorized him as a migrant-patron.[266] During our interview, he told me at my request, how he had come to Russia and how he started his own small business. At the end of his personal account I asked him if I could know more about his workers. For Faridun, remitting cash to families plays a central role in the entire process of labor migration, so that he himself feels responsible for making the bank transfers on behalf of clients within his patronage. Excerpts:

Delia: You said at the beginning of our conversation that you were a brigadier[267], you even referred to yourself as a master (*usto*) ...

Faridun: (interrupts) Look I am everything: I am an architect of these villas since I draw plans and make sketches, I am a brigade leader or human resources manager, it is called these days: I hire these people.

Delia: How many ... how many people are there working for you?

Faridun: I don't want to answer this question. (looks around) I can't tell you, sorry.[268]

Delia: I understand. As I told you earlier, when I ask you something and you don't feel like talking about it, please feel free to tell me to carry on with the next question. So, how much do your people, well, you referred to them as your workers... how much do they earn? What is their average salary?

Faridun: It depends on the Russian contractors, the size of the house, the time limit we have. What is really important is the fact that I help these people!

Delia: (nodding) Help?

Faridun: Absolutely! They are happy because they send money to their families. With the money they earn here, they feed their wives and their children, invest in housing back home, you know all that!

Delia: Yes, yes...

---

265 Studies on such remittances exist in literature as early as Thomas and Znaniecki's *The Polish Peasant*, Chapter 3, Volume 5, and Goldring's studies of collective remittances in US/Mexican migration and development context (Goldring, 2004).
266 See more on Faridun in Chapter 10.
267 Meaning 'team leader' in Soviet construction terminology.
268 At the wish of the interlocutor, this interview had to take place in his car. During the interview he was worried about being watched or listened to. Given such circumstances, I did not record the conversation but was allowed to take notes.

Faridun: I am the one actually who sends the money. You see how much I care that their families are helped?
Delia: But...uh...if you pay them here, then send money to Uzbekistan and Tajikistan? Or how do you arrange all that? What do you mean you send money to their families?
Faridun: My workers don't need money for here. They know what they earn. I give them enough to get by for their minor expenses here but I really believe their families should get the money.
Delia: Are you implying that your workers don't get to see their earnings as such? I mean in form of currency?
Faridun: Right! I make a list and make one single cash transfer. I then come back with the list of how much I transferred to whose family. There is one single tax payment involved, as there is only one cash transfer for a group of say 4-5 people. There is one recipient that gets the code[269] and I tell them, "Now here is a list of whose family is getting how much. Call your wives and tell them to go and get the cash." You know and every time I do that...they call, then they verify that their wives got their earnings. They then come to me and say "Thank you so much, boss, that you help us."

It becomes obvious from these excerpts that the remitter is not the migrant himself but his employer, job broker, or patron. While we know a considerabe amount about the use of remittances in the households, we know little about the mechanisms involving sending money.[270] Following the 9/11 attacks, informal transfer systems attracted more attention worldwide and scholars became more aware of the importance of assessing the outflow of informal cash transfers and the network of *hawaladar*.[271] The case of Faridun and his workers demonstrates that there is a hybrid collective cash transfer system where neither the remitter nor the receiver can be entirely identified.

What should also be mentioned is that families living in migration share remitting obligations. Kayrat, a native of Kyrgyzstan, is a co-owner of a company which produces mattresses in St. Petersburg. Together with a Georgian entrepreneur he employs 42 people, among whom six are Kayrat's closest relatives. His workers send 200-250 US dollars to Kyrgyztan every month. Whenever his family in Kyrgyzstan needs money, they call him. Then he and his two brothers, who work for him, gather 50 dollars each and send it. The share of sending remittances is distributed more evenly among unmarried siblings. The situation gets much more complicated when siblings are married, share the same household in migration, and have to send money to their husbands and wives as well as their parents. Disputes occur among

---

269 The MTCN, the number the Western Union sender needs to give the recipient.
270 Itzigsohn 1995, Stark 1989.
271 El Qorchi *et al.* 2003, Maimbo 2003.

migrant siblings on the basis of unfair distribution of obligations, and may cause the siblings to stop sharing households and accommodations.

5. 4. Receiving Remittances

After having taken a closer look at how cash transfers from the country of destination can imply more complex social practices than the research on migration has so far addressed, it is worthwhile turning attention to the country of origin. Evidence from observations and interviews in two provinces in Tajikistan, namely Sughd in the North and Khatlon in the South, as well as Buxoro in the South of Uzbekistan, has been taken into account.

When one goes to a Western Union counter in the provincial town of Buxoro in Uzbekistan, he or she may experience that about a dozen people are waiting for the counter to be opened. Western Union banks are usually located at branch offices of the national banks. Recipients of the remittances present their identity documents (usually their passports) and give their ten digit number (MTCN) to the teller. They may witness, while waiting, how another customer cuts in line with his passport containing bills in local currency to grease the teller's palms. Amidst the tumult of customers counting their cash, sorting out the order of the queue, and others waiting and naming the place and the name of their senders out loud, it becomes clear that the majority of the people are recipients of remittances from migrant workers in Russia. In this case, the formality of the transaction, which was discussed at the beginning of this chapter, is defined by the use of a banking system. A careful observation of the receipt of cash transfers indicates that informal ties are of additional value for the target persons to obtain the money allotted to them. Those customers who do not engage in the practice of bribing the bank personnel or those who do not have any ties to them are likely to be served last. Interestingly, as the case in Uzbekistan shows, formal transactions such as wiring through Western Union are not necessarily likely to reduce corruption nor do they always function as means to expedite transaction processes and alleviate bureaucracy.

After the fieldwork in St. Petersburg, an attempt was made to trace the families of the migrants in Tajikistan. In the province of Sughd I encountered the family of the migrant called Mahmud who works as a street-sweeper in Russia. His parents told me that they had just received money from him. Mahmud did not wire the cash through the bank as he had told me in the interview. The same female broker who commutes between Isfara and St.Petersburg by van and transports laborers had brought a small package from him. He sent some cash and a mobile phone to his parents. For the sake of convenience, as it turns out, migrants also send money with commuters or job brokers. Being aware of the delicate situation of the job brokers, I decided for personal security reasons not to talk to them in the country of origin.

In the remote village of Darai Havash on the outskirts of the town of Kulob (TAJ) the situation was different. In the village itself there were no Western Union booths. Furthermore, when I arrived there to carry out my fieldwork, the daily consumption limit of two hours on electricity had just been lifted and the cell phone connection was very poor. It became clear to me how much social interaction receiving money from abroad may involve. During a group discussion with women in the Southern province of Khatlon in Tajikistan, I inquired how they receive cash since there are no banks in the village.

> When my husband sends me money, he usually sends it to his brother who lives in downtown Kulob.[272] My brother-in-law goes to the bank and picks it up. He receives it in US dollars and exchanges a small portion into Tajik somoni and brings it to us. Every month he comes over here and brings a portion of it so that I have enough cash for household expenditures. Since I have no idea what the currency rate is, my brother-in-law does everything for us.[273]

In this example we see that siblings and family members assist each other in receiving, delivering, and managing remittances. In some cases, those family members who bring the cash to its ultimate receiver keep a certain portion for themselves, but this is usually arranged with the migrant who sends it and the ultimate receiver of the cash. Remittances are important not only between the migrant and his immediate dependent family, but also because they contribute to the sustaining of kinship ties among other family members in the absence of the labor migrants as this example suggests. In the same province in the rural district of Sovetsky, it was interesting to find out that there are special couriers involved in cash deliveries. The family I interviewed told me that their father who is in Russia wires the money through the local Agroinvestbank to his brother in the capital city of Dushanbe. The migrant's brother gives the money to the taxi driver, who is known in the village itself as a cash courier from Dushanbe. Located about 200 km southwest of the capital city, Kulob can be reached within three hours by car. The person who gives the driver the money to deliver pays him about a 5 somoni (roughly 2 US dollars) service charge in advance for the delivery of 100 somoni (29 US dollars). By comparison to Southern African countries such as Zimbabwe and South Africa, where taxi drivers are engaged in similar cross-border cash deliveries for roughly 20 percent of the overall sum, the amount of 2 dollars within Tajikistan seems rather low.[274]

---

272   Power outages are less frequent and telecommunications are better in provincial centers.
273   Interview with Shirinmo, Kulob, May, 2007.
274   Genesis, 2004 and Maphosa, 2004 as quoted in Pieke *et al.* 2005. Furthermore, in the province of Khatlon in Tajikistan, taxi drivers can deliver consumer products as well. It is a common practice for relatives living in urban centers to send deliveries for a small amount of cash with taxi drivers. It is not unusual for a taxi to be an investment in long term (ongoing) seasonal migration to Russia.

It is also essential to consider the practice among migrant families in the countries of origin of requesting that cash be sent. It is important in this study for the following reason: concerning migrants' remittances, the adherents to the theory of the *new economics of migration* tend to side with migrants and explain their motivations for remitting, highlighting the situation more from the migrants' perspective. Thus, according to Lukas and Stark, one of the rationales behind sending cash home is the mutual altruism between the person abroad and the families in the country of origin.[275] The research goes deeper into analyzing the propensity linked with sending monetary resources and focuses on the importance of contractual agreements between the migrants and their families. While families are represented as being passive in receiving cash to manage households, or in participating in decision making, their endeavors to request cash and efforts to claim their share go unnoticed. Empirical findings from Central Asia may reveal significant practices from individual to collective behavior of the family members in the homelands.

In rural Tajikistan, electricity and landline telecommunications are scarce. Women have to make small trips to urban centers in order to be able to make phone calls as mobile telephones are not only costly but also often have only poor connections. Nozima, who is a teacher of Tajik literature at a high school on the outskirts of the city of Khujand, takes her children once every two weeks on a Saturday to the city telephone station so that they can talk to their father.[276] Depending on the distance of the rural areas from the urban center, the telephone is usually the only means for families to communicate with their significant others abroad. The exchange of letters that the scholars of migration know from the study on *The Polish Peasant* [277] is rare for Central Asian migrants in Russia due to the educational backgrounds of the migrants, time constraints as a result of household chores in women-headed households, and unreliable and slow postal services. However, the pleas of the migrant families to send cash, as meticulously documented in Thomas and Znaniecki's volumes, can be heard in the telephone conversations and be read in text messages sent via mobile phones.

The village of Darai Havash in Khatlon was one which had never been supplied with telephone lines during the Soviet era. Upon my arrival I was asked by the women in the neighborhood if I had a mobile phone. Unfortunately, my mobile telephone had no service during my entire stay in that village, but I was able to observe that the one cell phone, which had a different provider than mine, did have service and was used by several households exclusively to call Russia. Women in this village walk together in small groups for several miles to the top of a hill in order to get a connection.

---

275 Stark and Lukas, 1985 as quoted in Lianos, 1997; Stark and Bloom, 1985.
276 Interview with Nozima in Sughd, Tajikistan
277 Thomas and Znaniecki, 1927 (*cf.* for example Borkowski letter series pp.343-375 and p. 117 in Barszczewski letter series).

They dial the number in Russia, let it ring, then hang up, otherwise they would have to pay long distance charges to the owner of the cell phone. Seeing the long distance number displayed on their telephones, the migrants in Russia will call them back. Sometimes it can take up to several days for the communication to take place.

Discussing the impact of remittances on economic development, as well as the reasons for migrants choosing informal remittance systems, Pieke and associates conclude that the lack of accessibility to services and infrastructure makes it difficult both for senders and recipients of monetary resources to use banking systems, especially since not all the migrants have a legal status and hence are not able to provide the banks with their addresses.[278] While this is true in the context of African, Caribbean, and Pacific countries, the situation of undocumented migrants of Mexican origin in the US has undergone some changes in the last few years. They now need a so-called *matrícula consular* in order to open a bank account. This identity document is issued by Mexican or US authorities upon the proof by a migrant of his or her Mexican nationality. Amuedo-Dorantes and others are skeptical about whether undocumented migrants benefit fully from such seemingly improved procedures, as their study indicates that informal ties or personal transportation of cash are still a much preferred method among some migrants.[279] In this respect, I agree with Amuedo-Dorantes, and contend that the legal status of migrants still predetermines which remitting practice and social ties they will use to send money.

5.5. Conclusion

This chapter has dealt with migrant cash transfer practices involving transnational social interactions that are essential to analyze from both ends of migratory movements, namely that of the senders as well as their receiving families. One might argue that if more and more migrants from Central Asia are opting to send money through banks, it might have negative implications on the kinship and friendship ties existing in the country of destination, as remitters then benefit to a lesser extent from such ties. Data gathered from Central Asia and Russia show that kinship ties are not completely replaced by banking systems, but rather migrants' relatives and friends can act as facilitators in monetary transactions. In other words, kinship and friendship ties are indispensable to "fill the gaps" in transactions.

In those places where telephone connections function well, verbal communication is expedient to keep the ties between the two ends of migration strong. It cannot be repeated too often that modern technologies

---

278   Pieke *et al.*, 2005:26.
279   Amuedo-Dorantes and Bansak, 2006.

play an important role in sustaining transnational ties.[280] But despite the development of modern means of telecommunications, we should be cautious about concluding that their existence is the main reason for maintaining close transnational ties between migrants and their family members. While the most recent technological developments play an important role for long distance communication, it is not great enough to attribute the global tendency of increasing transnational ties to their existence. Rather, social interactions in transnational social spaces, decision making, managing remittances within families, and the changes in the priorities of remittance-related expenditures are worth of paying attention to. In the next chapter, we shall move further away from remittances as means of household survival *per se* and look into the changes in the life cycle practices of migrant dependent families. We shall see how remittances are used initially to finance matrimonial projects. It is often with the aim of celebrating a wedding that able-bodied men leave for Russia. Many of them realize, however, that they need to stay longer than planned. Their one-time matrimonial project turns them into transnationals as they feel the obligation to pay for further celebrations and support their young families.

---

280 Faist, 2006:3-4.

6. Toil in Russia to Tie the Knot: Weddings and Other Life Cycle Practices in the Context of Transnational Migration

Why do we come to Russia? We must marry off our children! It is getting more and more expensive to celebrate a wedding!

A market worker in Astrakhan (RUS)

My daughter-in-law left a long time ago...ten years ago. Both she and my son left their four children for me to take care of. Thank God, now the oldest child has just been married off. My daughter-in-law married her off. She spent the money she had saved from her earnings in Russia on this wedding. The second child is 18 years old. She will be turning 19 soon. Next year, my daughter-in-law will come back to marry this one off too.

Masturaxon Opa, Jalalabad (KYR)

I don't understand these people. They work so hard in Russia, and instead of investing their earnings in a sophisticated way, they celebrate a big wedding and spend all their money in one day. Can you believe, all of their remittances are then gone in one day! Then everyone says this country is poor, uneducated, and underdeveloped...no wonder.

An international employee at a humanitarian organization in Tajikistan

Migration scholars who focus on migrant weddings and other family celebrations at both ends of the migratory path do so to emphasize the significance of family events for migrants to maintain their social ties across multiple nation-states. In her research on a large-scale wedding that took place on a Caribbean Island, Olwig shows how an extended kinship that is scattered across the globe finds it crucial to reunite for this family occasion in order to underline solidarity among kin members in the large family's 'home.'[281] Elsewhere in the literature, the transnational dimensions of these celebrations are explained as enabling migrants to continue with practices to which they were exposed in their homelands and to develop social personhood in the places of destination. In her study on split ritual practices of migrants between Morocco and Italy, Salih demonstrates the importance of celebrations for the maintenance and reconstruction of membership in the sending countries. On the other hand, she shows how migrants need to split practices such as weddings between the countries of origin and destination. In the latter place they register their marital bonds to be provided with legal protection.[282]

---

281 Olwig, 2002.
282 Salih, 2003:82-84.

In the case of Central Asian migrants, the picture is somewhat different. Financing weddings and circumcision parties are often a reason for a journey that turns into long-term transnational labor migration, although this is not to deny that a large group of people migrate in search of employment and provision for their families. I will discuss two types of labor migrants to Russia whose projects involve matrimonial festivities. In the first pattern of labor migration, workers leave for Russia determined to stay, as they admit, 'only' as long as they need to manage to save enough for a wedding or a circumcision ceremony. In the second pattern, workers leave for Russia after a lavish wedding, which they celebrated by borrowing money from family, friends, or cash dealers on an interest basis. In both categories, on which I will elaborate, what starts as a one-time or a short-term trip develops into an entire way of life as a migrant and leads to the development of transnational migration. Beside weddings, there are other life-cycle celebrations and rituals that often either force people to migrate or make those who already commute reconsider their permanent return home due to the expenditures the life-cycle rituals involve.

6.1. Labor Migration and Weddings

> Working in Russia is good, of course. People are building houses, marrying off their sons and daughters, young people are getting married thanks to having made money in Russia. Without working in Russia all this would be impossible.
>
> Orolbay, Jalalabad (KYR)

In the village of Lavova in the Province of Khatlon (TAJ), I was accompanied to migrant dependent households by Nazokat, a young Tajik woman who managed a UN-sponsored development project. Nazokat needed to see some family members of labor migrants and invite them to attend a seminar she planned to organize on micro-financing two weeks later. She said that it would also be a good opportunity for me to meet with these families. Nazokat and I went to the house of a migrant who commuted between Kulob (TAJ) and Lensk (RUS).[283] It was May and Saidali, a long-term commuter, had come home a month earlier to celebrate his wedding. Nazokat told me that the wedding had taken place three weeks earlier. When we entered Saidali's house, neither the young bride nor the other family members in the house gave the impression of having recently celebrated a wedding. The atmosphere did not make it apparent that the bride was new to the home or that the family had just initiated her. When I wondered about the solemn expressions of the women who served us tea and sweets, Nazokat whispered to me that Saidali's

---

283 Lensk, a small town of approximately 25,000 inhabitants located in the Republic of Sakha (Yakutia) in Russia, is the farthest geographic place that I have recorded as a place of destination of Central Asian migrants.

younger brother had been working with him in Lensk. It had been planned that Saidali would come to Kulob early so that he could help remodel the house and prepare his wedding party. Saidali's brother would have come from Russia on the day of the wedding, but he did not make it. He bought his ticket, but had a fatal accident at the construction site where the two brothers were employed. Saidali had been told that his brother had fallen off the scaffolding of a tall building. The body of his deceased brother arrived on the day of his wedding. Out of respect to the deceased, Saidali's wedding had to take place without a band and dancing, since neither the bride's nor the bridegroom's family could afford to postpone the wedding and waste the groceries they had bought from their hard-earned savings.

The price for celebrating a wedding by working hard in Russia and saving money from physically strenuous jobs in spheres such as construction, agriculture, and street maintenance can be very high. As the story of Saidali's brother shows, in some cases it can even take human lives, as men engage themselves in high-risk physical work. Employers in Russia often do not pay for health insurance or work accidents, nor do they provide assistance to fulfill basic security requirements such as wearing helmets and security belts. Saidali showed me the pictures he had taken in Russia. He told me about how hard it was to make money in Russia, but because he and his younger brother were so hard-working, docile, and loyal, their employer had provided them with a small room and even a bathroom with running hot and cold water for them to wash themselves. There were some pictures of buildings that were taken at stages before and after Saidali and his coworkers renovated them. Along with photos of his coworkers, Saidali had taken pictures of Tajik food that his younger brother had been good at preparing. "He had professional training as a cook here in Tajikistan," Saidali added as he turned the pages of his photo album.

Saidali left the room and his mother started telling me about how difficult it was to save money and organize a wedding. Saidali's mother showed me and Nazokat the dowry that decorated her daughter-in-law's guest room, as she counted the most basic items that the bride and groom's families have to collect by the time the actual wedding takes place. I noted them down for the purpose of providing a general impression.

Figure 2: A list of items to be accumulated for the wedding of an average peasant family in the Province of Khatlon (TAJ)

Items to be accumulated	
By the bride's family to be taken to the groom's house after the wedding (dowry)	By the groom's family for the wedding party
6-8 mattresses (*ko'rpa*) to sleep on 8 mattresses to be laid out along the walls of the guest room 10 mattresses to be used as blankets 20-22 pillows to be used both as cushions and pillows 100 cups 12 large teapots 40 large soup bowls 100 plates At least 7 sets of clothes for members of the groom's family[284] Set of furniture for the living room A stove and an oven Sets of clothes to be worn after the wedding and jewelry[285]	1 cow 1 sheep 7 sets of clothes for the bride (dresses and pants, sweaters and coats) jewelry 6 sacks of flour (four sacks of hand-milled and two sacks of machine-milled flour, each sack containing 50 kg) 25 kg oil 25 kg sugar 30 kg candy 40 kg rice $100 qalym (bride price)

This table is only one example among many and represents the expenditures for a wedding in a rather poor rural Khatlon family. Depending on the wealth of the would-be couple's family, the demands for the dowry may vary as do the expenditures for the wedding celebration. A complex gift exchange (comprised mostly of enough fabric for one dress) takes place between the female relatives and friends on such occasions. The costs for the wedding also depend on the number of guests to be invited and the amount food that is served.

A woman, with whom I spoke during fieldwork in rural Sughd (TAJ) in 2006, mentioned that she had first sent her elder son to work in Russia. Her second son had followed a year later to earn money for his own wedding. Her

---

284 Known as *saripo* or *sarpo* or *sarupo* (Taj. literally *sarupo* 'head and toe,' meaning from head to toe, also *sarpo* in Uzb., a Persian-Tajik loan word), it is common in Central Asia to provide family members with sets of clothes on large celebrations such as weddings, ceremonies of circumcision, *beshik to'y*, the festivity of putting a newborn child into the cradle, and *muchal*, the celebration of the birth year on March 21st (*Navruz*) according to the Chinese calendar.
285 The type of fabric and the amount of clothing and jewelry depend on the family's economic situation and social status, and the position of the bride vis-à-vis other siblings.

husband had died during the Civil War in the mid 1990s, so she had to raise her two sons and a daughter alone. The money and the dowry she had saved for her sons had to be spent on her youngest child – her daughter – whom she had married off before her sons, despite her young age. She said that her eldest son sent money regularly, which she either saved in cash or would use to buy some of the textiles and goods for the future bride she did not yet know. She mentioned that she needed to save at least $3,000. This sum did not include the expenses for textiles, jewelry, and other gifts that parents gather over a lifetime.[286]

As far as Saidali in Lavova is concerned, he did not stay in Tajikistan as he had initially planned. The reason was that in Russia he had found a relatively stable place to work and an employer who knew his skills. He also had accommodation – a room which he used to share with his brother and he would now have to share with another person. He seemed to have no interest in losing the social capital he had accumulated in Russia.

To migrants such as Saidali, whose case represents the first of the two categories of labor migration I mentioned above, the life-threatening conditions of his workplace in Russia were less of a worry than the risk of being unable to feed a family in Tajikistan. A newly-married woman in Central Asia is expected to get pregnant in the months following the wedding. When the young wife gets pregnant, the husband who had planned to stay in his country of origin permanently or at least for a longer period, changes his mind, as he starts losing hope of finding a job that pays well enough to provide for his family.

The cohort of migrants who leave for Russia for the purpose of a wedding are mostly male. Young unmarried women almost always leave only when their close relatives (usually mothers) are also working in Russia. Both in Russia and Central Asia, I also encountered brothers and fathers who migrated to Russia specifically for the purpose of saving money for the weddings of their siblings and children, respectively. Sotvoldi, a 50-year-old construction worker from Marghilon (UZB) in St. Petersburg, narrated as follows:

> I came to St. Petersburg on April 1, 2005. I then stayed until December and came back in January [2006]. We had celebrated the wedding of our daughter and had so much debt to pay that I had no other choice than coming to Russia to work. As you know, we are Muslims and we have inherited traditions from our ancestors that we marry off our children and provide them with housing, etc. Other religions don't have that. Thank Allah, after having worked here since April last year, I have been able to pay back all my debts. You have to have these kinds of celebrations in our culture. You see how others celebrate weddings and see the gifts that come to the newlyweds and of course, you can't neglect your children either. You want to have a wedding just like the others and your children would like to have a fancy wedding like the others.

---

286 Interview with Mehri, Khujand (TAJ), October 2006.

Sotvoldi's story represents the second pattern of migration in which the marriage is first celebrated more lavishly than the hosts can actually afford. Family and friends lend large sums of money but also help by arranging the place of celebration and groceries that are needed for meals for the invited guests. Financial assistance from family members can also be part of an unwritten exchange custom where money is expected to be returned at a similar family event.[287] Depending on the position of the hosts, the number of guests invited to weddings can reach a thousand people. Cash dealers lend money to such families at a rate of around 20% interest per month. For those who do not migrate to Russia, it is extremely hard to pay back the money borrowed with interest.

What Sotvoldi shared during the interview reflects the region-wide phenomenon related to life-cycle rituals and celebrations, particularly weddings. With the growth of economic inflation that creates more hurdles in the lives of impoverished rural people, the costs for weddings are growing even more. Kandiyoti and Azimova, and Louw explain that celebration of weddings and the exchange of gifts reflect the growing gap between the 'new rich' and 'the new poor' in post-independent Central Asia.[288] Scholars of area studies rightly point out that in the context of a market economy, the exchange of gifts is becoming more difficult and more expensive, and that this contributes to further stratification of the society.[289] In this context the dynamics with which the global movements of goods, finances, and services grew after the fall of the Soviet borders should be borne in mind. Having been shown the dowry boxes of many brides and having observed some bridal shopping during fieldwork, I was able to observe that the expensive clothing the brides or their families insist on are imported from Turkey, Iran, and/or Saudi Arabia. Kitchen appliances can be imported from China, extravagant leather furniture is imported from Arab countries, and textiles are usually brought from China, Turkey, Iran, and Dubai.[290]

The celebration of weddings and expenditures of the families should be seen within the social, economic, and political contexts of the countries. One day, while I was in the Province of Khatlon (TAJ), I witnessed the mullah of the small community gathering all adult men and women to hold a talk on the state of the community. He repeated the critical remarks that President Emomali Rahmon had made about limiting the expenses of weddings and funerals. He emphasized that he supported the Tajik president's concern about

---

287 This is similar to the situation of families studied by Scott in Southeast Asia (1976:168).
288 Kandiyoti and Azimova, 2004:337, Louw (2007, 207).
289 Kuehnast and Dudgwick, 2004 and Louw, 2007.
290 Unfortunately, I was not able to attend a wedding financed by migrants during the fieldwork in Central Asia. There were several reasons for this: first, I intended to spend sufficient time accumulating data in Russia. Second, during the months of late September and October 2006, no weddings were taking place in Tajikistan due to the Muslim fasting month of Ramadan. In Kyrgyzstan in February and March (the weeks I was there in 2008), it is simply not wedding season. Furthermore, an ethnographic description of a wedding at each field site would lie beyond the scope of this research.

families not managing their incomes in a sophisticated way. He made the following remark that caught my attention: "And this taking away of plastic bottles? Aren't you all ashamed of doing such things? Don't you think about the poor family that has to organize the wedding?" The women from the village who were sitting next to me looked at me, feeling somewhat abashed. I did not understand what the mullah was alluding to and whispered to my neighbor to explain. She said that in her impoverished village for the past several years, the residents have adopted a practice where the guests of the wedding drink all the soda beverages, cut one third off the large plastic bottles with a knife, then fill them with savory food, pastries, or sweets to take home. The remarks of the mullah then became clear. In view of the humanitarian crisis that occurred after the civil clashes in Tajikistan in the 1990s, in the provinces of Khatlon and Badakhshan that had been economically challenged even during the Soviet era, the population's strategies for coming to terms with food insecurity should be taken into account in addition to the factors described above.

Status symbols should not go unmentioned either. Shortly after the fall of the USSR, hosts of wedding celebrations began hiring cameramen to video record their festivities. In addition, some well-off people began giving their bridegrooms expensive gifts such as keys to a new apartment or a car as presents during the wedding. What we can observe now is the practice of digital video recording not only of large family rituals, but also of smaller-scale birthday gatherings. Purchasing of DVD players is becoming more and more common.[291] On the last day of my fieldwork in Sughd Province in 2006, I hired a taxi driver to take me to the airport of Khujand. As soon as I got into the car the taxi driver started it, and a couple of minutes later, yanked out a foldable monitor from the dashboard and turned it on. He inserted a CD and started playing the video recording of his own wedding while driving. My driver accelerated, turned the volume on, and made dancing movements the entire ride to the airport, often watching dancing guests on the monitor and snapping his fingers instead of keeping a steady grip on the steering wheel. I was able to recognize him as the bridegroom and his wife in a white European-style wedding gown.

After this experience in the car, and later, during several other long-distance drives between different towns I took in the region, what became clear was how drivers were merging practices of their *home space* into their *work space*.[292] Some of the drivers with whom I talked were seasonal mi-

---

291 During my fieldwork in Tajikistan I visited very poor families whose family members would sell their only cow to migrate to Russia. They could barely afford three meals a day, yet a DVD player and CDs of Tajik popstars had become the center pieces of their modest guest rooms.
292 In Giddensian terms, these would be *locale*s that may include a host of places such as a room, a house, a street, a village, a city, and/or a geographic territory of a nation-state. Giddens would probably term this merger of home and professional space as *internal regionalization*. Regionalization is explained as localization of space in terms of routinized social practices of agents in connection with time-space zoning. Regions are of great sig-

grants. For instance in Osh, Jalalabad, and Bishkek (KYR) where I had similar experiences during the months of February and March in 2007, long distance cab drivers told me that they had bought a car from their savings from seasonal work in Russia and were making money by giving people lifts during their off-season periods in Central Asia. Comparing my experiences in Central Asia with video recordings in cars to those in both Russia and Central Asia in living rooms in which I was often welcomed, I became aware of the fact that not only were practices of a private space (i.e. living rooms) sometimes extended to a working space, but also of how much it mattered for people to watch their wedding parties and show them to others. It must be said that in Central Asia it is customary to turn on the TV set for guests, as hosts feel that they should entertain them. This is especially true when the hosts themselves are busy cooking for guests. There is therefore nothing new about turning on a TV set. Now, families of migrants more and more prefer to turn on the DVD player and play the recordings of celebrations. Labor migrant families who hosted me in Russia, also proudly played their family and friends the video recordings of the weddings that they had helped finance. When such recordings were lacking, the hosts turned on the DVD player and asked which video clips of (ethno) pop stars I would like to watch.[293]

In the excerpts of the interview with Sotvoldi he relates the wedding of his daughter to Islam. At the same time, Islamic scholars of the region have reiterated that high wedding expenditures should not be linked to Islam. For instance, the Institute for War and Peace Reporting, which covered the problem of wedding expenditures in a short report, cited Umarali Nazarov, the rector of the Islamic University in Dushanbe (TAJ), as arguing that: "The laws of Islam do not prescribe large outgoings. On the contrary, the Koran says that Allah does not expect a person to exceed his capabilities, but people are scared of censure from relatives, neighbors and acquaintances, so they hold lavish celebrations."[294] While scholars focusing on post-Soviet Central Asia repeatedly argue that it is since the demise of the USSR and the revival of traditions and customs that life-cycle rituals in the region have begun being celebrated in such dimensions, historians elaborating on such practices during the Soviet era present a different reality. Relying on archival data,

---

nificance for the contexts of interaction (1984:118-119). In a routine manner, agents such as this taxi driver were practicing the activities, that once used to be confined to the territory of their homes, in the space of their professions. Without a doubt, it was also a way of getting involved in social interaction with customers. Sadly, I became too concerned about the dysfunctional seat-belts to observe the content of the video-recording.

293 "Nima ko'rasiz, klip yoki kino? Ujas qo'yib beraymi? Yoki Shakirani ko'rasizmi?" (*Uzb.*"What would you like to watch, a [music] clip or a movie? Would you like me to turn on a thriller? Or would you rather watch Shakira?") Shakira's "Hips Don't Lie" has been one of the most favorite hits in Central Asia since 2006 (Field observations, August, 2006).

294 *Keeping Up with Neighbours.* Article published by the Institute for War and Peace Reporting, on March 27th, 2006. Available at http://www.iwpr.net/?p=rca&s=f&o=260558&apc_state=henirca2006 (last consulted on February 27th, 2009).

they explain that notwithstanding state control over such ostentatious gatherings, families made every effort to spend as much money as they could.[295] The Spiritual Directorate of the Muslims of Central Asia and Kazakhstan (SADUM) even issued a *fatwa* in 1952 encouraging Muslims to refrain from ostentatious weddings and large-scale expenditures on weddings and circumcisions. Of course, this institution was under the control of the Soviet state and cooperated with the state to 'protect' the proletarian society from ideologies that were not in accordance with the state dogma.[296] Considering the state's control over life-cycle rituals during the Soviet era as analyzed by Ro'i, the attitude of the authoritarian presidents in Central Asia after the disintegration of USSR might not seem very surprising. In their decrees, President Karimov of Uzbekistan and President Emomali Rahmon of Tajikistan prohibited ostentatious festivities in 1998 and 1999, respectively.[297] Despite these presidential decrees, families have continued such expenditures in the same way.

As emphasized by Nazarov, the rector of the Islamic University in Dushanbe (TAJ), the social pressure on the kinship and community levels forces people to maintain the level of expenditures, if not to exceed the expectations of the members of their social networks. In the three Central Asian countries, migrants who succeed in fulfilling these expectations have gradually been influencing those families not dependent on the remittances of their family members. As one informant stated:

> I know this guy, this neighbor's son who works in Russia. Karimjon is his name. He married a relative of mine, so I was present at their wedding. His wife gave birth and he recently came to visit his first child. He came back from Russia, sold his new car, added $12,000, and bought a new Mercedes. He left the car here and left again for Russia. You know he built a new house, got married, paid off his wedding, bought a car, and still he left to go back to Russia. These people think that it is useless to stay here in Kyrgyzstan. They think that it is a waste of time. So I can imagine that with such revenues it is affordable to commute between Kyrgyzstan and Russia. When I see this, I feel like commuting too.
>
> Tursunoy, Jalalabad (KYR)

The sense of obligation and responsibility of parents to marry off their children and finance their weddings in Central Asia are similar to the South Indian rural example. Velayutham and Wise, in their study on translocal family ties between a South Indian (Tamil) village and Singapore demonstrate the strength of moral economies of obligations and responsibilities. They explain the concept of *nandri-kaadan* ("thankful indebtedness") and demonstrate that children are called to show responsibility towards their parents and choose to

---

295   Ro'i, 2000:530-535.
296   More on *fatwa*s condemning sumptuous life-cycle celebrations during the Soviet era, cf. Ro'i, 2000:150, 534-535.
297   More on President Karimov's decree, *cf.* Kandiyoti and Azimova 2004:337 as cited in Louw, 2007:77 and President Rahmon's decree, see section 9.2 of Chapter 9.

marry within their caste. Disrespect of the expectations of kin members and the village often results in loss of reputation, shame, and ostracism in the home communities.[298] In the Ferghana Valley, especially in Osh and Jalalabad, the burden of parents to provide for the would-be brides seemed enormous. Xolmurod, who commutes between Nijny Vartovsk (RUS) and Osh (KYR), explained that the expenses of a daughter's parents do not end with the celebration of a wedding. Indeed, as many informants in Osh and Jalalabad explained, after marrying off a daughter, parents and close relatives of the bride are expected by the bridegroom's family to prepare warm meals three times a day and bring them to her new family. For the period of forty days, the bride's family is expected to provide the newlyweds with warm meals, baked goods, and sweets to create a sweet and festive atmosphere for the new couple. It goes without saying that the portions are meant not only for the married couple but for the entire family with whom the couple shares the household, that is the bridegroom's parents, grandparents, and siblings.

While some informants who complained about the situation with competitive wedding parties did not mention the Soviet era in the interviews, others expressed nostalgia for this period in which weddings were, according to them, less expensive. Shohidaxon, with whom I stayed for a week in Jalalabad (KYR), had graduated from Moscow State University in the early 1980s. She and her fourteen-year-old daughter speak Russian at home. Having a Kyrgyz mother and an Uzbek father, she did not seem to make any ethnic-based distinctions about matrimonial practices. Shohidaxon told me that she had started preparing her daughter's dowry from the time she had given birth to her. She told me how much she despised these customs, giving the situation of her friend as an example.

> Shohidaxon:
> My friend recently married off her daughter. Can you believe what she had to do for her? She had to fully but really fully (Rus. *polnost'iu*) equip the rooms that were allotted to the newlyweds by the bridegroom's family. Does this exist in Buxoro?[299] No. I don't think such madness exists anywhere! Then guess what! The wedding was over and two days later, the mother-in-law of her daughter called and said, "Actually the little runner you bought for the corridor is a bit too short, so we would like it to be replaced. And oh, the nightstand in their bedroom does not have a matching color, so would you also bring a different one?"
> I find it so...so absurd, so primitive, you know. Why is it the mother-in-law's business anyway? You spend so much money on the wedding, and then, what I find insane is that you pamper your new son-in-law. You flatter the bridegroom's family. You do so much for, you give so much...excuse me...but it is as if...as if you pay this young guy, you do all this to your new son-in-law to beg him to sleep with your daughter. It is so absurd.

---

298 Velayutham and Wise, 2005.
299 Here Shohidaxon was referring to my hometown.

To a certain extent Shohidaxon's Soviet world view has not changed much. Seeing the most recent trends in wedding celebrations, she uses the adjective *primitive* as can be read in the excerpts of the interview. It is precisely this notion of 'primitiveness' that Soviets applied in their ideology and used to justify modernization of the society.[300]

Shohidaxon: I hate these traditions. It was not like this here before. People brought it here from other places.
Delia: Oh yeah? Where do you think they brought it from?
Shohidaxon: Toshkent, it all came from Toshkent.

In Uzbekistan and the south of Kyrgyzstan, the Uzbek capital Toshkent is known as the source of reinvented traditions such as extravagant equipping of the bride's future abode.

Transnational migrants play an interesting role as *victims* of and, at the same time, *catalysts* for these practices. Once faced with the challenge of financing their own wedding or that of their close kin, they leave for Russia. Through hard labor they become senders not only of monetary remittances, but also of consumer goods such as boxes of candy, cheese and sausages for the actual wedding celebrations, and kitchen and bathroom appliances. Washing machines and dryers as well as ovens and stoves are seen as practical gifts. Ideally, the latter has to be equipped with both gas and electric ranges. Such stoves are usually produced in China. In the current times of energy crisis in Central Asia, it is common to have massive electricity and gas outages. Stoves equipped with gas and electric burners are very practical since they make cooking possible in case one of the two heating sources is turned off.[301] Toasters, electric kettles, and microwave ovens are brought from Russia as gifts as well, although these gifts are typically given in urban areas.

In Khatlon (TAJ), as I sat in Saidali's guestroom listening to his mother's descriptive inventory of her daughter-in-law's dowry, I wondered if any of the requirements about the dowry, the costs of the wedding, and/or the number of guests were changing at all after the presidential decree. Many people I talked to mentioned the tougher measures that the government was taking on the organization of lavish weddings, but the hosts themselves did not think of them as lavish at all. Saidali's mother said:

> Well, all these things, we brought in small portions of course. We hired a smaller truck and brought a small portion before the wedding...otherwise Emomali

---

300 With the implementation of the First Five-Year-Plan in 1928, Stalin was committed to eliminating "backwardness," put an end to poverty and slavery, and strive towards industrialization (Hirsch, 2003:696). As Hirsch also demonstrates, the discourse of primitive cultures of the Soviets had traces in the British cultural evolutionist Edward B. Tylor's book *Primitive Culture* which had appeared in 1871 (Hirsch, 2003:706).

301 The fall and winter of 2007-2008 were severely cold and long. Both urban and rural residents in all three Central Asian migrant sending countries had to use firewood, kerosene, or manure for heating due to scarcity of gas, water, and electricity.

would have become furious.[302] After the wedding, we brought the remaining dowry home. Before, it was different. We used to hire a huge truck, load everything on it, and bring everything on a single ride. Now things are changing.

6.2. 'The Bridegroom Works in Russia': Representation of Migrant Workers in Marriage Arrangements and Wedding Negotiations

How has migration to Russia changed the process of arranging marriages and similar practices? What are the opportunities for young migrant men in the marriage market in Central Asia? These questions arose as families shared their stories of weddings celebrated or the search for brides for their migrant family members.

Arranged marriage is practiced almost everywhere in Central Asia. The parents of a future bridegroom already start looking for a suitable bride for their son when he is in his late teens. There is no typical age for marriage in a strict sense, for the social, economic, cultural, and educational circumstances for marriage of young men and women can be different from one family to another. Some parents wait until they have saved enough money, or have found a suitable girl, or until their son has finished his education – or all three. The usual scenario is that the mother, or in the case of her absence, the closest senior female relative of a young man, takes several other women whom she knows well (usually relatives) and goes to the house of the girl recommended by relatives, neighbors, or friends. These (mostly) female delegates are known as *khostgor* (Taj.) or *sovchi* (Uzb.). At least one of the women in this delegation of middle-aged women must herself be an experienced mother-in-law and a good negotiator. Over the course of several visits, exchange of sweets, food, and gifts are made. These visits involve complex discussions about the background of the young man who is represented by the female envoys, his parents' professions, and his position in the family vis-à-vis other siblings, in order to assess the future of the couple in case of marriage. Depending on the stage at which the decision-making process is – whether the bride's family has come closer to acceptance or refusal – they may return the gifts in the identical form they received them in or replace them with other items. Through gifts they make gestures of their position on the proposal, either by showing that the proposal is unacceptable for them, or by demonstrating that they have not yet made a final decision or come closer to accepting the offer.

Every province in Kyrgyzstan, Tajikistan, and Tajikistan has its own widespread practice of *sovchilik* or *khostgori*, i.e. carrying out visits to a girl's house to make marriage proposals. In some southern provinces of Uz-

---

302 In the Province of Khatlon I heard people refer to President Emomali Rahmon as Emomali.

bekistan, women have lengthy poetic and metaphorical sayings with which they express the purpose of their visit to the house of the girl. These are recited upon stepping over the threshold of the girl's parents' house. In other provinces, such visits that involve the initial request for the hand of the girl might not even take place. In some provinces of Kyrgyzstan, for instance, there are many cases in which young girls are first abducted, then forced to marry the person who organized the kidnapping.[303]

In the families I have studied in southern Kyrgyzstan, Tajikistan, and Uzbekistan, marriages take place quite similarly according to the pattern of what Bourdieu termed a "matrimonial game."[304] Bourdieu explains the matrimonial strategies among the Kabyle peoples in terms of a card game in which the results of the game depend on the actual cards that players have, the rules of the game, and the skills that players apply. Very much similar to the Kabyle, the positive outcome of the proposal negotiations in Central Asia (i.e. the approval of the bride's family of the proposal made by the groom's) depends on two factors: the material and the symbolic capital of the families involved and the ability of the parties to apply this capital.[305] The parties that enter into the negotiations, if we were to analyze the process from the bridegroom's perspective, do so with a fund of information about the bridegroom's family.

The matrimonial game has taken an interesting turn in cases of migrant-grooms that I have been able to observe. One of the most important types of capital to win the girl's hand is the bridegroom's profession, which has as much value as the reputation and the profession(s) of his parents. During the Soviet era, the educational background of the bridegroom was important capital as it was an indicator of his ability to hold a job in a state-owned institution, which meant a stable monthly salary. At the end of the 1990s, when the first waves of seasonal labor migration started, families showed reluctance about marrying off their daughters to migrant workers. Labor migration was associated solely with (a) near constant absence of the would-be husband as a bread-winner, (b) low and unstable income since almost all migrants were employed illegally and electronic wiring of remittances was not yet popular, and (c) living with parents-in-law on scarce means that involved

---

303 This aspect of matrimonial practices lies beyond the scope of this study. The so-called "bride kidnapping" (*kyz ala kachuu*) is indeed a major problem in Kyrgyzstan. Justified as an old Kyrgyz tradition, a man abducts a woman against her will and brings her to his house where his close relatives carry out a marriage ritual and celebrate a wedding. The woman is forced to agree to marry her abductor by her own parents or face rejection by her home village. In rare cases, a bride is kidnapped by her boyfriend with her own consent if her parents do not allow her to marry the man of her choice. International human rights organizations, NGOs, as well as the Kyrgyz government have condemned the practice of bride kidnapping and called for bringing abductors to justice. (For more on this topic, see Russ and Salimjanova, 2007, Human Rights Watch Report, published on September 27th, 2006 http://www.unhcr.org/refworld/publisher,HRW,COUNTRYREP, KGZ,45389b942,0.html).
304 Bourdieu, 2007:58.
305 *Ibid.*

frequent family disputes, partially due to unpaid wedding debts. Over a period of about ten years, however, there has been a major shift in which male migrant candidates are no longer treated as weak bread-winners; quite the contrary, in fact, as in many cases the parents of brides prefer them to those who do not migrate but have a lower income.

There is a concatenation of several factors which account for this shift. First, parallel to inflation, the costs of weddings have increased and so have the number of migrants. Second, Russia's demand for low-paid unskilled labor has grown and during the final years of Putin's first presidency, stricter measures towards curbing undocumented migration and illegal employment of foreigners were applied. More and more employers introduced written contracts and took responsibility for registering their foreign workers. Those who were reluctant to formalize working agreements have at least made verbal agreements with their seasonal workers which have contributed to the relative 'stability' of employment for many migrants. Third, with the gradual increase of migrant wages in Russia, the disparity between salaries of non-migrants in the sending countries and migrant earnings has grown larger. Fourth, neighbors have witnessed that weddings in the families of migrants are more likely to be debt-free than in those not supported by them. Ultimately, in some rural areas it is non-migration that has become the exception to the rule rather than migration itself, so families wishing to marry off their daughters might not have any alternatives.

Dilsifat, whose family I shall describe in more detail in Chapter 8, mentioned that she had been married off *because* the bridegroom who proposed to her was working in Russia. Her own father had been migrating for several years. He had heard of the young man who was asking for his daughter's hand because he was from his wife's native village. He had explained to his daughter that since the young man had been migrating for six years, he had to have a stable employment in Russia. The bridegroom's family made full use of their candidate's status as an experienced labor migrant. His status as a migrant worker was brought as social capital during negotiations as a whole, and ultimately played a key role in Dilsifat's father's decision to marry her off. Dilsifat's father himself had known how to appreciate the value of what his would-be son-in-law had accumulated over the years. It goes without saying that Dilsifat's husband's position in his own family vis-à-vis siblings was also important. As the only son of the family, he would inherit the house and the plot of land that his parents owned.

In a village of ethnic Kyrgyz in the outskirts of Osh I have encountered two interesting cases. On one occasion, during a group discussion with four male migrants, one of them admitted that he had not revealed his true occupation to his bride's family. Almaz was about 25 years old and had been a peasant in his village before leaving for Russia. He said that if he had told the girl and her family that he worked in Russia, he would have never received permission to marry her. His neighbors were present in the room where we discussed this topic. They worked together with Almaz in the same town in Russia and commuted together with him. They confirmed that the marriage would not have taken place if he had told the girl and her family that he was a migrant labor. Almaz's marriage had taken place a month prior to my visit. Only after the wedding did he tell his wife that he had booked a ticket and would have to leave for Russia eight weeks later. He did not mind telling in the presence of his neighbors that his wife got very mad at him first, but later insisted that she leave with him. She was a university graduate and knew Russian well. Almaz said that this would make it easier for her to find a job in Russia. From his native village in southern Kyrgyzstan, Almaz was trying to arrange a job at a small grocery store so that his wife could start working the day after their arrival. In the case of Almaz, his parents did not tell the girl's family about their son's job situation. Almaz was the only son among several daughters. Almaz's position vis-à-vis other siblings in his family, rather than his long-distance employment, had been brought to the foreground during the process of arranging his marriage.

Almaz's neighbor Anara, a 50-year-old woman and a mother of six sons and a daughter, was aware of such negotiations. During the interview that took place in February 2008, she said that she was planning to marry off her 27-year-old son in the fall of 2008. Her son had been migrating for several years. Together, we had a small tour of her house and she allowed me to take photos of the rooms in which she would welcome her future daughter-in-law. An entire set of three rooms had been freshly painted and decorated, as her son regularly wired cash from Russia. Similar to three or four other neighbors in the same village, Anara knew fairly well what she would say to the girl's family.

> Well, I will say, "We have everything ready for the wedding, the rooms for the future couple and all, so we are ready to receive the bride." To the parents of the girl I will tell the truth about my son...that he works in Russia and makes a living by working there seasonally and that he has been doing it for several years now. I will explain, "Look, my son is hard-working and honest. Your daughter and he will marry and after the wedding my son will leave for Russia. The young daughter-in-law will stay with me until she gives birth to a child. As soon as the baby is born, she will join her husband." You see, I don't want my son to live there [in Russia] all alone. He and his wife should work together and I will be happy to look after their baby. Really, why should I keep my daughter-in-law? I will raise the baby and let my son and his wife live in Russia.[306]

Anara and some of the neighbors of her age indeed represent a different generation of future mothers-in-law. We see from these interview excerpts that migration is brought up during negotiations and the girl's family is informed about the prospects of her life after the marriage. Women like Anara do not rule out that – as in the case of her own son – she might even be dealing with

---

306   Interview with Anara. Osh Province (KYR).

a long-term project. For the girl's parents who choose between several different candidates who may all be migrant workers, the option of their daughter being able to join her husband in Russia can be attractive. Unlike Almaz's parents, Anara is determined to enter the 'matrimonial game' with a handful of different cards, to use Bourdieu's terms. She is convinced that by proposing to the girl with a set of truthful information and beneficial offers such as child-rearing and permission to migrate, she will succeed in choosing the suitable bride. Such changes in marriage negotiations, too, become significant factors that turn short-term seasonal employment projects (that had been planned earlier) into long-term transnational migration.

Marriages are being arranged across nation-states as well. Anara's male neighbor Urmat mentioned that he was cautious when it came to making choices for his 21-year-old son. Urmat, who was about the same age as Anara, had been working in Russia for six years. Over the course of six years he had become a loyal employee as a grader operator. Urmat is a professional in grading and repairing roads, parking lots, and driveways for shopping malls and supermarkets. He was now teaching his son how to operate a grader, as they had both recently settled into their own rental room in the outskirts of St. Petersburg. He was planning to marry off his son in the fall as well. However, he said that people in his village were aware of his success as a migrant, so he had to be careful about making a proposal where the bride's side would take advantage of his socio-economic status. He said that while in Russia, he had to have long phone calls with his wife to discuss the details of whom their son should marry. Despite Urmat's absence, he and his wife continued familiar social practices using telecommunications as if both of them were in Kyrgyzstan. To begin with, he admitted that he was having difficulty deciding which girl's house he should allow his wife to go to. He mentioned that he wanted to avoid a situation in which the girl's parents would require too much for the dowry and the wedding. Urmat was on his way back to Russia where his son was waiting for him. During his stay in Russia, his wife would make the necessary visits and enter into negotiations with a suitable girl's family. Their son would then first meet her or them, if there are several girls to choose from. He would go back to Russia and come back in the fall to get married. Nothing was mentioned about plans to help the newlyweds in Russia, however.

On one occasion, in Kyrgyzstan, a 67-year-old woman told me how she had been raising her grandchildren for ten years while her daughter-in-law commuted between Perm (RUS) and Jalalabad (KYR). Her eldest granddaughter Shohsanam was 11 years old when her daughter-in-law first left. Shohsanam had just turned 21 when her mother came home from Russia, married her off, and took her and her husband back to Russia. Interestingly, the initiator of this arranged marriage was Shohsanam's mother, the transnational migrant parent. Typically, in Central Asia, the bridegroom's mother would make a request to marry her son. However, Shohsanam's mother, who owned a stall at a large retail market in Perm, knew her 23-year-old vendor well since she was his supervisor. She had offered him a job and after observing him for quite some time, decided that he would make a suitable husband for her daughter. Shohsanam and her husband had been offered the opportunity of getting to know each other before their wedding. Her mother had explained to her and her relatives that the bridegroom whom she had found had Russian citizenship. The two people then met, liked each other, and got married. They were meanwhile in Perm and working at the same retail market. Shohsanam was preparing her documents to get Russian citizenship through her spouse. In this example, the female transnational migrant applied the matrimonial customs of her country of origin in the country of destination with a difference, in that she initiated the process of negotiations. The social capital that she possessed in the country of destination, i.e. her entrepreneurial skills, as well as her ability to calculate the costs and benefits of matchmaking her daughter with her employee and her knowledge of the customs of her country of origin that was intact due to maintaining transnational ties, were all activated in the entire matrimonial game taking place across two nation-states. The importance of the bridegroom's initiation of the proposal as a tradition, as we can see, became secondary.

6.3. Life-Cycle Rituals of Migrant Workers beyond Marriage

While marriage as a life-cycle ceremony plays an important role in the decision-making process to migrate, the expenditures of other life-cycle celebrations such as circumcisions (*sunnat to'y*), cradle parties (*beshik to'y* Uzb./ *gahvorabandon* Taj.) but also funerals (especially in Tajikistan) are important factors for the continuity of working abroad.

The second important large-scale life-cycle festivity after marriage is the circumcision ceremony, *sunnat to'y*. Celebrated for the occasion of circumcising young (until the age of seven) sons, this religious ritual retained its significance even during the Soviet era.[307] In Buxoro, *sunnat to'y* and *gahvorabandon* often include the rite of *sallabandon*, a sort of an initiation of women into motherhood and adult married womanhood. A mother having her first child is crowned by a female religious elder with a turban. The relatives of the woman give her jewelry and expensive textiles as gifts.

A party organized in honor of the circumcised boy(s) requires expenditures almost equal to wedding ceremonies that may vary from $800-$2,000. In a similar way, marriage expenditures and circumcision parties, particularly

---

307   For more on this topic, see Krämer, 2002:165. It is not the primary objective of this research to focus on the procedures of Islamic rites or secular and/or religious ceremonies. It is critical, however, to include these life-cycle rites as they are part of the transnational lives of labor migrants. For many migrants who undertake yearly home visits lasting one to four months, these life cycle rites require thorough preparation to which they often commit themselves while working in Russia.

in families with multiple sons, either influence the decision for migration or force people to migrate. Those who engage in labor migration to get married and fulfill their matrimonial projects feel the obligation to their parents of bearing a son. With the birth of the first child, regardless of the gender, a large celebration is organized dedicated to tying the child to the cradle. When a boy is born, the young family is expected to organize a circumcision party. Quite often, a person who plans to support his younger sibling's wedding after his own combines the circumcision of his son with his younger sibling's wedding to save costs. The same saving strategy may apply to the combination of a cradle party with a sibling's wedding or his or her son's circumcision celebrations.

A circumcision party either follows the actual religious rite or precedes it. In the parties attended by men and women, religion tends to play a subordinate role. Such parties include several course meals, a fairly large amount of vodka, and dancing.[308] There is, however, a ceremony of serving *plov*[309] to male relatives, friends, and neighbors to which representatives from the community mosque are invited, who say prayers and bless the family of the circumcised child. During such ceremonies, several respected guests and family members such as the hosts' male parents are clothed in expensive robes as a gesture of honor and respect. While I was in Moscow, my hosts Saida and her husband Firuz played the video of their son's circumcision party which they had celebrated the previous year in Uzbekistan.[310] As mentioned elsewhere in this study, it is common for labor migrants and non-migrants alike to keep a video recording of such events to show to their guests.[311] Saida turned on the video player, started the party recording and then fast forwarded specifically to show me something which meant a great deal to her and her husband. The couple had invited their Russian employer, who was the owner of the restaurant where they worked, to Uzbekistan. The recording showed how in the presence of several hundred guests, Firuz took the microphone and asked their honored guest from Moscow to proceed to the stage where the band had been playing. He then took a hand-made expensive gold-embroidered robe and threw it over the shoulders of his boss, who thankfully accepted the gift. Saida told me how crucial it had been to invite their boss to Uzbekistan and show him their culture, customs, traditions, and hospitality which they hoped would contribute to their mutual understanding and employer-employee relationship.[312]

---

308 Krämer, 2002:167.
309 Also known as *palov, palav, osh,* or *pilav*. A traditional Central Asian dish with meat, onions, carrots, and rice. Depending on the region, season, economic scarcity of household, and the occasion at which it is served (weddings/rituals), variations of *plov* may include raisins, quince, garlic, and pasta (as a substitute for rice).
310 Saida and Firuz hosted me during my first fieldtrip in Moscow. Their story will be told in fragments throughout this book.
311 Chapter 6, section 6.1.
312 Field observations, September 2005.

Gendered religious events such as *xatm* (for men) and *bibi seshanba* (for women) take place on a more regular basis than weddings and circumcisions. Fewer guests are invited to such events, however due to their frequency, the organization of these gatherings entails a significant portion of migrant earnings. Many seasonal migrants organize a *xatm* each time they return home. A sheep is often slaughtered as a sacrifice and a mullah is invited along with men from the mosque community, neighbors, and relatives. The mullah recites from the Qur'an, giving thanks for a safe journey home, and the meal is served to guests. Although meant for men, many female relatives accompany their male family members to this event but stay outside the guest room in which male guests are received. The migrant as a host sets a large *dasturxon* (literally 'table cloth'), filling it with warm and hearty food, pastries, and groceries in large quantities (the latter often brought specifically for such purposes from Russia). Some close relatives are also given individual gifts with a handful of Russian sweets. Sweets are also kept aside by the migrant's family for late-comers who visit the migrant on the days and weeks following the *xatm*. As far as I have been able to observe in sending countries, a *xatm* is organized on a larger scale than usual when, apart from returning home safely, the migrant also manages to buy a home or completes a major house renovation project after having commuted for several years. This is done as a sign of gratefulness to God, the saints, and the souls of the deceased family members for such an accomplishment, and out of respect for and honor to the family, relatives, and neighbors. A *xatm* is also regarded as a sign of blessing to a newly constructed home.

Oshi Bibi Seshanba (literally "Lady Tuesday's Meal")[313] is a religious gathering of women in the Ferghana Valley and parts of Uzbekistan, although it is probably a more significant ritual in Buxoro than anywhere else. During *Bibi Seshanba* gatherings that take place on Tuesdays, as the name of the event suggests, a religious female elder (*otin, oymullo, bibi-otin, otinoyi*) recites the story of a poor orphan girl who suffers from the cruelty of her stepmother and finds protection by a female saint.[314] The ritual of *Bibi Seshanba* also includes prayers and recitations from the Qur'an. Reasons for the commitment to carrying out *Oshi Bibi Seshanba* can range from the fulfillment of a wish to a request for a wish to come true, such as the birth of a child after a long period of infertility, the birth of a long-awaited son (or daughter), successful treatment of a disease or finding a healing therefore, or a husband quitting his alcohol/drug habits.[315] Nasiba, a 35-year-old woman from Uzbekistan, worked several years in Russia, bought an apartment in Buxoro, and after finishing a thorough makeover of her new home, organized *Oshi Bibi Seshanba*, thanking the female saint (*Bibi Seshanba*) for her successful real estate project.

---

313   Also known as *oshi bibiyon* ("ladies' meal") in Buxoro.
314   Selected sources on *Bibi Seshanba* are Krämer, 2002; Fathi, 2004; Louw, 2007.
315   Krämer, 2002:201.

Funerals as life-cycle rites play an important role in the lives of many migrants. Certainly migrants feel that they must attend burials of deceased relatives in the country of origin and help organize and finance the events afterwards. At the same time, many male migrants are employed in places where the risk of a fatality is high. Not only would death of a migrant mean leaving his dependent family in a devastating situation, but it can also involve immense financial loss. During the fieldwork in St. Petersburg in 2006, when a migrant worker I had interviewed was murdered two days later by an organized criminal group, I was able to observe how his entire earnings for the season, which amounted to $1000, had to be spent on the transportation of his body home.[316] This amount does not include the airfare and accommodation of his close relatives who had to travel from Uzbekistan to St. Petersburg.

In the same way that expenditures for weddings are observed to have risen in the years following the fall of the Soviet power, funerals are also reported to have become more expensive. According to my data, this has notably been the case in Tajikistan.[317] Shamigul's family, whom I met in a village not far Kulob (TAJ), was one of the rare cases in which the male bread-winner was working in Moscow following the death of both of his parents. Shamigul's husband, a 37 year-old former police officer, decided to leave when funeral expenditures became a heavy burden for his family. In Tajikistan, the costs of the burial, services of the mullah(s), and large-scale meals for visitors immediately after the death of a close relative are considerable. Hundreds of visitors show up mostly during the first few days. Then, a week after the death, another gathering takes place, followed by those being held twenty and forty days after. At these three main gatherings at which the greatest number of guests is expected, warm meals are served by the mourning family. Shamigul implied that the death of both of her parents-in-law resulted in a financial crisis in her extended family. In her village, as she told me, all her neighbors followed the custom of inviting twelve male guests to their homes every Thursday for the period of twelve months to have a hearty warm meal and say a prayer for the soul of the deceased person. She said that she felt obliged to follow the same pattern as her neighbors, otherwise her neighbors would have developed a negative attitude towards her. At the same time she felt bitter that her twelve weekly guests would demand lunch with meat, which is expensive all over Central Asia. Shamigul had to borrow a large of amount of cash from her own siblings, since the siblings of her husband had no more money left. Her husband then left for Russia.[318]

---

316 According to the result of the police investigations, the migrant had been involved in drug-related activities in addition to his regular work. The murder was connected solely to his drug activities, in particular outstanding payments which the victim had neglected; he was avenged by his accomplices.
317 *Keeping Up with Neighbours*. Article published by the Institute for War and Peace Reporting, on March 27th, 2006. Available at http://www.iwpr.net/?p=rca&s=f&o=260558&apc_state=henirca2006.
318 Interview with Shamigul, April 2007.

6.4. Conclusion

This chapter has taken a look primarily at young male labor migrants from Central Asia who leave for Russia to earn money to get married in their home countries. I have shown how their one-time 'wedding project' often becomes a reason for a short journey to turn into long-term migration. I have pointed out two patterns by which such marriage-induced labor migration comes about. In the first instance, male migrants of marriageable age leave for Russia to stay long enough to save money for their celebration. In the second pattern, migrants leave for Russia immediately after their wedding, having borrowed large sums of money. In this case, working in Russia seems the only way to pay back their debts. In both cases, male migrants plan a short-term trip to Russia which then evolves into a long-term transnational migration.

A further interesting insight gained from the analysis is that labor migration, which used to be perceived as low quality and an unreliable source of income, has, over time, come to be looked upon as stable and well-paid employment. This change in the perception of labor migration has affected families' decision-making in arranging the marriages of their children. The representation of unmarried male labor migrants during marriage negotiations has been altered both for parents wanting to marry off their daughters, and those with similar intentions for their sons. In many cases the parents on the girl's side have begun to give preference to labor-migrant bridegrooms, since the bridegroom's household income in form of remittances means that the family is not only likely to be debt-free, but also enjoy regular cash being sent from Russia.

Life-cycle rituals such as weddings, circumcision celebrations, religious rituals, and funerals in home countries contribute greatly to the continuation of working abroad and should, therefore, be seen as crucial for maintaining transnational mobility. In this chapter I have also discussed how, over a period of several years, the costs of life-cycle rituals accrue not only due to the inflation rate in the home countries, but also due to the fact that remittances are increasingly being spent on such celebrations. Labor migrants who initially intend to stay abroad for a short time are expected to finance the family events that follow their weddings. At the same time, because these family events are increasingly being covered by remittances, we can conclude that labor migrants could be perceived as victims, but also as catalysts, of life-cycle rituals.

7. Documenting Transformation and Transnational Migration: Filial Relations in Central Asian Families

Studies on transnational families have, until now, focused on various topics such as motherhood, old-age care-giving, transformation of gender roles, conflicts between different migrant generations, post-colonialism, industrialization, and religion.[319] This chapter takes a closer look at the everyday lives of the families of labor migrants in the countries of origin and destination and focuses on the roles of the migrants within their families. In this respect, it has some similarities with the study carried out by Parreñas on transnational Filipino migrants and their families, in the sense that it distinguishes them according to their membership roles in their families. Parreñas makes a distinction between the households with *parent(s) abroad* and *child(ren) abroad*[320], however I consider the families within their cultural/traditional contexts and focus on the multiple roles the migrants play at both ends of migration. It will be shown that transnational migrants can be involved in their family lives simultaneously in various functions as sons and daughters, as well as siblings and parents.

7.1. Transformational Factors of Labor Migration

I met Orolbay, a Kyrgyz in his mid-50s, in March 2008. He owns a small modest store not far from the central market of the town of Jalalabad (KYR). When I entered his store to interview him, my attention was caught by three studio pictures of a little girl that decorated the shelves of groceries. The photos were placed in front of a dozen bottles of alcoholic beverages, cans of beer, potato chips, sunflower seeds, candy, flour, and sugar, I later learned from Orolbay that these were pictures of his little granddaughter, the daughter of his daughter who had left for Russia to earn money. When I introduced myself to Orolbay and mentioned that I was originally from Uzbekistan, he immediately told me about his great time as a student at the Industrial Pedagogical School in Toshkent (UZB) during the 1970s. Since Orolbay associated the country of my origin with the place where he obtained his degree, it created a warm atmosphere for him to tell me about his life as the father of two children who live in Russia as labor migrants.

In 2005, Orolbay quit his job as a teacher at the government-owned school for vocational training, a profession for which he had been qualified

---

319 Here I refer to monographs by Parreñas, 2001 and 2005; edited volume by Bryceton and Vuorela (2002); Baldassar, Baldock and Wilding (2007) and Coles and Fechter (2007).
320 Parreñas, 2001, Chapter 4.

after his studies in Uzbekistan. He opened a small grocery store that has since then served as his main source of income. Orolbay's son Munar (b. 1978) graduated from law school in the late 1990s. Munar followed a friend of his to Moscow and was working there, like many people of his generation. Orolbay used to own a small truck which Munar drove to Russia. He used the truck as a means of transportation to reach his destination and upon his arrival, drove around the Russian capital to transport goods until he found a more profitable job. Munar's friend soon helped him find employment at a large market, so Munar rented out his father's truck to have extra income. Several months after Munar left for Moscow, Orolbay's daughter Aygerim left to join her brother.

Orolbay's children had not planned to leave Kyrgyzstan, as their father told me. They were trying to live with a decent income that they earned by working for the government and Orolbay's shop. Orolbay noted that his shop was located in a rich neighborhood of Jalalabad, so his business was not too bad. However, there were some political changes that influenced Orolbay's family. Following the mass protests in March 2005 that resulted in the toppling of President Akaev's regime (the so-called Tulip Revolution), there was a large-scale power shift in Kyrgyzstan. President Bakiev who succeeded Akaev soon started distributing power and resources within the confines of his own network. Oralbay's daughter Aygerim's husband used to work for the customs office. As his boss "was replaced from above," he lost his job too. Aygerim, like her brother Munar, had obtained a degree in law and had been working for the attorney general's office in Osh. She gave birth to a little girl at the end of 2005 and left for Russia while still at the beginning of her maternity leave from her state employment. In Kyrgyzstan, a woman can take up to three years of maternity leave to raise her child. Aygerim, like many women in Central Asia, left her little daughter with her parents and migrated to Russia. She hopes to save money by working in Russia and still be able to resume her career at the prosecutor's office when she comes back.

Orolbay takes the photos of his granddaughter and tells me about how he and his wife are raising their granddaughter. He works in the store the entire day and says that he does not receive money from his son or his daughter. He said that it would be embarrassing in Kyrgyz families to accept money from a daughter, and that sons were more responsible for sustaining their parents financially. Munar was working in Moscow to save money to marry and invest in his own small apartment. Aygerim and her husband were determined to buy a house. Orolbay proudly tells me that as an educated person, he had insisted that both children obtain a degree from a higher education institution. Both of his children obtained degrees in law. Orolbay hopes that they will be able to resume their professions when they return from Russia, especially since he had difficulty financing his children's education in Kyrgyzstan. When asked if it was not difficult for him and his wife to look after his granddaughter, Orolbay assured me that it is his duty to support his children. Sarcastically, he mentioned a Kyrgyz saying: "Kyzdan ongoi kutulasyng, nebereden ölgöndö kutulasyng" ("You get rid of your daughter easily but you get rid of your grandchild when you die"), meaning, as a parent you are free from your duties when you marry your daughter off, but you still have obligations to your grandchildren.

I have chosen the story of Orolbay to illustrate a typical Central Asian family, which is being shaped and influenced by social, political, and economic changes in the region. Labor migration should be seen as part and parcel of such processes, through which relations within kinship are challenged and redefined. As mentioned in earlier chapters of this study, labor migration to Russia is closely connected to post-independence transformation processes, particularly the transition to a market economy. Faced with financial hardships, family members see themselves as left with no other choice than leaving for Russia to make a living. Reports and articles on labor migration from Central Asia to Russia may leave us with an impression that the Central Asian population migrates because it is poor. I too had assumed that labor migration would primarily have an economic reason. While I do not deny that poverty and unemployment are the prime push factors, as most quantitative surveys indicate, I find it important to take a broader approach to the decision to migrate. Personal narratives of the respondents, as we shall see, show us interesting details about the circumstances under which migrants leave. My inquiry into the decision to engage in labor migration revealed more about the socio-cultural and political contexts that were of equal importance to the economic aspects which prompted migration.

Individuals interviewed for this research often voluntarily shared information about the circumstances in which they or their family members migrated. During the interviews, I also asked my respondents to tell me more about their decision or that of their family members to migrate. One category of individuals, which I generated from the data, left for Russia because they had a large amount of [financial] debt. They left due to economic changes or the corruption, which is endemic in the entire region, or also because of disputes within the family. By "economic changes" I mean not only region-wide factors such as inflation or crises with convertibility, but also policies of individual states towards medium and small-scale business, such as the informal sector trade. For instance, the Uzbek government's arbitrary decisions to close down or remodel markets led a number of private small traders to leave because they were no longer able to make a profit. Some migrants told me that such policies have caused social discontent and affected those who made their daily livings.

Migrants whom I interviewed had difficulty paying back their debts in their countries of origin, and sought a solution in labor migration to Russia where the wages are higher. Respondents implied that, with the rule of law being absent in their countries of origin and with corruption increasing, they had no choice other than to migrate.[321] Indeed, according to the latest report released by Transparency International, Tajikistan was ranked at 152nd place, while Kyrgyzstan and Uzbekistan were ranked as 164th and 177th respectively in the Corruption Perceptions Index.[322]

As one of the significant factors in the context of migration, respondents throughout the places of origin and destination mentioned *tirichilik* (Kyr.), *tirikchilik* (Uzb.), or *zindagi* (Taj.), meaning 'life' and 'survival.' No direct equivalent of this concept exists in English, and the way in which individuals explained their situation as migrants or dependents makes this concept even more difficult to translate. Whether highlighted during the long conversations with Orolbay, the quinquagenarian Kyrgyz in Jalalabad whose daughter migrated leaving her 6-month-old baby, with an ethnic Uzbek woman with three children in Jalalabad (KYR) whose husband is a migrant, or with a Tajik construction worker in St. Petersburg with serious marital issues back home, the meaning of this word is best interpreted as a combination of concepts such as life, existence, subsistence, and survival.

The examples upon which I will draw in this chapter are in many respects similar to that of Orolbay's family. To better understand the relations between kin members, the perspectives of both migrant and non-migrant members will be taken into account. There were two types of male migrants that derived from the data: a) the type of an *eldest son* who leaves to the fulfill his obligation to salvage his family's economic situation and b) *youngest or only son* who is torn between the expectations of his homeland society to stay and take care of his family and, at the same time, to carry their financial burdens alone. Male migrants as *sons* will be juxtaposed to female migrants as *daughters*, for whom migration to Russia is an opportunity to leave their difficult situations back home and offer long-distance support to their families.[323]

---

321 Interview with Shahodat, St. Petersburg, August 2006.
322 *Cf* Corruption Perceptions Index released by Transparency International. http://cpi.transparency.org/cpi2011/results/. See also *Central Asia: Corruption, Lack of Vision Seen as Stunting Economic Growth*. Article published on EurasiaNet on October 10th, 2004 (available online at http://www.eurasianet.org/departments/civilsociety/articles/pp101 004.shtml), *Corruption Getting Worse in Central Asia*. Article Published on EurasiaNet on January 10th, 2007 (available online at http://www.eurasianet.org/departments/insight/articles/eav100107a.shtml). Further sources, http://www.transparency.org/news_room/in_focus/2008/cpi2008/ cpi_2008_table, *Tajikistan: On the Road to Failure*. Report by the International Crisis Group released on February 12th, 2009 (available at http://www.crisisgroup.org/home/index.cfm? id=5907&l=1), Corrupt Kyrgyz Courts. Report by Institute for War and Peace Reporting. RCA No.57, on June 22nd, 2001 (available at http://www.iwpr.net/?p=rca &s=f&o=176120&apc_state=henirca2001). See also Erica Marat's extensive analysis on corruption in relation with the state-crime nexus in Kyrgyzstan and Tajikistan (Marat, 2006) available at (http://www.silkroadstudies.org/new/docs/Silkroadpapers/ 0610EMarat.pdf).
323 On construction of types, see Kluge (2000) Empirically Grounded Construction of Types and Typologies in Qualitative Social Research, *Forum Qualitative Social Research*, Vol.1, No. 1, Art. 14.

7.2. Migrants as Sons and Daughters

7.2.1. The Eldest Son – The Rescuer of the Family

Mansurjon from Jalalabad (KYR) arrived in Russia with his close friend in the mid-1990s. After the fall of the Soviet Union, his father established a small private textile company to produce silk and cotton fabric. A number of family disputes arose between Mansurjon's father and his uncle, his father's younger brother, until the latter allegedly perpetrated fraud. One day, Mansurjon's father's company was raided by the police. He was then charged with fraud, had to pay a large sum of money as a fine, file bankruptcy for his company, and bribe his way out of a long-term prison sentence.[324] The family experienced a deep financial crisis and Mansurjon's father broke ties with his younger brother permanently. Mansurjon left for Astrakhan with the intention of saving his family from economic crisis and paying off his father's debts. He started making a living, first, as he admitted, by doing odd jobs for a small criminal group that extorted money from labor migrants, then later as a petty trader.[325]

During the interview, I inquired about his siblings and their whereabouts to learn whether his other family members were living in Russia as well. I asked him to name his siblings and tell me more about what they did in Astrakhan. Most interviewees would start listing their close kin ties and say whether they live and work in Russia or Central Asia. Mansurjon, however, first took a deep drag from the cigarette which he was smoking and exhaled a long sigh. He stated that it had been his fault that his two younger brothers had followed him to Astrakhan. I listened, waiting for him to elaborate.

Mansurjon had a strong desire to pay off his father's debts. As the eldest son, he felt responsible for the financial security of his entire family. He

---

[324] The money paid as a bribe and administrative fine may overlap. The subject of corruption in the judicial systems in the countries where this research was conducted cannot be discussed here.

[325] When I met Mansurjon at one of the largest markets in Astrakhan, he suggested that we eat breakfast and drink coffee at a decent café. I was at first surprised, because having explored the market for two weeks, I was aware that there were no suitable places where he and I could have an interview over breakfast and a cup of coffee. The cafés that I had visited were usually full of porters, vendors, and small businessmen. These were places that served rather simple and hearty meals and expected their customers to consume fast and leave. When we met, Mansurjon told me that he knew a special place and led me through the back alleys of market stalls and storage rooms to which I would have never been allowed access. Within ten minutes, I found myself with my interlocutor in a different world. The café to which I had been led had a different atmosphere. It was quiet and was not frequented by market workers, but rather by men who represented a much higher hierarchical position in the market network and were presumably seriously responsible for the protection thereof. It was the atmosphere in which the interview took place and the confidence with which Mansurjon was speaking about the underworld he had become acquainted with during his stay in Astrakhan that led me to think that he was not lying about many facets of his life as a migrant.

scraped together the little money that had been left from his family's business and gave half of it to his friend who was on his way to Russia, so that he could save it for him when he joined. Once in Russia, his friend suggested that he and Mansurjon should make a profit on the money and lend it to people for interest. He and his friend got involved in a criminal group that threatened and blackmailed Central Asian shuttle traders. He was charged with racketeering, extortion, and participation in organized crime, and received a prison sentence of 18 months in Astrakhan. His friend had run away without paying back the sum that he had borrowed from him. Mansurjon's parents came from Jalalabad to visit him in prison. They told him to stop robbing people and return to Kyrgyzstan, if that was the way he was making a living in Russia. When Mansurjon was released from prison, his family back home had even more expenses because of him. Mansurjon's younger brothers had to leave for Russia. As the eldest son and elder brother he felt responsible to organize their travel and accommodation in Astrakhan.

At the time of the interview with Mansurjon, he and his younger brothers were sending approximately $200-250 a month to Kyrgyzstan. His parents' joint pension is not even enough for their basic household needs. Mansurjon underlines that his family used to be part of the Soviet intelligentsia. His grandfather used to have a supervisory position. His uncle worked as chief architect for one of the economically well-off cities of the Ferghana Valley. Mansurjon is above all proud of his mother's employment during the Soviet period. OBKhES, the Soviet Department for Combating Theft of Socialist Property[326] where his mother used to work, was the institution responsible for the protection of socialist property and no one ever succeeded in cheating, as Mansurjon argues. Meanwhile his parents are fully dependent on the remittances sent jointly by Mansurjon and his brothers.

The interviews conducted with migrants and families show a pattern in which a close family member gets involved in or causes a severe financial crisis that has implications for the entire family. The eldest son then migrates to Russia. Once he settles in the country of destination, he tries to solve the short-term problems such as paying off debts and alleviating the family's financial crisis. He then sees opportunities in staying over a longer term. He arranges jobs for other siblings.[327] Usually it is then up to the father of the family to approve or disapprove of his child's decision to migrate. For example, 30-year-old Mashrab from Tajikistan left for Russia and shortly after arriving, arranged a job for his younger brother Mirzo. Upon their return to visit their parents, their father did not allow Mirzo to leave again, because his help was needed on the farm as the family planned to lease more land from the government.[328] A similar pattern was observed in the family of Bahriddin,

---

[326] OBKhES, the Russian acronym for Otdel po bor'be s xishcheniem socialisticheskoi sobstvennosti.
[327] Faist, 2000a:152-153.
[328] Interview with Mashrab, Kulob (TAJ), April 2007.

23 years old. When I visited his family in the village of Dahana in the outskirts Kulob (TAJ) in the summer of 2007, he had been migrating for three years. He had been home for four months during the late fall and spring to get married. He was paying for his younger brother's education and wanted to invite him to Russia as well.

Among the siblings for whom elder sons organize jobs, there are often elder or younger sisters. Nasiba, a 35-year-old woman from Uzbekistan, is one of them.[329] She followed her younger brother to Moscow. Her brother Umar left for Moscow in September 2003, after their father was charged with fraud and Umar had to sell his apartment to bribe their father's way out of a long prison sentence. His father had bought him the apartment as a wedding gift. Umar was a doctoral student, living in Toshkent with his wife and children and about to finish his degree. The troubles Umar's father was facing put him into an even more difficult position when his doctoral supervisor suddenly died. In the corrupt educational system in Central Asia, Umar had neither the financial nor the social means to set up a new Ph.D. committee.[330] Falling short of the expectations of his family and friends, Umar saw no reason to stay in Uzbekistan. Once in Russia, he first worked as a porter in a storage compound for construction materials in the outskirts of Moscow. Three months later, Umar called his sister Nasiba and told her that she could come to Moscow too.[331]

Upon her arrival in Russia, Nasiba looked forward to finally paying off her debts and saving money to buy an apartment in Uzbekistan. Unlike many other migrants in a similar situation, however, it took Nasiba and her husband Toshpo'lat longer – almost five years – to save $14,000 to buy an apartment. By comparison, other respondents, depending on their earnings and family situation, worked approximately three years to be able to make an adequate investment in housing. The longer it took Nasiba and her husband to save money, the more the real estate prices went up. Within the first two years of their stay in Moscow, the couple managed to save $6,000. Just when they were prepared to buy a small house, Toshpo'lat's younger brother Nodir, who was in Uzbekistan, became part of a large plot in Uzbekistan that involved financial fraud. Toshpo'lat's entire family expected help from him, not only because he was the eldest son, but also because he was the only close kin who had saved money by working in Russia. Toshpo'lat, as the

---

329 Participant observations with Nasiba, Umar, and Toshpo'lat in Moscow in September 2005 and their family members in Buxoro, Uzbekistan, in October 2006.
330 For more on corruption in the education sphere in Central Asia, see Heyneman and DeYoung, 2004, and *Central Asia: Buying Ignorance – Corruption in Education Widespread, Corrosive*, Article by Radio Free Europe Radio Liberty, published on July 7th, 2004, available at (http://www.rferl.org/content/article/1053724.html). Among the three sending countries on which this study focuses, only Kyrgyzstan has recently showed some signs of improvement in fighting against corruption, see e.g., Kyrgyzstan: *Officials Strive to Curb Corruption in Education System*. A report by EurasiaNet on January 22nd, 2009 at http://www.eurasianet.org/departments/insightb/articles/ eav012209b.shtml.
331 Conversations with Umar and Nasiba, Moscow, September 2005.

eldest son of the family, also felt responsible to save his younger brother, who, in his view, had become a victim of slander. The prosecutor who was in charge of Nodir's case demanded $10,000. Having spent their joint savings, that is $ 6,000, on bribing the prosecutor, Toshpo'lat and his wife Nasiba asked Nodir to pay them back gradually by working in Russia. When the trial was over, Nodir and his wife left for Moscow, where Toshpo'lat had found him a job and a place to stay.

In October 2006 I visited the family of Sohib, one of my respondents, in a small village called Kuchkak in the northern province of Sughd (TAJ). I had met Sohib three months previously during my fieldwork in St. Petersburg (RUS). Sohib had mentioned that he had to leave for Russia because his younger brother Sulton was in prison for having deserted his mandatory military service. Sohib wanted to earn enough money to buy Sulton out of prison. When I visited Sohib's home, his father had been weeding his vegetable garden. We drank tea and waited for his wife to come back from the market in Khujand where she had brought 20 kg of dried apricots to sell. In the absence of remittances, Sohib's parents had no income other than their miniscule earnings as private farmers. Sohib's parents welcomed me with great joy and told me that their second son Sulton had just been released from prison. Sulton and his parents were happy to tell me that with the remittances that Sohib had been sending from Russia, they not only had managed to get Sulton out of prison, but also Sulton had engaged himself in a large-scale remodeling of their house. His parents told me that they were planning to marry Sulton off before the end of the year.

Elder Brother in Migration – A Fatherly Substitute

While in migration, due to his role as the initiator and first breadwinner of the family, the eldest son often acquires enough authority to make him almost equal to the father, vis-à-vis his other siblings. Firuz (UZB), with whose family I stayed in Moscow, landed a job as a chef in a small restaurant in Moscow. It was through a conversation with his wife that I heard that he had come to Moscow to pay off $2,000 of his father's debt. Firuz's wife was not particularly clear about the details of the family's delicate economic situation. She mentioned that her father-in-law in Uzbekistan had borrowed money to marry off Firuz in 1999 then borrowed more money to start a small business. In September 2005, when I studied this family while renting a room in their apartment, Firuz had been living in Moscow for four years with his wife, son, and two younger brothers.

Within the first two years of his stay in Moscow, he had paid off his parents' debts. Firuz's authority, his fatherly affection, and his care towards his younger brothers were interesting to observe. Besides remitting cash regularly to his parents in Uzbekistan, Firuz was helping to sustain his youngest brother, a young man who was about six years his junior. He was regularly giving his brother cash, despite the fact that the latter was employed and had his own income. Furthermore, unlike Firuz, his youngest brother who was married to a Russian citizen had legal status. Firuz often addressed him as "my child." While it is not uncommon in Central Asia that an elder sibling refers to his or her younger siblings as their "children," provided that the age difference between them is greater than about 5-6 years, in the context of transnational migration in which family relations span across nation-state borders, the roles of the siblings are reconsidered in the country of arrival. Maintenance of close ties between siblings and the substitute for parental care in such cases gain importance.[332]

7.2.2. The Uneasy Situation of Youngest and Only Sons

Certainly, not all the male migrants analyzed in this study are first sons of their families. Age and adequate physical condition are also important factors in migration.[333] In some families, when elder male siblings are middle-aged, are married, and have grandchildren, they often choose to stay and send their youngest brother instead. This is especially true in families in which elderly parents are still around. When their elderly parents die, it is the responsibility of the sons to bury them. Absence from funerals or burials can be harmful to the social position of the sons, not only within the extended family, but also in the neighborhood. Hence, in order to continue to enjoy their reputations as senior members of their neighborhood or community, older persons might choose not to migrate and instead send their sons. In the family of Nasiba and Umar, their younger brother Usmon, the youngest child of the family, showed a strong desire to leave for Russia to work. Usmon is married and has two children. Having seen his elder siblings improve their financial situations, he too wanted to work there. Usmon's father, however, did not approve of his youngest son's intention to migrate to Russia since he needed at least one of his children present in case of his death. Usmon left for Russia to work but returned a month later due to sickness. His elder siblings and parents arranged that his family would benefit from remittances in exchange for his permanent stay in Buxoro. It must be mentioned that the father's decision was influenced by the rumors in Buxoro in the fall of 2006 that in a village not far away, an old man had died and, allegedly, since they were all in Russia, there was not a single adult male relative present to attend and carry out the burial. According to traditions derived from Islamic law, only men are

---

332 Already on our way to his apartment from the airport where he picked me up, Firuz told me that he had married off his youngest brother in Moscow to a Russian girl six months previously. Being the eldest of three siblings, he called his brothers several times a day and referred to his youngest brother as "bachem," Tajik for "my son," or in the Bukharan Tajik dialect "my child," which can be used to refer to one's child regardless of gender.
333 According to the report released by the World Health Organization, the life expectancy among men in Kyrgyzstan is currently 64, in Tajikistan 65, and in Uzbekistan 66. (www.euro.who.int/ document/obs/pophealth.pdf).

allowed to attend burials, yet this old man had to be buried by his female relatives.[334]

The societal expectations notwithstanding, there are cases in which the only son leaves for Russia with the intention from the outset to work and reside there for a long period, while maintaining close ties to the country of origin. Born after four girls, 26-year-old Muhammadyusuf from Jalalabad (KYR) was 22 years old when he left for Moscow after his father's death. During the interview with his mother Marghubaxon Opa, it became clear that Muhammadyusuf's older sister, the first daughter of the family, had been working in Odessa with her husband for three years. However, as a son, Muhammadyusuf did not follow his oldest sister. After his father's death, Muhammadyusuf took over his role as the bread-winner and the decision-maker of the family. At the time of the interview the following family members were dependent on his remittances: his grandmother (his deceased father's mother), his mother, his divorced sister with her seven-year-old child, and his wife whom he married three months prior to the time of the field research. Muhammadyusuf's mother said that her son was likely to stay in Russia and work, as the family had no other source of income.[335]

7.2.3. Daughters and their Search for a New Start

Similar to the situation with an eldest son, if the family has only one son, he takes the responsibility as the breadwinner, providing not only for his parents but also for unmarried siblings and divorced sisters as illustrated in the example above. It must be noted that in more traditional residential settlements such as rural areas and *mahalla*s, women are expected to return to their parents' home after a divorce.[336] Some single mothers manage to live alone in apartment houses with their children. Settlements with concrete multiple-storied houses, which were, for the most part, erected during the Soviet period, offer more anonymity to divorced mothers than neighborhoods where houses have courtyards and are adjacent to one another, and social interactions between residents are more frequent. In the latter residential situation, a

---

334   Observations in Uzbekistan, fall 2006.
335   Interview with Marghubaxon Opa, February 2008, Jalalabad (KYR).
336   As observed also by Krämer, residents in Central Asia discriminate between houses and apartments (2002:169). There is a distinction between living in a *mahalla* with one- and two-storied family houses and in a *dom* with multiple-storied apartment houses. *Dom* is a Russian loanword for 'house' which is also known as *seksiya* (Russian loanword 'section') in some parts of Tajikistan. Depending on the amount of savings, the type of real estate may vary in price, making a house with a courtyard in urban centers more expensive than an apartment. A house (depending on region and dialect, in Uzbek *uy*, *hovli*, or *uchastka* [Russian loanword *uchastok* for 'lot of land'], in Tajik *xona*, or *havli*, and in Kyrgyz *zher uy*, or *zher tam*) is usually shared by a large family and typically has a courtyard and/or a small garden for growing fruit and vegetables. A less expensive type of real estate is an apartment in a multi-storied building known as a *kvartira*, which is a Russian word for apartment.

divorced woman soon becomes the subject of rumors and judgment by the neighbors.[337]

Women in Central Asia seem to show an increased tendency towards engaging themselves in labor migration after a failed marital relationship. As will be discussed in the next section, they move to their parents' home with their belongings and children so as to demonstrate to their community that they follow social/traditional norms, then they leave their children with their parents and migrate. While the next section illustrates the category of women who play the role of daughter in the family, the next chapter will elaborate more on conjugal relationships in the context of migration.

To many women whom I studied, labor migration represented far more than an economic opportunity. Parreñas introduces the term "hidden causes" to labor migration, stressing that although labor migrants strive to sustain their families in their countries of origin, economic factors can be only one part of the picture.[338] The women encountered in Russia often confided that they had had family problems besides financial difficulties. Migrants' wives in the countries of origin expressed their strong desire to either join their husbands or get divorced and leave for Russia as well, because their situation was becoming difficult. This is especially true of those who have to share the same household as their in-laws. Particularly in rural areas, when the husbands leave, in compliance with the social norms, women move to their parents-in-law's or parents' home in order to avoid rumors that would in any way raise doubts about their fidelity. This would apply more to young newly-married wives who do not yet have children or have small children. For divorced daughters who have to move back to their parents' house, migration offers an opportunity to no longer be a burden to their parents.

Nargiza, a 27-year-old woman from Andijon (UZB) left for Russia soon after she got divorced. Our interview took place in a small bakery stall at a food market in St. Petersburg where she was simultaneously selling bread products and talking to me about her situation. She had graduated from the State University of Andijon where she obtained a diploma with honors. Her professors proposed that she pursue an academic career. She was married, however, and had a daughter, so she decided to teach at a school and remain more of a traditional obedient wife than a career-pursuing modern woman, as her family would otherwise have referred to her. Her marriage did not last long as her husband became increasingly abusive. Nargiza got divorced, returned to her parents' home with her daughter and then left for Russia. On her way to St.Petersburg in the train she got acquainted with a young married man named Akramjon. Akramjon and Nargiza fell in love and started an

---

337 As observed also by Bourdieu in his explanation of matrimonial strategies among the Kabyle, a divorced or a widowed man can remarry without difficulties on the marriage market. A divorced woman, however, loses her status or becomes of secondary value (2007:69).
338 Parrenas, 2001:65-66.

affair.³³⁹ Akramjon convinced her that they should be together and that he would help her settle in Russia which "was not a place where a woman should be alone."³⁴⁰ Nargiza soon persuaded Akramjon to let her bring her four-year-old daughter with her to St. Petersburg where they would live together.

The interview with Nargiza was an interesting experience. It was Nargiza's aunt Shohida Opa who had wished to introduce me to her. Shohida Opa had worked in Uzbekistan as a literature teacher in a high school prior to migrating to Russia. She immediately showed great interest in my research when I told her about it. She insisted that I should get to know Nargiza, her "intelligent niece" (*aqlli jiyanim*), as she referred to her. Nargiza worked in a small bakery shop at one of the food markets in St. Petersburg.

In the sending countries, I was exposed to the different roles that a single woman may play in her social context in Central Asia. Through a short trip to the bakery shop and a conversation in the labor migrant's working atmosphere it became clear that in migration, the roles of a female labor migrant become more complex as they span multiple social and cultural fields. I was accompanied to the bakery by Shohida Opa, whose entire trip had been arranged by her niece who was about 30 years younger than she. During the conversation, Nargiza was carrying out complex business-related calculations and at the same time reporting them to the owner of the bakery, who was an Azerbaijani with a Russian passport. Her aunt Shohida Opa had told me earlier that her Azerbaijani boss was very satisfied with the quality of Nargiza's work. Given that she had been a math and physics major in Uzbekistan, Nargiza's reliability in accounting was not surprising. To her boss she was good at math, fast, and friendly to customers, so Nargiza's role at the bakery shop could not have been fulfilled better.

Between selling bread and entering the sales into her ledger, Nargiza narrated her life as a migrant and a single parent.³⁴¹ She mentioned that several times a day she had to call her four-year-old daughter from her cell phone since she was home alone. It seemed quite unbelievable to me that a mother would leave a small child alone at home, but Nargiza was convinced that "the proximity of the store makes it easier to leave her alone in our apartment, call her several times a day, and have a lunch break with her."³⁴² It became obvious that she was not at ease as far as her role as a mother was concerned, but she still preferred to have her daughter with her than with her parents back in Andijon.

While I was still in the store, her boyfriend Akramjon dropped by to say hello to us. Immediately, Nargiza jumped into the role of an obedient wife, as they exchanged words on how the day should proceed. Shohida Opa and I

---

339 Issues of extramarital relationships and polygamy in migration will be discussed in a separate chapter.
340 Interview with Nargiza and her aunt Shohida Opa.
341 Her boyfriend was living with her, but Nargiza was the sole caregiver of her daughter.
342 *Ibid.*

went and strolled around the market for quite a while, as the number of customers grew in the bakery and we did not want to disturb the work. By the time we came back, there was an 18-year-old adolescent sitting on the same stool as I had sat earlier, eating bread with tea. This was Nargiza's younger brother who had just arrived in St. Petersburg. He had not passed the entrance exams to study at the university in Andijan and therefore came to Russia to work. Nargiza had already found him a job as a porter at the same market where she was working. Her earnings were primarily meant to sustain her parents and siblings in Andijon. Besides being the breadwinning daughter, this woman was fulfilling the role of a mother, an older sister, a wife, and a niece.

Nasiba, part of whose story was told in the last section, had been remarried for just a year when she left for Moscow to follow her brother Umar. Before her remarriage, she lived in her parents' house for almost two years. She was employed in a higher education institution. Her salary was low and she had to provide for her parents, not only since her brothers were also earning little, but also because they were not living in the same household. Due to this delicate situation, Nasiba, as a divorced woman, played the role of the eldest son in that she felt responsible for taking care of her parents. She would make extra money every year during the months of February and June, when students had their final exams, and also in August. By making arrangements for students who would pay bribes to pass their finals in February and June, she would earn her share. August was the month in which new students would be admitted to the program and Nasiba would "help" them to succeed. During other months, Nasiba's income was just enough to buy food for her parents. Her low salary was one of the reasons why she engaged herself in small-scale trade with her ex-husband. She and her ex-husband had borrowed a large amount of money from family, friends, and acquaintances that they were unable to pay back. Domestic abuse and disputes over loans led the couple to get divorced.

In early 2000s, at the time when Nasiba left for Russia, not only was corruption in the area of education getting worse year by year, but also the non-convertibility of the national currency in Uzbekistan was a major problem. The inflation rate was 24% in 2003; the black exchange market was flourishing despite strict measures against it by the government.[343] The interest rate for borrowing cash through informal channels was 20%. By the time Nasiba left for Moscow, she had large debts. After her divorce, she returned to her parents' house. Her lenders started coming to her parents' house, threatening her and demanding their money back. Nasiba almost committed suicide. Migration to Russia, which started as an opportunity to pay off debts and live independently from her parents, turned into long-term employment for Nasiba and Toshpo'lat, whom she had meanwhile remarried. Since then,

---

[343] Information on the inflation rate is taken from by-country and by-year charts provided by Index Mundi (http://www.indexmundi.com/g/g.aspx?v=71&c=uz&l=en).

Nasiba's daughter from her first marriage has been living with Nasiba's parents. The couple has managed to entirely pay off Nasiba's debts and save enough money to buy an apartment in Buxoro, where they plan to live together upon their return. In a personal conversation, she shared that she was satisfied with her situation as a migrant worker in Russia, as she had no longer been able to tolerate the dishonest way in which she was making a living in Uzbekistan.

We can see that, figuratively speaking, both Nargiza and Nasiba were stretching their hands across nation-states to their extended family back in Uzbekistan. Perhaps there too, the two women would have developed skills to shift constantly among several roles. Migration to Russia, long-distance relationships with their families and their positions as significant breadwinners have given these women skills to adjust to different challenges of life.

7.3. Female-Headed Households: Introducing Gulruh and Shohistaxon

In their analysis of Bangladeshi women, scholars Hussain and Huda describe migration as one of the most common processes by which women come to be in charge of their households. The authors explain that in the case of a rural Bangladeshi family, the conditions for women to take over the household is that they are neither living with their parents-in-law nor are adult sons living in the household. Under these circumstances, the wife fulfills the tasks of the absent male head of the household. The husband who is in migration, however, is still fully in charge of providing his family with finances and making the major decisions, while the wife left behind does not work outside the home.[344]

While this may be true for many migrant wives in Central Asia, we shall see in two examples that some women opt for additional sources of income despite the remittances. I shall first take a look at an example from rural Tajikistan and move on to the case of a migrant wife in an urban center of southern Kyrgyzstan.

7.3.1. Gulruh

Gulruh was introduced to me by an authoritative woman in her village. During the field trip in southern Tajikistan, on the outskirts of Kulob, I visited the rural district of Dahana. I was told that if I wanted to stay in the village for several days and talk to village inhabitants, it would be better to talk first to the deputy head of the village council (Taj. *raisi jamoa*). In Dahana, I encountered a courageous woman in her early 50s who held this post. She in-

---

344 Hussain and Huda, 1997.

vited me to stay at her place for several days and interview migrant families during the day. "This way you don't have to worry about any men in the house. I have no man. Got rid of him a long time ago," she added sarcastically. "I have two daughters living with me and two granddaughters temporarily visiting." She later told me that she had been a politically active woman during the Soviet period and that her husband found it hard to cope with her higher social position in the village on the one hand and her career in the village council on the other. The deputy head of the village encouraged me to talk to Ayub, who travels back and forth between Russia and Tajikistan, and his wife Gulruh, as they were "one of those families in the village whose living standards had reached [sic] an excellent level (Taj. *ba darajai olii*)."[345]

Gulruh has been managing her household for at least ten years. Her husband Ayub has been commuting between Moscow and Kulob. Gulruh and Ayub are in their late 40s and have six children. During the Soviet period, both of them obtained degrees from higher education institutions prior to settling as teachers in the village of Dahana. Ayub received his degree with honors from the State University of Dushanbe as a teacher of history and law but was only able to practice his profession until the late 1990s. Gulruh studied education and psychology in Kulob. During the field research I encountered a great many women who completely depended on migrant remittances. Due to lack of education, their sole option for employment was farming, from which they did not derive much income. Some of them were housewives with no additional external source of income, either because they were too busy managing their households and carrying out chores such as cooking, baking bread, cleaning or the physically strenuous chores which would be otherwise carried out by the male family members who were in Russia. This especially concerned those women who did not have an elder or adolescent male family member. Transportation, storage, and preparation of a large amount of fodder for cattle have been taken over by women in many families where male migrants are absent. The same applies to *ogorod*s, in-house plots of land for growing produce. There are some male members from the extended kin who assist them, yet physically challenging tasks such as plowing, sowing, and harvesting have been added to women's tasks. In one of the families where I was staying, I joined my host sister Marambi in driving cattle, which would otherwise have been done by one of her two elder brothers had they not both been in Russia. Every evening her family would release their chickens from their small cage. These chickens would immediately start eating the freshly planted potato seeds. In such situations, male members of the family would have put up a fence around the vegetable garden.

Such circumstances did not apply to Gulruh. Unlike many migrant-wives whom I encountered in rural Tajikistan, Gulruh strove to earn her own cash despite the fact that she had a large family to take care of, low wages from her jobs in Tajikistan, and a husband who received a decent salary in

---

345 Field notes, Kulob, April 2007.

Russia. One of the arguments women often tried to advance during the interviews was that the wage difference between Russia and Central Asia (especially in rural areas) was so great that it was not worth working in Central Asia.[346] Ambitiously, Gulruh expressed her eager wish not to be completely dependent on her husband's support, as she distanced herself from those who are in a similar situation.

> I am not like other women. I have a neighbor whose husband is in Russia. She doesn't work anywhere! She walks around the village with her cell phone. Every time her husband calls, she quickly says, "Hi-how-are-you-send-me-money!" – just like that. I couldn't do that. The last time I remember specifically asking my husband for money was when our daughter gave birth and I had to take over the medical costs.

Unlike many other inhabitants of Dahana, Gulruh and her husband do not lease any land for farming. Instead, Gulruh has three different jobs. The village where she lives has a school for vocational training that was built during the Soviet period and still functions as such. Gulruh works there as a part-time teacher and a cook at the canteen. In addition, in the afternoon, she works as a teacher for an elementary class at the village's only secondary school. I went to the school for vocational training looking for her. Gulruh later told me that when she had seen me, she had first thought that I was looking for an apartment. It turned out that Ayub and Gulruh had bought a 2-room apartment in the city of Kulob from Ayub's earnings in Russia. Real estate is one of the most common kinds of investment of the financial remittances in Central Asia. Gulruh said that the apartment was meant for her eldest son, who she would soon marry off, and eventually for his young family to move into. Since the couple purchased the apartment, however, they have been renting it out to students and young skilled workers coming from rural areas. Hence, besides the three jobs, Gulruh carries out the tasks of a landlady as well.

This is how she explained her attitude about being a labor migrant's wife:

> I have to work. I can't wait for the Russian money (*sumi Rossiia*) to be wired.[347] The Russian money is not enough since we have to educate our children. Everyone is talking about Russian money but if you don't make efforts here in addition to that, the Russian money is nothing. The first time my husband came to visit –

---

346 Some female respondents stated during interviews that they had a strong desire to work, but the salary offered to them was hardly more than the costs of public transport to get to their workplace. Other women simply preferred to rely on their husband's support and stay at home, taking care of children and household rather than seeking low-paid employment. There were also women who did not work because their in-laws did not allow them to.

347 Monetary remittances were often referred to as 'Russian money' by migrants and their dependents (Uzb. *Rossiia puli*, Taj. *sumi Rossiia, puli Rossiia, or puli Rossiano*, depending on the linguistic and regional contexts).

and you can ask him yourself when he comes back home later – he'll tell you the details when exactly it was, he is intelligent and educated, he remembers all the details... Well, yes, the first time he came to visit he brought $600 with him. We had debts to pay off. He paid off part of the debts then we had to receive guests and throw a party. You know what it is like when someone comes back from a long journey. The money was gone pretty soon.

It is common in all three sending countries that every time the migrant visits home, the migrant's family invites their extended family as well as neighbors. In small villages, there is greater social pressure to invite as many guests as possible, as the ties between community members tend to be denser. Those who cannot manage to come to the large-scale gathering, to which Gulruh was referring, come to visit the migrant on other days. When I visited Gulruh, her husband Ayub was visiting from Moscow for two weeks, so I had the opportunity to interview him as well. During our talk, several people came to visit Ayub. Gulruh received them and ushered them into another room, so that Ayub and I would not be disturbed during the interview.

Gulruh is the mother of six children. She has two daughters and four sons. Two of her sons (23 and 18 years old) were in Moscow. She said that both of her sons were studying at the State University of Kulob. The Soviet system of education, which continued after its demise, and the adoption of the so-called Bologna model (two-tiered B.A. and M.A.) in some of the USSR's successor states enable students to engage in the education by correspondence. The Russian term *zaochnoe obuchenie* is applied to those educational institutions where this kind of education is still available. *Zaochnoe obuchenie,* a typical heritage from the USSR's education system, requires that students that be present to sit exams and tests twice a year for about a month. The rest of the year, students fulfill the assignments from their professors and lecturers on their own. Education by correspondence is convenient for migrants like Gulruh's sons who work in Russia. Gulruh's elder daughter was married off at the age of sixteen in 2004, so she does not live with her parents any more. Gulruh's fourth child, an adolescent who is fifteen years old, studies at the Turkish lyceum in Kulob. This is a prestigious high school where tuition costs $200 a year.[348] At home, when her husband is away in Russia, Gulruh takes care of her 11-year-old son, her 7-year-old daughter, and her elderly parents-in-law.

A further point which should not go unnoticed is that Gulruh plays a central role in the upbringing of the children. Following her advice, her hus-

---

348 Founded by Fethullah Gülen, Turkish lyceums were already established in the earliest years of independence. Due to the Islamic affiliations of the schools, the Uzbek government became wary about the rise of Islamic fundamentalism in Uzbekistan, which led to the closing down of the Turkish schools in this country in the late 1990s. In Kyrgyzstan and Tajikistan, however, these schools have become more prominent for their quality and affordability of education (classes taught in Turkish and English), their non-Western backgrounds, and the strict discipline and order which parents of the lyceum students seem to appreciate (Balci 2003).

band's stay does not exceed two or three weeks when he visits his family twice a year, for their two eldest sons work in Russia as well. Gulruh is anxious about her sons being out of parental control in Moscow during her husband's absence, even though her sons are adults. She gave me a short tour of her house, which she said had been built in 1984. She pointed to the rooms that had been recently remodeled, thanks to her husband's earnings in Russia. Keeping in mind both that her husband does not stay for a long period each time he visits and her confidence in explaining the details of their remodeling projects, I have understood that Gulruh is in charge of managing the home improvement plans in her family. In a traditional sedentary male-headed household, these tasks would be fulfilled by a man instead.

I would like to elaborate on several aspects of women-headed households and the shifting of gender roles in the context of transnational migration. First, the status of migrant families in transnational social spaces needs close attention. I had not known Gulruh prior to visiting the village of Dahana. The deputy head of the village, who herself is a respected person in the community, chose to introduce Gulruh and Ayub to me. Drawing on Goldring's work on Mexicans in the US, it can be seen that this family is clearly regarded as one that has achieved economic success and maintained close ties to the community.[349] Goldring also emphasizes the significance of shared meanings in a community. He points out that as a result of migration, shared meanings within the community of origin may be challenged and new meanings and practices can emerge. These new meanings and practices are reflected in the way migrants dress, act, or speak.[350] Goldring contends that, in addition, these "new" practices are transmitted to non-migrant women. Although no "new" practices can be identified as being "imported" from Russia as such, this can be seen in the way Gulruh judges and distinguishes herself from other women, whom she identifies as a certain category of migrant wives. This can be seen, in particular, in the way she judges her neighbor who is in a similar situation, but who, unlike her, does not have employment and is not dedicated to educating her children, but is dependent on her husband's remittances.

7.3.2. Shohistaxon

In her community (*mahalla*) in the urban center of Jalalabad, Shohistaxon is admired for her traits such as diligence, modesty, honesty, and politeness, as well as her decorum as an Uzbek woman and her good attitude towards her neighbors. Similar to Ayub, Gulruh's husband, Shohistaxon's husband, Muhriddin, works in Moscow. By contrast to Ayub however, Muhriddin does not have a contract with his Russian employers and makes less than Ayub from the merchandise that he sells in the Russian capital's Cherkizov Market

---

349 Goldring, 1999:168.
350 Goldring, 1999:168.

(*Cherkizovskii Rynok*). Muhriddin visits his family approximately once a year. When his revenue is too low for an airplane ticket, which happens quite often, Muhriddin travels home by train.[351]

Shohistaxon is 36 years old and a mother of four children: three boys and one girl. Shohistaxon's children are younger than Gulruh's. Her eldest son is twelve years old and her second one is eleven. Her daughter is seven and her youngest son only two years old. Shohistaxon and her husband never received degrees from a higher education institution. Muhriddin used to make a living as a carpenter. After watching his neighbors and his brothers leave for Russia one by one, he too decided not live from carpentry any more. Shohistaxon, Muhriddin, and their four children share two small rooms. Their house consists of seven rooms that surround a large courtyard. Shohistaxon's parents-in-law had three sons. They married off all three but rather than letting them move out of the house, they distributed the rooms among them, which is not unusual for a traditional Uzbek family. At the beginning, the brothers used to argue over their portion of the property. Starting from the beginning of the 2000s, all of them left for Russia, each with his own project of saving money to buy his own place.

Shohistaxon's delicate economic situation is noticeable from the moment one enters the house, which she still shares with her sisters-in-law and their children. She starts by admitting that it is *tirikchilik* (life, subsistence, survival) that led her husband to leave for Russia. With four young children to raise, Shohistaxon does not work outside the home. The money sent by her husband, which is on average $150 per month, is spent mainly on food and clothing for her children. She tries hard to save for remodeling. She admits that it would be hard for them to buy a new apartment or house. However, they would like to demolish the two small rooms in which they live and rebuild them. They would like to add another room, a kitchen, and a bathroom. For the time being, the wives of the three brothers living in the same house have to share the toilet facilities. Each small family has its own small gas and electric stove in their living rooms where they cook.

Similar to Gulruh, Shohistaxon is fully in charge of managing remittances since her husband wires them directly to her. Shohistaxon's mother-in-law passed away several years ago. Her father-in-law lives with her brother-in-law's family. If he lived with Gulruh and her children, he would be in charge of managing the resources. Her situation as a kind of a single mother makes it extremely hard for her to seek employment. Her neighbor who in-

---

351 This market, located in Moscow, was the biggest retail market where most Central Asian small vendors and porters used to work. According to some estimates, around eight to ten thousand Tajik citizens used to be employed there. Due to alleged violations of international trade and quality regulations and an increasing crime rate, the market was closed down on June 29, 2009, per decree of Yuriy Luzhkov, the Mayor of Moscow (Source: http://www.ferghana.ru/news.php?id=12318&mode=snews).

troduced her to me told me later that Shohistaxon bakes *somsa*[352] and sells them at her neighbor's canteen in order to earn some money.[353]

As seen in the previous example, Gulruh, who had obtained a professional degree during the Soviet period, has still been able to maintain her employment in the formal sector. Whereas during the Soviet period and in the early years of independence she had only one full-time job, she has now tripled her working hours in the formal sector. Shohistaxon, by contrast has had to turn to the informal sector to make additional money. She did not receive a professional degree, which would have enabled her to earn monthly wages. She attended a vocational school and worked at a factory in the years immediately before and after the fall of the USSR. And, as she rightly argues, wages are not paid on time. Muhriddin's earnings are so limited that she cannot afford anything more profitable than baking *somsa*. I encountered families in the region (both urban and rural) who first invest migrant remittances in a small grocery store so that wives and children are not completely dependent on those remittances. Sometimes goods are sold in a separate store, but those who cannot afford the lease arrange shelves of groceries at the entrances to their own houses. In addition, it is not rare to see grocery windows, built into either the kitchen or the living room, that open to the street and blur the spaces of informal trade and family ambience. Shohistaxon, since she does not have the financial means to establish a store, uses her relatives' trade domain to sell her pastries.

Shohistaxon's family situation should be noted as well. During the interview, Shohistaxon complained that it was getting harder for her to raise her children alone. As a mother of three boys, she said that her husband's presence would have made a difference in the family. Her 12-year-old son had thrown a tantrum when his father Muhriddin left for Russia after having visited in Kyrgyzstan, because he wanted to work in Russia as well. Often, Shohistaxon complains to her husband about their sons' behavior when he calls. She says that when she has Muhriddin scold their sons on the phone, they change.[354]

It would be not unusual for a woman in her situation to turn to her close kin for help. Other examples have shown how either parents or siblings of the migrants help raise the children. Some may volunteer to foster the child [ren] temporarily or host them on weekends. Parents of the migrants can often look after all the children so that couples can migrate together. However, Shohistaxon's large family of origin – ten children – is affected by labor migration to such an extent that her burden cannot be lightened by her siblings. During the interview, she named her siblings to me in the order of birth and told me where they live. I illustrate Shohistaxon's family in Figure 3. We can see in this image that the first son of the large family who is deemed to be the most

---

352 Central Asian puff pastry filled with meat and onions.
353 This is similar to women in the Dominican Republic observed by Levitt (2001:104).
354 On challenges of transnational parenting, see Levitt (2001:76).

senior of all the children has stayed in Kyrgyzstan. This is not to rule out the possibility that in the case of a severe economic situation or a unique job opportunity, this person would leave for Russia as well. Given his age, this person would likely be able to work for 2-3 years, arrange jobs for his children, and then return to his homeland permanently. All Shohistaxon's other male siblings, that is Qudratjon, Mansurjon, and Sattorjon had left for Russia. Her brother Mansurjon became a Russian citizen and had to renounce his Kyrgyz citizenship. He and his family are determined to stay in Russia permanently. Among her female siblings, Shoiraxon and Munisaxon's families are not affected by migration. Out of ten children in this large family, seven have been involved in labor migration to Russia and in the case of Shohistaxon's sister Gulchehraxon, she has a son who works in Kazakhstan. After Russia, this country has become the second destination country for labor migrants from Central Asia.

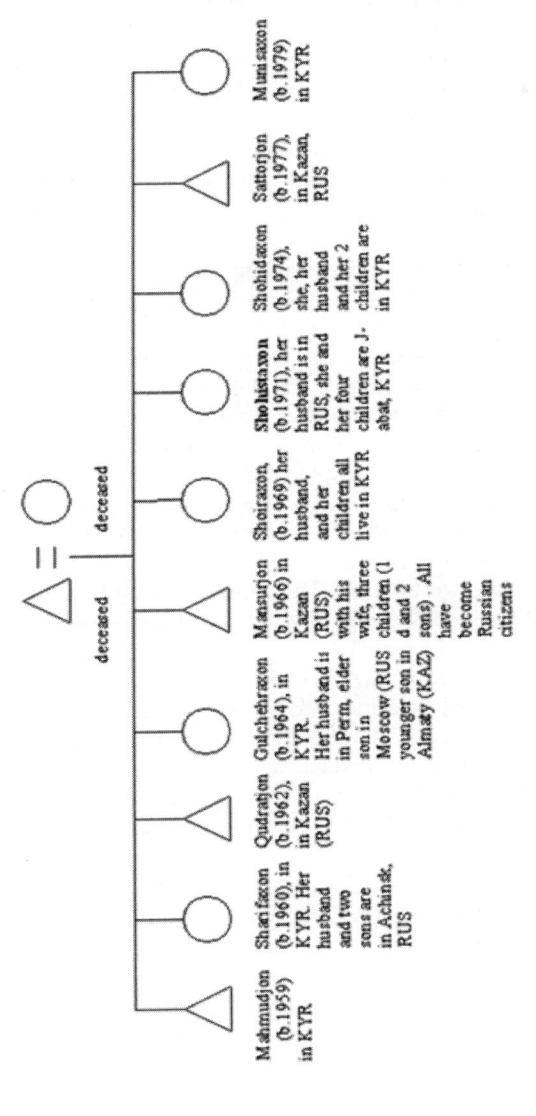

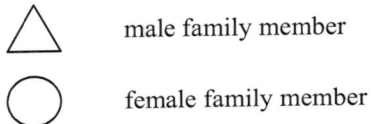

Figure 3: Genogram of Shohistaxon (in bold) and her Siblings

- △ male family member
- ○ female family member

Parents: △ (deceased) = ○ (deceased)

Siblings (left to right):
- Mahmudjon (b.1959) in KYR
- Sharifaxon (b.1960), in KYR. Her husband and two sons are in Achinsk, RUS
- Qudratjon (b.1962), in Kazan (RUS)
- Gulchehraxon (b.1964), in KYR. Her husband is in Perm, elder son in Moscow (RUS), younger son in Almaty (KAZ)
- Mansurjon (b.1966) in Kazan (RUS) with his wife, three children (1 d and 2 sons). All have become Russian citizens
- Shoiraxon, (b.1969) her husband, and her children all live in KYR
- **Shohistaxon** (b.1971), her husband is in RUS, she and her four children are J. abat, KYR
- Shohidaxon (b.1974), she, her husband and her 2 children are in KYR
- Sattorjon (b.1977), in Kazan, RUS
- Muniaxon (b.1979) in KYR

7.4. The Impact of Changing Citizenship on Kinship

This challenge particularly concerns migrants from Tajikistan and Kyrgyzstan. The Russian Federation and Tajikistan have had a bilateral agreement since 1995 that allows their citizens to hold passports of these two countries. The situation in Kyrgyzstan, however, that has yet to reach an agreement with Russia on citizenship issues, is becoming more and more delicate. On January 3, 2006, the Russian Federation adopted a new law on citizenship. According to the amendment to the 2002 Russian citizenship law, all citizens who formerly held Soviet citizenship or individuals who were registered in Russia before July 2002 as well as holders of temporary residence permits were made eligible to obtain Russian citizenship by January 1st, 2008.[355] Following the adoption of this amendment, the Russian Federation placed consultants representing its Federal Migration Service in their consulates in the republics of Kyrgyzstan and Tajikistan, where the citizens of these countries could apply to get a Russian passport in addition to their Kyrgyz or Tajik one. Since dual citizenship is not allowed in Uzbekistan, and the country has taken a cautious approach to Russia's new citizenship law, Uzbek citizens wishing to apply for the Russian citizenship have to renounce their Uzbek citizenship in order to obtain a Russian passport.

One of the ramifications of the 2006 legislation, which allowed citizenship in the Russian Federation to be acquired in a so called "more facilitated manner" (in Russian legislation *v uproshchenom poriadke*), has been that hundreds if not thousands of migrants and non-migrants from Central Asian countries have applied for it. In addition, the Kyrgyz Republic changed its law on citizenship on May 21, 2007 to allow dual citizenship. Some sources claim that in 2005, that is even before such legislation was adopted, 38,000 Kyrgyzstanis obtained Russian citizenship.[356] During the fieldwork that took place prior to the adoption of this law, migrants told me that they dreamed of a Russian passport. In January 2006 when the Russian government created a legal framework, many Central Asians saw it as an opportunity for their dreams to come true. By the time I visited Kyrgyzstan in February/March 2008, these developments were having a great impact on families of migrants.

The 52-year-old Kyrgyz woman, Cholpon, whom I interviewed in Osh, is the mother of six children. My host family introduced me to her as a supportive mother who "even got her children Russian passports." Cholpon

---

355 Given the ongoing demographic crisis in Russia, Putin's successor President Medvedev signed a new amendment that postponed the deadline of applications for citizenship from January 1, 2009 to July 1, 2009. (Federal'nyi zakon Rossiiskoi Fedracii ot 20 dekabria 2008 g. N 201-F3 O vnesenii izmeneniia v stat'iu 14 Federal'nogo zakona "O grazhdanstve Rossiiskoi Federacii" available at http://www.rg.ru/2008/12/31/grajdanstvo-izmenenie-dok.html last consulted on January 23, 2009).
356 *Citizenship Plan Seen as Flawed.* Briefing of the Institute for War and Peace Reporting on August 26, 2006. (http://www.iwpr.net/?apc_state=hrubbkg323447&l=en&s=b&p=bkg&o=323448, last consulted on January 22, 2009).

owns two houses on the outskirts of Osh and a small apartment in the city, but lives alone with her husband because all of her children are away. She teaches history at a Kyrgyz school.[357] In our interview, Cholpon immediately started telling me about her herself and her family. Excerpts:

Delia:	So you say you have six children. Can you please name them for me in the order of their date of birth?
Cholpon:	(1) Ermirza (male), born in 1979, (2) Gulzada (female), born in 1981, (3) Elnura (female), born in 1983, (4) Zarema (female), born in 1985, (5) Ramazan (male), born 1987, (6) Emil (male), in 1992.
Delia:	Which ones are in Russia?
Cholpon:	All of them are away, all in Russia, only Ramazan is studying at Bosphorus University in Turkey. He just left yesterday. He is studying international relations there.
Delia:	Can you tell me who went first and who followed whom?
Cholpon:	First Ermirza left. He then invited Gulzada. Gulzada invited Elnura who invited Zarema. Then my youngest son was invited. They (my children) invited each other. This other son of mine is in his third year in Turkey. All others are in Russia.
Delia:	Who did Ermirza follow?
Cholpon:	Someone from the family. He is married and lives in Nijny Udensk. It is between Krasnoyarsk and Irkutsk. Elnura, Zarema, and Emil live in the same place, they also live in Nijniy Udensk. Gulzada and her husband live near Krasnoyarsk.
Delia:	Since when has Ermirza been in Russia?
Cholpon:	Since 2002. You see I have not gotten Russian citizenship for my sons, but only my daughters. They have Russian citizenship, not my sons because we need to buy property here. Only my girls have Russian passports.
Delia:	How is it that you got them Russian passports?
Cholpon:	What needed to be done here, I did. The rest they got done in Russia. I de-registered them from here. I took care that they got out of the registration (*propiska*). The girls work in the market in Russia. Last year in April they were all driven out of the market. As for my son Elmirza, his wife has Russian citizenship. We have land here. If I de-register my sons, they will lose their rights to own land and housing here in Kyrgyzstan.[358]

---

357 In addition to a Kyrgyz school, there was also an Uzbek and a Russian school in the village where I interviewed Cholpon.

358 Cholpon was referring to the new law on the status of foreign citizens in the Russian Federation and the order of the government of the Russian Federation of November 15th, 2006 to limit the engagement of foreign citizens at retail markets, in tents, and outside of stores to 40 percent. This order foresaw the gradual prohibition against foreign citizens selling merchandise on April 1st, 2007. This date has been remembered by most labor migrants as massive police raids took place at Russian wholesale markets. (*We tried our best...Changes in the situation for foreign citizens in the Russian Federation.* Article by

Delia: Do your children plan to come back?
Cholpon: Yes, I hope they will return to Kyrgyzstan. I don't want my daughters to marry Russians. No, I don't need that. I had them change their passports only so that they can sell in the market again. The Russian authorities strictly forbade them to sell in the market and told them to go get Russian citizenship. They came and had difficulties getting their documents ready. Each of them had to pay about 1000-1200 dollars.[359]

Cholpon's situation illustrates the changes in which the sending societies find themselves: the era of mass migration and processes of adoption and implementation of citizenship policies and regulations by sending and receiving states. Due to these changes, Kyrgyz, Tajik, and Uzbek citizens have been applying for Russian citizenship. Cholpon's approval and support of Russian citizenship for her daughters on the one hand and, on the other hand, disapproval of the same for her sons reveals interesting political and socio-cultural aspects. Again, we should link Cholpon's rationale behind supporting her daughters, but not her sons in the process of changing citizenship, to the societal/familial expectations of the sons mentioned at the beginning of this chapter. Similar to some women of her generation, Cholpon alluded to the responsibilities that her sons should bear in mind. She said she would like her sons to return to Kyrgyzstan some day. In the time during which the new Kyrgyz government that took over power in March 2005 has been changing regulations on citizenship, migration, and property rights, the population in this country, notably migrant dependent families, find themselves in a confusing situation.

According to Article 5 of the citizenship legislation of 2002, Kyrgyz citizens were not allowed to obtain the citizenship of a foreign country without renouncing their original citizenship. Hence, when Cholpon's daughters obtained Russian citizenship in early 2007, they had to renounce their Kyrgyz citizenship. One may argue that Articles 6 and 22 of the amended citizenship law of May 2007 could have changed Cholpon's daughters' situation, as it states that the acquisition of a different citizenship does not imply the loss of the Kyrgyz citizenship.[360] The same law states further, though, that a citizenship in addition to Kyrgyz citizenship is only allowed when the country of the second citizenship allows it, which in this case Russia does not.[361] The new citizenship law has indeed created confusion among the population and

---

Svetlana Gannushkina for Polit.Ru Available in Russian at http://www.polit.ru/author/2007/01/23/ migranty.html and in English at http://refugee.memo.ru/For_ALL/RUPOR.NSF/450526ab8b3e4d91c325702e0065b29f/e41f265e28b95e85c3257 26a00813b46!OpenDocument).

359 Interview with Cholpon, Osh (KYR), February 2008.
360 Law on Citizenship of the Kyrgyz Republic, May 2007 (*Zakon Kyrgyzskoi Respubliki o grajdanstve Kyrgyzskoi Respubliki. May, 2007*).
361 Article 22, Law on Citizenship of the Kyrgyz Republic, May 2007.

Kyrgyz policy makers have meanwhile become aware of the scenarios that the so-called dual citizenship legislation has created. Having heard of the possibility of retaining a Kyrgyz passport, Kyrgyz citizens have been holding two passports without thinking about the consequences this might involve while they are in the territory of the Russian Federation.[362]

A further point is that the new citizenship law that allows dual citizenship in Kyrgyzstan does not mention anything about what it may imply for property rights. Neither the Land Code nor the newly adopted Property Law clearly limits the usage of property in case of dual citizenships. Article 5 of the Land Code prohibits transfer or access to ownership of agricultural land to foreign citizens. As far as non-agricultural land is concerned, foreign citizens can either have temporary access or purchase land using the services of a mortgage company as defined by Kyrgyz regulations on credit facilities.[363] Situations such as Cholpon's reflect the convolution of a series of amendments and reforms in the legislation of the receiving and sending states.

Ultimately, the term dual citizenship itself opens up an interesting argument. The new citizenship law in Kyrgyzstan implies that through acquisition of a second citizenship, the Kyrgyz citizens maintain voting rights, but lose their rights to be politically active.[364] Note that the word 'dual citizenship' used in the legislation text is a direct translation of the Russian term *dvoinoe grajdanstvo* as it is employed in the Kyrgyz legislation. Having analyzed the conditions of the legislation on the dual citizenship, it should be remembered that, in this case, we are dealing with *dual nationality* rather than *dual citizenship*. Faist points out that contrary to *dual citizenship*, the rights of the holders of *dual nationality* are more limited. He draws our attention to the example of the holders of Mexican nationality IDs who do not have voting rights and are not eligible to get involved in homeland politics, which is similar to Kyrgyz citizens.[365] Elsewhere in a joint publication, Faist and Kivisto argue in favor of an analytical differentiation between nationality and citizenship in the era of modern citizenship. While nationality implies

---

[362] Ryskulova, Head of the State Committee for Migration and Employment expressed her concern about Kyrgyz citizens carelessly traveling with two passports and urged Parliament to sign a bilateral agreement on dual citizenship with the Russian Federation. *Ryskulova: "Tysiachi kyrgyzstancev, poluchiv grazhdanstvo RF, prodolzhaiut xodit' s dvumia pasportami v karmanax."* [Ryskulova: "Thousands of Kyrgyzstanis are Walking Around with Two Passports in their Pockets After Having Received Russian Citizenship. AkiPress, January 23, 2009. available at http://kg.akipress.org/news/66294 last consulted on January 23, 2009.

[363] *Kyrgyszkaia Respublika. Zemel'nyi kodeks.* [The Land Code of the Kyrgyz Republic] October 17, 2008.

[364] Article 22 of the Law of the Kyrgyz Republic on Citizenship states: "Citizens of the Kyrgyz Republic who hold dual citizenship may not become President of the Kyrgyz Republic, a member of the Jogorku Kenesh (parliament) of the Kyrgyz Republic, or a judge of the Kyrgyz Republic. He or she may not be employed by the law enforcement agencies or by the Ministry of Defense of the Kyrgyz Republic, nor can he or she hold leadership posts in government institutions." (my own translation) (Law on Citizenship of the Kyrgyz Republic, May, 2007).

[365] Faist, 2000a:271.

full membership and submission to the legal system and state power within the territorial confines of a state, citizenship is perceived in terms of membership in a nation-state with defined universal rights and obligations.[366] In the case of former Soviet republics, the equivalent of the Russian term *citizenship* is applied in citizenship laws. As was explained in this study's chapter on the historical background of migrations, the concept of nationality has a different connotation. To reiterate, in the early years of the USSR's existence, Soviet leaders were eager to contribute to the evolution of clans, tribes, and communities into 'developed nationalities' (*natsional'nost'*) which in turn would merge together in the era of communism. In the 1930s, Soviet ethnographers created an official list of fifty-three nationalities. The early Soviet censuses understood nationality as "a population group united into a nationally self-conscious community." The Soviet identity documents had an entry where citizens were required to define their *natsional'nost'*. [367] I assume, that for these reasons, there may not be a concept of dual nationality in the post-Soviet context as an analytical distinction would require. Rather, the concept of a *dual membership* with restricted rights is perceived as *dual citizenship*.[368]

Moving beyond the legislative settings of this example of changing citizenship and filial relations, we can look at its practical use in migration. Social historians such as Tilly regard citizenship as a kind of a tie "between persons and agents of a given state in which each has enforceable rights and obligations [...] by membership."[369] A tie in this context stands for a series of transactions that involve understandings, memories, rights, and obligations that agents share with one another. Tilly argues that citizenship could then be seen as a *thin* or *thick* tie depending on the degree of rights and obligations.[370] However, rather than joining Tilly in taking the state perspective on practices and state-citizen relationships, I would like to take a look at Cholpon's family and consider citizenship from the perspective of its usage in the context of transnational mobility. In doing so, I agree with Horstmann's observation that people themselves become significant actors in reconfiguring the notion and practical use of citizenship.[371] As Cholpon argues, she supported her daughters' intentions to obtain Russian citizenship because Russia's strict regulations led them to take such actions. At the beginning of 2007, foreign citizens were no longer allowed to engage in selling goods in Russian markets and shops. As a result, migrant workers were either deported from such places, or forced to change employment or pay a large bribe to receive a Russian passport in an expedited process.

---

366 Faist and Kivisto, 2007:49-50.
367 Hirsch, 2005:106-112.
368 For more on distinctions between nationality, citizenship, and dual membership debates, see Faist *et al.* 2004.
369 Tilly, 1995:8. For more on citizenship as a contract between a state and a citizen, see also Faist 2000:271.
370 Tilly, 1995:8.
371 Horstmann, 2006:159.

Cholpon is certainly aware that if her sons acquired Russian citizenship the consequences would not be limited to a loss of property rights. She and her husband would like to have at least one of their sons living with them in the same house to take care of them when they get older. In the age of transnational mobility, the younger generation's ambitions to live and work in Russia contradict the social norms and expectations that families have of their sons. The daughters, however, are in a different position, as some middle-aged migrant parents told me. Although they too are expected to take care of their parents when they are old, the parents who raise them do so with the awareness that they will belong to the families of their future husbands. During the interview, Cholpon assured me that she was pinning high hopes on her son Ramazan (born in 1987) who, at that time, was studying at the Bosphorus University. Cholpon, the mother of six children, highlighted the difference in her youngest son's behavior and respectful attitude towards his parents. She said that Ramazan had been a diligent and disciplined student in Turkey and would make a different career than his other siblings. He would certainly not go to Russia to earn money, she said. According to her, Ramazan had attended the Turkish lyceum funded by Fethullah Gülen and that thanks to this school her son had not only received a good education but was also disciplined and did not share the same world view as his other siblings.[372] In this respect, Cholpon is reminiscent of Gulruh who invested in her son's secondary education in a Gülen-funded school. Such parents hope that their children will not have to work as labor migrants in Russia, but rather can obtain a higher education degree, find well-paid employment in their homeland, and fulfill the expectations of their society by abiding by their traditions.

7.5. Conclusion

This chapter has looked at family relations in transnational migration. It illustrates how labor migration is intertwined with transformational factors of the sending countries. It considers the roles which migrants play as family members and projects them onto the social and political conditions which cause family members to leave for Russia. It explains that beyond the commonly analyzed economic reasons, causes such as regime change and redistribution of power in clan structures of sending countries may result in loss of employment and prospects. This chapter distinguishes between male and female migrants as sons and daughters of their parents and siblings vis-à-vis other children in the family in Central Asia. The status of young male migrants as eldest sons and youngest or only sons within their families determines not only their responsibilities and obligations to migrate, but also the period of

---

372 For more on Fethullah Gülen schools in Central Asia, cf. section 7.3.1.

time they should stay in Russia. As has been seen, the length of stay in the country of destination has implications on the transnationalization processes. Similarly, female migrants as daughters are shown to be in search of a new start in Russia following broken marriages. Contrary to the societal expectations that require that they live with their parents after divorce, daughters choose to migrate to Russia and provide for their parents back home.

Portraits of two women and their situations as heads of households have been included to illustrate the gender dimension of labor migration. Such women are often challenged, on the one hand, by sharing obligations as heads of their families, not only managing and saving remittances, but also acquiring additional resources so they need not fully depend on their husbands' support. On the other hand, however, they find it difficult to be full-time mothers and bear the responsibility of raising their children alone since their husbands are away most of the time.

A further finding of this chapter is the most recent trend of Central Asian labor migrants obtaining Russian citizenship and the implications of this change of citizenship on family relations. The example of a Kyrgyz woman, the mother of six children, describes how the mother of the family chooses to support, if not actively assist, her daughters in applying for Russian citizenship by procuring the necessary documents. For fear of her sons' losing their property rights in Kyrgyzstan, she decides not to allow them to change their citizenship. Amidst reforms of citizenship, property, and land legislations in the Kyrgyz Republic and new citizenship legislation in Russia, this chapter tries to illustrate how families deal with such circumstances in their everyday lives.

8. Conjugal Relationships in a Migration Context: Interaction of Mobility and the New Mode of Life with Cultural Values and Mores

While it is important to bear in mind the economic incentives for labor migration, it is equally essential to consider that labor migration creates new opportunities for female migrants from Central Asia. This chapter will bring back the families already introduced in the previous chapters and will look specifically at conjugal relationships in the context of migration in both places of origin and destination. Paying close attention to everyday practices of migrant spouses at both ends of migration, it will highlight the changes that spousal relationships undergo when migrants live abroad and when their spouses remain in the home country. We shall see that long-distance mobility offers migrants, above all, more room to maneuver and liberate themselves from social norms, authority, pressure, and expectations of their kin members and, in particular, parents-in-law. At the same time, labor migration of male spouses may create mechanisms that enforce mores and values, which in turn may place their dependent spouses back home under more social pressure. Conjugal relationships in the context of migration will be discussed against the backdrop of an increasing state-society gap in Central Asia and the diminishing role of the state, which was strong during the Soviet period. In particular, it shall be shown that in the absence of Soviet ideology, its family and labor values are gradually being replaced by 'revived' and 'reinvented' forms of cultural, traditional, and religious values.

8.1. The Struggle against and Retaining the Virtues of a Docile Daughter-in-Law

In this section I would like to reintroduce Firuz and Saida with whom I spent several weeks in Moscow.[373] During my stay, I was able to observe the struggles which the couple were having. To start with, the marriage of Firuz and Saida was arranged, but not in the strict sense of the term where there is often a situation in which the girl is forced by her parents to marry. Firuz had a Russified background and was the eldest son of a former Soviet functionary. He had two younger brothers, the younger of whom was married to a Russian woman. Firuz had arrived in Moscow with a near-native command of Russian and three years later, when I met him, he had acquired a Moscow accent. His wife Saida was from a traditional Uzbek-speaking family. By "traditional" I mean not as Russified as Firuz's family, which had also been part of

---

373 They were mentioned in the context of life-cycle celebrations in Chapter 6, section 6.3.

the Soviet intelligentsia. Having graduated from an Uzbek secondary school, Saida's Russian, unlike Firuz' was far from flawless. Before their engagement, Firuz and Saida dated for several months, and Saida knew and liked her future husband. In the old traditional part of their provincial town in Uzbekistan, the couple lived with Firuz's parents. As a traditional *kelin* (daughter-in-law), Saida was responsible for all the household chores. By the time Firuz, the eldest son of the family, got married, his mother had raised three sons including Firuz and had been doing all the housework alone. When Firuz got married, the family finally had a young woman who took over the work including cooking and laundry for the entire family. Firuz's mother was barely willing to help her daughter-in-law.[374]

When I met Saida in Moscow, she told me that she had been married to Firuz for six years. Two years after their marriage, Firuz left for Moscow. At the time when I carried out my fieldwork, Firuz had been in Moscow for four years. Saida and Firuz had a five-year-old son. When Saida joined Firuz, their son was 18 months old. Two years after Saida left their son with Firuz's parents, the couple decided to bring him to Moscow. The family shared a small two-room apartment with one of Firuz' younger brothers. The other younger brother who was married to a Russian lived separately. When Firuz' parents visited, they lived with Firuz and not with Firuz's married brother. At the time of the fieldwork I observed that Saida was torn between her role as an obedient *kelin* of her husband's family and the modern wife she strongly desired to be in Russia. The day I arrived, Firuz, Saida, and I talked over a cup of tea. Firuz told me how happily married they were. He had to promise his grandmother that he would marry only Saida. Firuz's grandmother did not live to see their wedding. According to Firuz, she died giving her blessing to Firuz and Saida's future unity and that it was thanks to this blessing that the couple was living happily. I soon noticed that in reality, Saida was frustrated. She compared her position to the relationship between her youngest brother-in-law Shukhrat and his Russian wife as well as to the lives of her Russian colleagues and Russified Uzbek friends. Several days after my arrival she expressed her feelings to me when I came home earlier and her husband was still at work.

> He never ever makes any compliments to me! Never! I get more compliments from our five-year-old son than from him. I put on a new dress the other day and

---

374 Conversations with Saida. The duties of a *kelin* and the control and authority of in-laws over her may vary depending on the background of the family, i.e. the extent to which the family had been Sovietized, whether or not she is a distant relative to her spouse, and the religiousness of her spouse's family. In some religious families, a *kelin* is expected to start her day as early as 4:30 AM and heat up warm water for the in-laws' ritual washing necessary for the morning prayers. In some families in the Ferghana Valley, for instance, she is obliged to wash her father-in-law's feet (*cf. Kyrgyz Women Suffer in Silence.* Article by Institute for War and Peace Reporting. RCA No. 47 April 10th, 2001, available at http://www.iwpr.net/?p=rca&s=f&o=176899&apc_state=henirca2001 last consulted on February 16th, 2009).

he didn't say anything. Our son said, "Wow, Mom, you look so beautiful!" And Firuz? Nothing! I don't receive the attention I deserve. You know when I come to work, my Russian boss [the owner of the restaurant] looks at me admiringly. He says, "You look great today, Saida! You look gorgeous!" I get many compliments from my boss, he would notice my new clothing, my new hairstyle, but not Firuz, not my own husband. He only knows how to give orders. I am tired of the way he treats me. He never says "please!" He goes, "Do this! Do that!"

The couple had an argument one day because, contrary to Firuz's expectations, Saida did not polish his shoes after he came back from work. Firuz worked as a chef at a Russian restaurant. Saida helped him in the kitchen. Saida had in fact studied at *meduchilishche,* a special college in the former USSR that trained young secondary school graduates to become medical nurses. Saida worked as a nurse before joining her husband in Moscow. Firuz had received his vocational training as a chef in a provincial town in Uzbekistan. Within several weeks after his arrival in Moscow, he became a specialist in Russian/European/East European cuisine. After a whole day of cooking non-Uzbek meals, Firuz would come home around 10 PM. Often the dinner that Saida had prepared would not suit his appetite so he would demand that she cook something different. Every month while receiving a salary, Firuz would sign on Saida's behalf, receive the cash that she earned, save her money, and give her some cash for her minor expenses. Their Russian boss did not care who signed and received the earnings. Saida had not brought up this issue to Firuz at the beginning stages of her migration. She was now realizing that these were *her* earnings that her husband received and managed as he wished.

In Uzbekistan, in a typical male-headed household, Saida would not have opposed such behavior. Saida's self-assurance was growing to the point that she not only made clear to Firuz that she wanted to receive and spend her earnings herself, but she also seriously considered approaching her boss concerning the matter. When we spoke, Saida brought up her friends' and her brother-in-law's family as examples and told me that she found her husband's macho attitude unacceptable. She told me that despite everything, she found her life in Moscow better than in Uzbekistan. Before following her husband to Moscow, she had to suffer under her parents-in-law's authoritarian rule. After the wedding the family had a huge amount of debt so they had only a little food. Saida was not used to such standards while at her parents' home. Saida's parents-in-law had strict control over where she went, what she ate and what clothes she wore. It seemed that in Moscow, Saida started wearing trousers, short skirts, and tank tops.[375] Her husband said that while in Russia, he preferred it if she wore Russian clothes and not traditional Uzbek garments. Through everyday communication not only with Russian-speaking Slavic migrants but also with Russified Uzbeks of the first and the second

---

375 I had seen her family photo album with pictures that had been taken in Uzbekistan prior to migration.

generation, Saida started admiring the lifestyle of women in Moscow to which she had not been exposed in Uzbekistan. Her interaction with the new lifestyle was not limited to people, however. Through television, media, and work at the restaurant she became familiar with the different culture in which Russian women lived. She would flip through the pages of the Russian edition of *Forbes* magazine and tell about her desire to learn how to drive, but that she would let her husband get his license first.[376] During the weeks I stayed with this family in Moscow, I became aware that Saida was already developing strategies to acquire more confidence, independence, and self-assurance not only vis-á-vis her husband but also towards her mother-in-law back in Uzbekistan. She explained her strategies to me as follows:

> Look, my parents-in-law have a house. Firuz has two younger brothers. One of them, the youngest, is already married to a Russian woman here in Moscow. The other one is flirting with someone who has a passport here. They'll definitely get married. My mother-in-law, with whom I had terrible disputes before coming to Moscow, is now realizing something...namely that if she does not change her attitude towards me, she'll be left all alone in that house. She came to visit us in Moscow earlier this year. She first stayed several days with Shukhrat, my youngest brother-in-law, and his Russian wife. Do you think she was able to give orders to her the same way as she would do with me? No way! This Russian daughter-in-law showed the kitchen to her and told her to feel at home and help herself to whatever she wanted. She did not even serve her a cup of tea! My mother-in-law then came to stay with us. I was serving her in the way that she realized that she had better appreciate what a good daughter-in-law I am. She took my hands and kissed them before leaving. She now knows that either she'll be good to me or she won't have any daughters-in-law to do her chores. And I am not afraid that they'll send me back to my parents and get another wife for Firuz. They can't afford another wedding, you see.

As far as Firuz was concerned, Saida told me that he wanted to have a second child. Shukhrat, his youngest brother, and his Russian wife had a four-month-old baby. Since they lived two blocks away from Firuz and Saida, we went to visit them several times. Before our first visit to Shukhrat's apartment, Saida mentioned that I should pay attention to the way Shukhrat treated his wife. According to Saida, Shukhrat had taken very good care of his wife during her pregnancy. During my visit I noticed that he shared household chores and helped his wife, which was quite unusual for a typical Uzbek husband. He would cook, wash dishes, change his baby's diapers, and go for walks with his wife. He was preparing his documents to change his citizenship and was living in the apartment which actually belonged to his Russian parents-in-law. Saida pointed out to me that Shukhrat was not only dependent on his

---

376 Focusing on Russia's richest people, *Forbes* covered news on Alisher Usmanov, an Uzbek-born Russian businessman whom Firuz and Saida admired. In November 2007, Usmanov became a major share-holder of the English Arsenal Football Club.

wife's family but also genuinely demonstrated his affection to his wife in the company of his friends and family.

Having observed Shukhrat's family, Saida tried to explain to Firuz that unless he started showing more appreciation and affection for her, she would not be willing to have a second child. She reminded him that during her first pregnancy when she had been in Uzbekistan and the couple had not yet migrated to Russia, she had worked hard and nobody in the family would help her. Firuz would not look after their baby at all. In Uzbekistan it is not unusual for fathers to distance themselves from child care especially at the early stage of childhood. Child care is rather the task of mothers and grandparents or often aunts, the younger sisters of the child's parents. Through migration, Saida's understanding of child care, division of labor in the household, and more equal distribution of household resources (earnings, for instance) was clearly changing. By contrast, as Saida later told me, Firuz would consciously demonstrate his authority over her in front of his colleagues. She showed me pictures of the couple at various gatherings and parties that colleagues at the restaurant organized. Since he had started working at the restaurant in Russia, Firuz had gained weight, which he had no desire to lose. As I was looking at those pictures, I became more aware of Firuz's physical shape vis-à-vis other colleagues and friends, and realized that both his height and weight symbolized power and authority in Russian and Central Asian cultures.

The changes in the relationship between Saida and Firuz were occurring due to their close interaction with Russians and transnational migrants of Slavic origin. Firuz's Russified background should certainly be regarded as an important factor. The married couples I encountered in Moscow and elsewhere in Russia who did not have Russified backgrounds functioned according to the norms of their homeland. I did not notice any major changes between the spouses *per se*, although migrants working with their spouses often stated that they enjoyed living separately from their parents-in-law no matter how difficult living conditions were in migration. My encounter with another Uzbek woman, Suluv, in St. Petersburg was a different experience.

When Suluv met me at her doorstep for an interview I almost forgot that I was in Russia and not Uzbekistan, but we were indeed in St. Petersburg. Our interview took place in the room she rented with her husband in a communal apartment. Suluv had been living in this city for five years but did not communicate much with Russian speakers. She was dressed in Uzbek clothes when I went to visit her. Her rental room was decorated completely in traditional Uzbek style. There was an Uzbek cradle that Suluv used for her baby daughter.[377] There were no tables or chairs in the room, but Uzbek silk mattresses filled with cotton (*ko'rpacha*) decorated her floor. We sat on the floor on the *ko'rpacha*s. Suluv brought a hand-made *dasturxon*, a table-cloth

---

377 Known as *beshik* (Uzb.) or *gahvora* (Taj.), cradles in Central Asia are made of wood. The cradle has colorful curtains that can be closed and opened and convex bottom rails like in a rocking chair. It contains a mattress board and two belts that are used to tie the baby.

157

where she served me tea using Uzbek teapots and Uzbek bread which she and her roommates took turns making regularly. It occurred to me that I had not seen a *dasturxon* at other migrants' apartments. In the middle of St. Petersburg's Vasilevskiy Ostrov, the TV set in Suluv's room was the only thing which reminded me that we were not in Uzbekistan.[378] My impression was that she fully obeyed her husband and her sisters-in-law with whom she shared a household. Suluv's sisters-in-law lived in a different room within the same communal apartment, so she would have been careful about what she told me about her husband's family. It was obvious, though, that within the communal apartment, Suluv and her husband's family created a social space that fully conformed to Uzbek family values, leaving virtually no room to maneuver for Suluv.

I have described two kinds of Uzbek migrant families in Russia. In the first family, through the changes in behavior and perceptions of the daughters-in-law, it could be seen how the values, norms, and traditions from the migrants' homelands and those of their places of destination impinge upon each another. Some families adopt certain elements of cultural values and habits while in migration whereas others reject them completely, as can be observed in the case of Suluv. It should be mentioned that in Saida's case, the precondition for the changes to occur was her husband's Russified background due to which she was allowed to dress herself more like Russian women. Suluv's situation stands in stark contrast in this respect.

8.2. A New Chapter in the Life of a Married Woman

Migration to Russia represents a new chapter in the lives of many married women. It has been noticed that some women migrate when their marriage is on the rocks if they are not divorced already.[379] Many of them, having distanced themselves not only from the authority of and dependence on their husbands and their parents-in-law and also from their own parents back home, gain independence and courage. In such cases migration and long-term absence lead to the end of the troublesome relationships that preceded the journey. For example, Nasiba, who was introduced in the previous chapter,

---

378 Fieldnotes, St. Petersburg, August-September 2006. On a historical note, having been designed originally as the center of the city by Peter the Great, Vasilevskiy Ostrov is considered to be the largest of the islands. In addition to its charming old residence districts, this island houses museums, exhibitions halls, the state university, and the city's educational center, for which it is known. As far as my informant Suluv is concerned, I was not able to live with her family, which would have enabled me to observe more about her life as a wife in migration. As will be discussed in a separate chapter, Suluv was part of a very closed network functioning under the aegis of a patron. The woman who introduced me to her had talked to her several times beforehand. Had Suluv had any doubts that the interview would not harm her husband or patron, she would not have received me at her place.

379 Silvey points out failed marriages of female migrants from Indonesia who are involved in domestic service in Saudia Arabia (2006).

left for Russia after her divorce. When I was at the final stage of this research, a neighbor from my hometown in Buxoro, who had gotten divorced two years previously, remarried and wanted to leave for Russia with her new husband. The court granted her custody of her three-year-old daughter, whom she will leave with her parents when she migrates. The category of female migrants who leave for Russia in search of a new start differs from that of migrant-daughters illustrated in the last chapter in that the former's sense of obligation is not as strong as that of migrant-daughters. Migration offers such women a rare opportunity to reflect on their lives and gain independence from their families. Among them are those who opt to stay in Russia for a longer term and may not necessarily plan to return to Central Asia permanently, yet they still maintain ties to their families.

In this sense, Central Asian married women who migrate to Russia are similar to their Filipina counterparts studied by Parreñas.[380] Analyzing Filipina migrants, Parreñas found out that migrant women are at first not familiar with managing their resources when they arrive in a new country, since they are not accustomed to making decisions independently from their husbands or their families.[381] While this may be true for some women from Central Asia, I have doubts about women's inability to manage their resources in migration. It should be borne in mind that often this involves with women who survived the early years of severe economic crisis in their homelands after the collapse of the Soviet Union. The period following the independence of the three sending countries was marked by losses of jobs in the state-owned institutions. Salaries were paid only after delays of several months. Moreover, instead of cash (and this practice is still being applied in some parts of the region), people used to receive a small amount of groceries. During this period, more and more women made efforts to bring their families out of the financial crisis by engaging themselves in the informal sector, practicing small trade with clothes, pastries, or domestic services. When women in this category leave for Russia, they do so with life experience, which they have gained prior to migration. With the combination of their previously acquired management skills and newly absent husbands, they gain even more independence in migration.

8.2.1. A Path to Freedom from an Authoritarian Husband

Sobira was in her mid-20s when I met her. I was introduced to her in St. Petersburg through her colleague Shohida Opa whose niece Nargiza I introduced in the previous chapter. Sobira, who was from Samarqand (UZB), shared a room with Shohida Opa from Andijan (UZB) in the back of the

---

380   Parreñas, 2001:67.
381   Parreñas, 2001.

kitchen of the Italian restaurant where the two women worked.[382] Sobira seemed quite depressed and was obese. She had initially left for Russia with her husband several years previously. They left their two children with Sobira's mother. The first thing Sobira started telling me in the interview was how she had lost her elder brother before she migrated. Sobira's brother and sister-in-law were living in her parents' house. After her brother's death, her sister-in-law and four children who were left behind did not leave her parents' house for they had no place to go. Sobira left for Russia with her husband, but shortly after they arrived he abandoned her as result of an argument. Sobira's husband disappeared and all her attempts to contact him failed. She soon heard from another distant relative who was living in the same neighborhood in St. Petersburg that her husband wished to have no further contact with her. Sobira and her elder sister were living in St. Petersburg and providing for a large family which included their parents, their widowed sister-in-law with four children, their younger sister, and the two children that Sobira's husband had abandoned. Although Sobira had planned to come to Russia for a short term, she was worried that it would be difficult if she went back permanently. Her relationship with her husband affected her plans about the duration of her stay. Her brother had been the only son in the family. Having lost her brother and been abandoned by her husband, Sobira along with her sister is now responsible for the entire family in Samarqand. "My husband is like dead to me, you know," she said repeatedly. "My children are small and every time they ask me about their father, I just tell them, 'Your father is dead.'"

Before leaving for Astrakhan (RUS) Zulxumor, a 50-year-old woman from Xorazm (UZB), used to work in a kindergarten. She left Uzbekistan for the first time in 2001. She has one son who is 25 years old and lives in the Caucasus and two daughters who are 20 and 17 years old. Zulxumor and her daughters work at one of the markets in Astrakhan selling clothes. She too left for Russia for a search of a new life. Here are some excerpts of Zuxumor's story:[383]

Delia: Tell me about your decision to migrate here with your daughters.
Zulxumor: My husband was the main problem actually. My salary was so small. We have a house and a car back in Xorazm but my husband is a serious drug addict. Towards the end [meaning before she took off for Russia], I would even buy his dose myself because his withdrawal attacks were unbearable. Until he fell asleep around one o'clock in the morning our life was a disaster. I would get up in the morning and go to work. My children were at home and I would

---

382 The owners and the chefs of the restaurant were Russians. I inquired from my informants whether any Italians were among the employers because I was curious if they had hired the two undocumented Uzbek women I interviewed. My informants told me that the Russian chefs cooked using cookbooks and that no Italians were working in the restaurant.
383 Interview with Zulxumor, Astrakhan (RUS) in June, 2007.

worry about what he would do to them when he woke up. He lived from one dose to another. I left, then shortly thereafter, I brought my son and my [elder] daughter Zukhra. My husband stayed with my younger daughter Ozoda. Then I invited Ozoda and him over here. I had no desire to live with him.[384]

I thought when he came here I would leave him at home and would go to work. I was ready to provide for the family on my own. Again, when he came here my life became miserable. He wouldn't work and he made my life so hard. By the time he came over here, I had gotten to know lots of people, partners I do business with. My husband was jealous. He started calling all the people whose numbers I have stored in my cell phone and asking them who they were. He gave me such a hard time. These were people I knew, drivers, my business partners. I go, bring merchandise, and sell it here at the market...My husband thought he could control me like before...Well, he left. I am not going back. I just can't live any more the way I used to live back home and obey him, no.

By saying "the way I used to live" Zulxumor herself is defining the boundaries of her life before and after migration. Even before migrating, Zulxumor was providing for her family on her own by working in the kindergarten. She left to join her neighbor in Astrakhan. She mentioned that it had been dangerous to leave her drug addict husband alone with her younger daughter, but she had had to do it because there had been no choice. During migration, she found the courage to set herself free from the social norms she had followed back in Uzbekistan. In Astrakhan she no longer wanted to show obedience to her husband or be a patient Uzbek wife and a good example for her neighbors. When Zulxumor said that she did not want to return to Uzbekistan, I tried to find out how she thought she would be able to stay permanently in Russia.

Delia: What are the possibilities for you to stay here permanently? You say that your papers are fake.
Zulxumor: I am thinking of applying for Russian citizenship, not only for myself but also for the sake of my daughters. My daughters may look very Uzbek, but if you look closely at my features you might notice that I am [only] partly Uzbek. I am partly Bashkirian.
Delia: Bashkirian?
Zulxumor: Yes, my mother was born in Bashkiria (Russia) and so was I. My father was Uzbek. My husband is Uzbek. Next time I go to Uzbekistan, I have to dig up the documents that prove the real place of my birth and my Bashkirian ancestry. With that document, I would like to get Russian citizenship.

---

384 Parreñas' informants share similar stories (2001:66).

The interview with Zulxumor took place in her house. On the day of my visit she, her two daughters, Faroghat, her neighbor from her home village, and I took a long walk from the market where the women worked. The women told me that I would have to spend the night at their place as it was off the traffic route and not easy to reach by public transport. Indeed, after walking through unbeaten paths and across abandoned railroads for a half an hour, there was a small hidden wooden house in very poor condition. While washing the dishes after the dinner, Zulxumor's elder daughter Zukhra told me that she had had a relationship with a young Chechen man for two years. When they separated, her boyfriend allowed the family to continue living in his house. This is when Zulxumor invited her neighbor Faroghat from Xorazm. Faroghat had just abandoned her husband and was struggling to make ends meet with three children. She left her eldest son who was 16 but brought her 14-year-old son and six-year-old daughter with her to Astrakhan. The house had two dilapidated rooms and an outhouse in the backyard. Zulxumor and her two daughters shared one room and Faroghat and her two children shared the other.

At the beginning of the evening, Faroghat was not in a good mood. She had to pay rent to Zulxumor which seemed unfair since Zulxumor was living there for free. Unlike Nargiza, the woman I encountered in St. Petersburg who had to leave her four-year-old daughter alone during the day, Faroghat would leave her six-year-old daughter alone only in the morning. Her 14-year-old son, a slender teenager whose height was barely 1,60 m worked at the market as a porter until about 1 PM. He would come home to have lunch with his sister. I tried to hear more from Faroghat, but she was not in the mood for sharing more than she already had. Faroghat and her children did not eat with us that evening. After we finished dinner, she came out of her room and seemed more relaxed. Then her son played a DVD with Xorazmi music. Faroghat, her children, and the two daughters of Zulxumor turned the music up and performed traditional dances from Xorazm for me. My hosts had a large collection of DVDs that consisted of traditional Xorazmi music, Uzbek ethno-pop, and Hollywood thrillers. It seemed that in order to forget about the troubles of her life as a single mother and an undocumented migrant and to relax after a long day of toiling in the market, all that Faroghat needed was her traditional folk dance from Xorazm. For me, coming from Buxoro, it became clear that Faroghat and Zulxumor's two daughters were demonstrating choreographic abilities they had mastered in their childhood.

Towards the end of the evening everyone asked Zukhra, who had been in the relationship with the Chechen man, to perform a traditional Caucasian dance called *lezginka*. Zukhra found a Chechen DVD and danced. She explained the technique to me and the order of foot movements one has to follow strictly while dancing *lezginka*. All the while Zulxumor, Zukhra's mother who was also the landlady of the house, refrained from dancing. While everyone in the house spoke Uzbek with me (or the Xorazmi dialect of Uzbek), Zulxumor spoke Russian. She spoke Uzbek with her daughter but switched to

Russian when she turned to me. This seemed her way of manifesting the traces of her non-Uzbek ancestry and perhaps therefore she chose not to dance with the others.

Despite a Bashkirian ancestry, based on her Russian knowledge, I was able to determine that Zulxumor did not have a Russified upbringing or education. In Central Asia, when children are brought up by ethnically mixed parents such as one Central Asian and one Tatar, Russian, Korean, Armenian, or Jew it is common to send children to a Russian school. Zulxumor was from a rural area and an impoverished part of Xorazm, which explained why she had been sent to an Uzbek school. It was striking that she was more open-minded than many other women her age that I encountered during the fieldwork. The way her daughters were dressed did not fully conform to the social rules of the Central Asian migrant community, which is surprising given that at the market, where the two young women worked, a large proportion of the stalls were occupied by Tajiks, Uzbek, and Kyrgyz migrants. Zulxumor had allowed her elder daughter to marry a non-Uzbek (Chechen) and her son was married to a Chechen woman as well. She said that she had been married off to her husband and was unhappy. Therefore she did not want to deprive her daughters of the liberty of making their own choices.

8.2.2. The Situation in Dependent Families of Breadwinning Wives

On two occasions, I was able to talk to family members of female migrants in sending countries. In both cases, the migrants' dependent families were intact in the sense that husbands remained at home and were fully in charge of their male-headed households. In both cases, the elder brothers of the women had been initiators of migration by inviting their younger sisters to Russia. The very first encounter with the family members was not as easy as it would have been in the case of female-headed households. In the first case in Timurmalik, a village outside of Kulob, I had the possibility of talking to the teenaged daughter of the migrant.

Zulfiya was seventeen years old. She quit school at the age of fifteen in 2005 when her mother left for Russia. Her mother had tried to open up a small store but became indebted. Zulfiya's father's salary was not enough to feed a family of eight people. The father of the family was a rather low-ranking government employee. He did not want to risk his state retirement benefits for the sake of migration. When Zulfiya's uncle [mother's brother] found Zulfiya's mother a job as a waitress in a small café in Moscow, her father To'ychi agreed, trusting that his brother-in-law would protect her. At first, Zulfiya did not want to talk to me because she was afraid that her father would scold her for talking to strangers. I tried to explain the purpose of my research to her and assured her that I was not a journalist. I asked her if she thought if it would be better if I talked directly to her father and she said that she would like to talk to me herself. Her mother had just sent 1000 dollars to the family so that they could save the money to remodel their house. I understood that she had already paid off her debts and was now trying to save cash for other purposes. Zulfiya explained that her father was in charge of receiving remittances from her mother. He would make regular trips to the capital of Dushanbe where Zulfiya's mother would wire money. Her father would do grocery shopping and make decisions concerning Zulfiya and her siblings. The entirety of work in the household was completely the responsibility of Zulfiya who admitted that she felt as if she were the mother of the family. She had two elder brothers who were 20 and 18 years old. Zulfiya's eldest brother had just followed their mother to Moscow. Zulfiya was in charge of doing the laundry for her father, herself, and four other siblings, of cooking for them three times a day, and of baking bread in their clay oven once or twice a week. She had three siblings who still went to school and Zulfiya had to take care of them alone. All the tasks and responsibilities of her mother had been shifted to her when she had left for Russia.

The husbands who had been left as dependent spouses generally felt ashamed about having their wives earn money for the family. I briefly met Zulfiya's father and accepted that he did not wish to talk to me about his life. A year later, in February 2008 in Kyrgyzstan, I met another male-headed family that had a female migrant mother abroad. Ghayrat, the father of the family, was 42 years old, about the same age as Zulfiya's father. My conversation with him was only 30 minutes long. Ghayrat was quite reserved. Having noticed that he did not feel comfortable I did not ask him any questions but drank tea and had a chat with his children and a female relative. Ghayrat's eldest daughter was seventeen years old and married. She was no longer living with her parents. There were three more children who lived in his house: his fourteen-year-old daughter, his eleven-year-old son, and his eight-year-old daughter. The household work was, as in the case of Zulfiya, the responsibility of his fourteen-year-old daughter. Unlike the family in Tajikistan, Ghayrat's family was very religious. His fourteen-year-old and eight-year-old daughters wore *hijabs*, leaving only a small part of their faces uncovered. I had visited other religious families in southern Kyrgyzstan where women would wear a veil when they left their houses, but Ghayrat's family was different. The two young girls were covered almost head to toe and only their faces could be seen. In the small village where male-headed migrant dependent households were rare, it seemed that through his devoutness Ghayrat was making up for having allowed his wife to leave for Russia alone. When I was leaving his home, he assured me that his situation was a temporary one and that his wife would be back soon. He would then leave for Russia himself to provide for the family.

8.3. Parents-in-Law and Their Leash of Morality

> They don't even let me talk to my husband on the phone. They talk to him every time as long as they wish, then towards the end of the conversation they give me the receiver. It is in that moment that my husband doesn't have enough balance any more to speak to me properly. I just say "Hi, I am fine. Take care of yourself. Goodbye."[385]

Dilsifat from Sughd Province (TAJ) mentioned this detail about her parents-in-law at the very beginning of our conversation at home. When I stayed with her at her parents-in-law's over the weekend, I was able to get more insight into her everyday life. While visiting the northern city of Khujand, the capital of the Northern Province of Leninaband (TAJ), I was told that it was worth visiting the small suburban district of Ghonchi for it was known to be the home of a lot of migrants in Russia. I got on the public taxi-van that was almost full with old and young women wearing scarves, long colorful Tajik dresses, and pants. The van was taking me to Ghonchi and I was soon asked by the twelve other women traveling with me who I was visiting and why, as my face was unfamiliar to them. I explained to them about my research and said that I was looking for families of migrants that I could talk to. A young woman who was in her early 20s immediately suggested that I come with her and be her guest as her husband had been migrating to Russia for seven years.

Dilsifat, who volunteered to talk to me, told me that her parents-in-law would not have an argument with her for bringing me home without warning them. I had noticed at which bus stop she had got on the van. As a sign of courtesy to my hostess, I told the driver the exact station where Dilsifat had gotten on and paid the ride fee for both of us. When we got off the van and started walking to her place, she pleaded with me not to mention that it had not been at Khujand main bus stop that she boarded the van. She told me later that she had been attending a vocational training to become an accountant in Khujand. The training would last six weeks. She had let her parents-in-law think that she had been in Khujand, but in fact she had secretly visited her mother who lived halfway between Ghonchi and Khujand. Dilsifat told me later that she had to beg her parents-in-law for permission to visit her mother every two weeks. Her father was working in Russia. If her parents-in-law found out that she had visited her without asking them, she would have faced serious problems. The training was a good opportunity for her to 'sneak out' earlier from class on Fridays, spend the night at her mother's, and come to her husband's house the next day. Dilsifat had an 18-month-old daughter. Her parents-in-law looked after her on weekdays when she was in Khujand.

I was welcomed warmly by Dilsifat's parents-in-law who were devout Muslims. As a traveller (*musofir*), I was their special guest for whom they

---

385   Interview with Dilsifat, Sughd Province (TAJ)

ordered Dilsifat to cook *plov* that same evening. This special dish made with meat, onions, rice, and carrots, as well as the dinner as a whole required laborious preparation. It was the month of Ramadan when the leftovers from a hearty dinner would be served at 4 AM the next morning to break the fast at dawn. I offered my help to cook with Dilsifat, which her parents-in-law accepted. As I set to julienne about a kilo of carrots and Dilsifat was gone to get the fire started, Dilsifat's mother-in-law sat next to me and told me how much she felt responsible for the behavior of her daughter-in-law. I had barely known the mother-in-law half an hour, yet she gave me more information about her daughter-in-law than I had expected. Excerpts:

> Her husband is in Russia. Everyone's eyes are on her now because of that. If something happens...if she is seen with another man, what will I say to my son? How will I live in this village? But this daughter-in-law of ours turned out to be *pochakash shurut* (Taj. 'loose'), you understand *duxtaram* (my daughter)?[386] Before the wedding...well I mean my son would have never fallen in love with her...her grandmother lives not far from here. She's actually from a different village. She came here and was walking around our streets. She came to see our neighbor's daughter with whom she is friends. Then my son, who was visiting from Russia, saw her and liked her. It is only because he liked her that we got her for him.
>
> We have to watch out what she does and where she goes. She used to dress herself differently before we got her. Then we had to intervene and forbid her certain things. When you live in this village, you have to suit your way of clothing to here. A couple of weeks ago, she was on her way to the city early in the morning on Monday to go to this training for the rest of the week. My husband took her bag from her and what we discovered was terrible! The clothes she was taking to Khujand...ask her to show, she probably has them in her wardrobe! She had a blouse that would expose her chest from here to here (*shows with her hands from one shoulder to the other*)! She had also packed a skirt that showed her legs to wear in the city! She would have left our house in these decent dresses, you see, and she would have changed in Khujand, can you believe! Shameless, completely!
>
> My husband scolded her and told her she would not go anywhere unless she left those clothes here at home. She cried but what could we do? She packed her clothes and wanted to leave our house to move to her mother's forever. She wanted to leave my son. My husband walked to the door and told her to get back to her room and that she was not going anywhere. We did not let her. We had paid so much money for a wedding. There was no way we could let her go and get another bride here.
>
> Our reputation will be over if something happens to her! We told everything to my son on the phone and he scolded her too. Upon my request, my husband went to Khujand and talked to the dean of her school. He also talked to the manager of her dormitory. He said, "Would you please watch out what she does, whom she

---

[386] She used Tajik to describe her character. The inhabitants of Ghonchi kept switching between the Tajik northern dialect and Uzbek.

sees, where she goes, and how she behaves. Her husband is in Russia and we are responsible for her."

This account highlights several processes of change. At one level, Dilsifat and her parents-in-law are going through intergenerational conflicts that could be happening notwithstanding migratory movements between Tajikistan and Russia. During the Soviet period, despite the Sovietization efforts, it was possible to see the population in Central Asia in 'traditional' clothes at home, at weddings, and during rituals or while attending religious gatherings. People were able to differentiate between *professional space* in which they were expected to be dressed according to the Soviet norms (such as pants and shirt for men and dresses or skirts for women) and *home space* in which they conformed to their social, cultural, and/or religious norms.[387] Usually the latter space required wearing a long, traditionally-sewn, loose, colorful dress and pants.[388] It must be mentioned that Dilsifat's in-laws insisted on her wearing a scarf to cover her head, but not a *hijab* where her head, her forehead, and her neck would be covered, leaving only her face exposed.

In some provincial urban centers and all rural areas the rules of abiding by dress norms are stricter than in the capitals. The disputes over dress norms between a mother-in-law and a daughter-in-law are not *per se* by-products of migration.[389] They can also happen between a mother and a daughter as a

---

387 Giddens applies the concept of *locale* regarding "the use of space to provide the *settings* of interaction." He draws on Hägerstrand's usage of 'place' that refers to "the body, its media of mobility and communication, in relation to physical properties of the surrounding world." (Italics are taken from the original text. See Giddens, 1984:118.) Dress codes are not only strictly implemented for work and home but also for running errands such as doctor's appointments, shopping, visiting friends and family, or visits to mosques. Krämer rightly mentions the Russian adjective *kul'turnyi* (cultural) that speakers of Uzbek, Tajik, and Kyrgyz apply to mean 'in a cultivated manner.' In her study on female religious elders in Uzbekistan, she points out the term *kul'turnyi* which is associated with Soviet culture and is used by religious women depending on the context in opposition to *eskicha* (old way). With this adjective, one of her informants implied wearing dresses with short sleeves opposes her notion of an Uzbek woman's virtues such as honor and shame (Krämer, 2002:357-359). In her book on the unveiling of Uzbek women during the early Soviet period, Kamp makes a similar distinction between modern and traditional clothing (Kamp, 2006:226-227).
388 The way dresses are sewn, they cover most of the chest and have sleeves that come half way down to the elbows. In more 'tolerant' families, women have them tailored shorter but so as not to expose their armpits. The pants are known as *lozim* (literally 'must' or 'necessary') or *ishton* in Uzbek and *pojoma, ezor,* or *pocha* in Tajik. Depending on the regions of southern Kyrgyzstan, Uzbekistan, and Tajikistan, they can be as long as below the ankle.
389 I am also critical of Levitt's 'social remittance' pattern that specifically concerns cross-pollination practices such as sharing of clothing between home and host societies (2001:58). While it is true that non-migrants are influenced by migrant practices and observe the way they dress at home, other conditions that are responsible for cross-pollination should also be taken into account. In the case of Central Asia, changes in clothing are not remitted through migrants from Russia *per se*. The Soviet modernization efforts to dress the Soviet people in certain ways had already brought certain hybrid social forms. The "modern" clothes that Dilsifat would have rather worn in Tajikistan had been imported directly from China. I could imagine this was also the case for the clothes that were imported through migrants to Miraflores in the Dominican Republic (Levitt's field

result of conflicting worldviews between different generations. In Dilsifat's case, her husband would probably have straightened out the terms between his parents and his wife about what his wife would wear. As it often happens, a son is in the position of protecting his wife although his parents are at the top of the hierarchical order. However, in his absence, the daughter-in-law can lose the modicum of rights she would otherwise enjoy. The mother-in-law of Dilsifat started her narration by emphasizing that *because* her son is away, she and her husband feel responsible not only for their own reputations but also for the reputation, role, and authority of their son in the village.

As she commutes between the city of Khujand and her village, Dilsifat is clearly aware of how she should be dressed and behave as she attends classes with those who come from other villages and urban centers. Between changing roles as a daughter-in-law during weekends and a student during the week, between the domains of authoritarian religious parents-in-law and a state-owned education institution, between the blurred boundaries of the city of Khujand and the rural area, Dilsifat constantly tried to position herself in a way that would accommodate everyone's expectations. This was probably the reason she admitted that she was having a crisis and cried after dinner until midnight. I, as a woman traveling alone, had been brought into the house in her company. It was therefore appropriate to share a room with Dilsifat in the part of the house allotted to her and her husband. Her parents-in-law could not hear us, which gave Dilsifat the opportunity to share her own version of the problem.

Dilsifat: Imagine a middle-aged man who is not your father taking your bag and going through your personal things one by one. It was so low...and it was embarrassing for me. He touched my clothes! He took my skirt and my blouse and both he and my mother-in-law criticized the style of the clothes I was willing to wear in Khujand. All this strict control and the visit to my college and talking to my supervisors. This was not necessary! Who am I, a prostitute or something? They treat me as if I would betray my husband as soon as I had the opportunity.

Delia: Did you marry your husband because you fell in love with him?

Dilsifat: I would not have married this guy. He liked me and started following me everywhere when he was visiting.[390] My father then married me off to him when his parents asked for my hand. My father works in Russia.

Delia: Oh, so did your husband and your father know each other from Russia prior to your wedding?

---

site) from the United States. Russian retail markets are full of similar Chinese products too, so I would rather highlight global flows of goods as bearing at least as much responsibility for the mixture of dress norms as 'social remittances.'

390 Even if she had fallen in love, it would not have been surprising for her to deny it, because some women are too proud or shy to admit it.

Dilsifat: No, my father, who is a migrant himself, thought it was a good idea to marry me off to this man since this was someone with a stable income. My husband is the only son of his parents. When they die, he will inherit the house. You know how our people prefer to marry off their daughters to someone who is the only son of his parents. Until my in-laws die, I will have to deal with them and their divorced daughter.

Delia: Where is your sister-in-law?

Dilsifat: She is in Russia. My husband invited her. She and I used to argue so badly. We used to fight and pull each other's hair. My husband and my father do not work in the same city in Russia, so my father did not know my husband before either...Now both of them are gone in Russia and I have to suffer...You see, I don't know my husband. I see him once year. We have arguments almost every day when he comes to visit. Our daughter is 18 months old. He was here when I gave birth to her and this is when I saw him last time. He'll be here in two months, stay about a month or two, and leave again. And me, I am expected to get pregnant again. When that happens I will never be able to leave this house and get divorced. I will be stuck with these people (parents-in-law) forever.[391]

On Monday morning when we left Dilsifat's house to go back to Khujand, her father-in-law insisted that he accompany us to the main stop where vans gather passengers. At dawn, the entire village was awake. He greeted his neighbors as we passed by homes and a teahouse which was frequented by village elders. As we were boarding the van, he discretely gave 3 *somonis* to Dilsifat, which was all she received for her food expenses for the entire week.[392] It was also her share of her husband's remittances which she saw only in this form of pocket money. Dilsifat did not know how much her husband earned. Her husband's earnings were directly wired to her father-in-law.

In Kyrgyzstan in the family of a migrant worker I encountered a similar situation, except that I only had the chance to talk to the mother-in-law. It must be mentioned that on several occasions I met families with young daughters-in-law who had been married only several months previously. As they were young, inexperienced, and new to the family themselves, they were too shy to speak to me. In a Kyrgyz-speaking family in the outskirts of Osh, I had been told by parents-in-law that when more senior people are available, young daughters-in-law should keep quiet. During the fieldwork in Kyrgyzstan in March 2008, I encountered a family in the center of Jalalabad whose situation was reminiscent of Dilsifat's except that the migrant had married only four months previously. It was impossible to talk to the daugh-

---

391 Interview with Dilsifat, October 2006.
392 Tajik currency which was equal to almost $1 in 2006.

ter-in-law. I sat on the *so'ri*[393] with Munojotxon Opa, the mother-in-law. The similarity between the ways young Dilsifat complained about her mother-in-law and Munojotxon Opa, who was 57 years old, complained about her own was startling. Munojotxon Opa told me how much she was suffering under the strict control and the ongoing mean behavior of her mother-in-law. Her mother-in-law was still alive, about 85 years old, and still making her life difficult even though Munojotxon Opa was near 60 herself and had grandchildren already. Usually women at her age enjoy far more freedom than before due to their age, demonstrated experience, loyalty, service, and respect to their parents-in-law. While she spoke, Munojotxon Opa's daughter-in-law brought us a table-cloth (*dasturxon*), tea, bread, jam, and sweets. Every time the young woman served us something, she left immediately again without uttering a word. While I was interviewing Munojotxon Opa, she kept busy in the kitchen where she was listening to a loud recording of Qur'an recitals.[394]

Munojotxon Opa's only son was a migrant in Russia. Very similar to Dilsifat's mother-in-law, she wanted her son to continue working in Russia since there were no other opportunities to earn money to provide for a large family such as hers. Something that struck me was the fact that the young daughter-in-law was wearing a *hijab* at home, whereas Munojotxon Opa who had just been to Mecca did not wear one. I ran into Munojot Opa in the street the next day and her large scarf was not tied as strictly as a *hijab*. I asked Munojotxon Opa a question about the age of her daughter-in-law and which district of Jalalabad she was originally from. After stating that she had turned 18 three months previously, Munojotxon Opa said the following:

> This *kelin* (daughter-in-law) of ours...she is not from this neighborhood. When she first came to this place, her way of dressing and behavior was somewhat Russian-like/Russified (Uzb. *kiyinishi, yurish-turishi o'rischaroq edi*). Then I said to her, "Look at this street, the way you are dressed does not fit in this neighborhood."[395] Before we brought you here, there were many people who wanted to marry off their daughters to my son. My son had many girls to choose from (Uzb. *xaridori ko'p edi,* literally 'many people wanted to buy him,' 'many people were interested in him,' or 'he had many admirers'). My son didn't like other girls because he liked you." This is what I said to my daughter-in-law. I said to her, "Do not embarrass me with your clothing and behavior now because these people might say, "Oh, you didn't want to have our daughter for a daughter-in-law, now is that the one you ended up having?"

---

393 Uzbek word for wooden patio outside in the courtyard where people sit on cotton mattresses, eat and drink during the day, and sleep at night during the summer.
394 For more on migration and religion, cf. concluding remarks of this book.
395 I cannot confirm Munojotxon Opa's description of her street that all women wear scarves and *hijab*s. Although Jalalabad, much like the rest of southern Kyrgyzstan, was becoming increasingly religious, there were still families in the neighborhood who were more secular. The family that introduced me to Munojotxon Opa, for instance, was a highly educated one, whose daughters I came to know, did not abide by the dressing norms that Munojotxon Opa had in mind.

So, I said to my daughter-in-law, "From now on you will put a scarf on, be decent, and start praying (Uzb. "Endi ro'mol taqasiz," dedim, "Namoz o'qiysiz," dedim). You will not go outside. You will not work. You will not have to earn money. You will have to put up with whatever material means we have here in this household." Then she said, "All right!" and from that day on started wearing a scarf and praying five times a day. When she gets bored, she might go outside with my daughter, they go to the pharmacy and come back [the distance was about 200 m from their house].[396] Or, if relatives are having a wedding, she goes and helps out, that's it, she doesn't go outside.[397]

Munojotxon Opa then complained about her own mother-in-law whose strict authority she still suffered under. Yet she was ruling her daughter-in-law in the same manner. In fact, in many ways Munujotxon Opa is stricter and her daughter-in-law might suffer more than she herself had in her youth. At the same time, there seems to be nothing all that surprising in her behavior. Analyzing Dilsifat's mother-in-law and Munojotxon Opa's attitude towards her daughter-in-law, each woman's anxiety about maintaining a good reputation becomes discernible. James Scott, in his book *Weapons of the Weak* in which he scrutinized peasant resistance in a Malay village, poses a question: "[...] what is the cost of a bad name?" He then explains that "[...] the cost of a bad name hinges directly on the social and economic sanctions that can be brought into play to punish its bearers."[398] Without digressing from these examples and falling into the trap of James Scott's class discourse, I would argue that in both examples and in both neighborhoods, family members (here parents-in-law) are wary about social sanctions that might be imposed on them. The parents-in-law automatically gain power over their daughters-in-law upon the wedding of their sons. In the absence of the latter, the power balance is tipped even more to their favor. In Dilsifat's neighborhood, there was not a single house that did not have at least one male breadwinner in Russia. The value of power and reputation for Dilsifat's mother-in-law, who justified her strict control with the absence of her son, is clear. Munojotxon Opa, by contrast to Dilsifat's mother-in-law, did not explain her control in terms of maintaining a good reputation in the neighborhood for the sake of her son. She explained how important it was for *her* to have a good name, a stable social position, respect, and authority in her *mahalla* (traditional neighborhood) in general, and among other mothers-in-law in particular. She

---

396 Saida, Firuz's wife in Moscow regularly asked her husband for money because she 'had to go to the pharmacy.' The pharmacy was one of the shops where Firuz allowed her to go in my company while I was visiting. Because of its proximity, Saida and Firuz saw little risk of getting controlled by the police, extorted for a bribe, or into other kind of trouble. One of the largest pharmacy chains in Moscow known as "36.6" was Saida's favorite place. She seemed to enjoy buying vitamins, foreign-made diet candy, and diet beverages. When I finished the fieldwork in Central Asia and Russia, I came to the conclusion that in addition to having health purposes, a pharmacy often represented an enjoyable place where women would go because it was an easy way to justify the necessity of leaving the confines of their home.
397 Interview with Munujonxon Opa, March 2008, Jalalabad (KYR).
398 Scott, 1985:24.

first celebrated her son's wedding to which she had to invite all her neighbors. She was able to afford a big wedding thanks to her son's earnings in Russia. A month after the wedding, using the same financial source, she went on a pilgrimage to Mecca.[399]

During the Soviet period, due to suppression of religious values and the state efforts to promote the emancipation of women, conflicts in the families had different roots and dimensions. Some efforts were made in the communities to solve family conflicts with the intervention of state administrative institutions. Especially during the Gorbachev era, the mass media used to cover reports on family conflicts.[400] Problems in families about relations between spouses, children's education, addiction of family members to drugs and alcohol, and conflicts between family members over various issues including disputes with parents-in-law or inheritance problems between siblings also used to be openly discussed at the workplace or at reunion meetings of the communities in which the conflicting parties resided. What is changing in post-Soviet Central Asia is the gradual decrease of state protection. The protection of the family through labor unions vanished as the USSR disintegrated, state-owned institutions let their employees go and the employable population increasingly sought undocumented low-paid employment outside the territorial borders of the newly established nation-states.

8.4. Conclusion

This chapter has examined conjugal relationships in the context of transnational migration. It elaborated on the changing roles of migrant wives vis-à-vis their spouses and parents-in-law, considering both migrant wives who joined their husbands in Russia and those who remained in the country of origin. Through a comparison of two couples in two different Russian cities, this chapter has shown how in the first instance, the female migrant's experiences could change the role she played as a woman in her family prior to

---

399 It must be mentioned that Saudi Arabia sets Kyrgyzstan a quota of 4,500 pilgrims per year and that applicants have to register and obtain permission well in advance. (On pilgrim quotas see *Kyrgyzstan: Government Religious Policies Fueling Societal Tensions*, article by Alisher Khamidov for Eurasia.Org on December 18, 2007, available at http://www.eurasianet.org/departments/insight/articles/eav121807.s html). Since Munojotxon Opa's permission to go to Mecca was granted for the same period of her son's wedding, she left for Mecca despite the high costs of the wedding, which only added to public respect for her.
400 A series of reports I remember watching on television and reading in newspapers were dedicated to the issue of self-immolation among young women in Uzbekistan through the 1980s. This kind of suicide has been on the rise again since the beginning of the 21st century throughout the entire region. In one of the villages in the province of Khaton (TAJ) where I conducted fieldwork, all the inhabitants appeared shattered by the death of a newly-married woman who had burned herself to death in her clay oven. For more on the description of domestic conflicts and violence, as well as self-immolation of women in Central Asia, see Ro'i, 2000:546-548.

migration as she gained more self-confidence and learned to challenge her husband's authority during migration. In the second example, the female migrant abided by the customs and traditions of her home country and made an effort to remain an obedient wife of her husband. This chapter has also cast a glance at multiple cases of married women from Central Asia for whom migration to Russia represented a new chapter in their lives. They left for Russia at the stage of life when their marriage was in trouble. In migration they often gained independence from their authoritarian husbands. Further, special attention has been paid to the situation of the families in which the female spouse has left to work in Russia to sustain her husband and children. In such cases, eldest daughters have taken over the role of the mothers by caring for their siblings and taking charge of household chores. It seemed that in their traditional societies, husbands were torn between the expected role of "breadwinner," which they had failed to perform, and the role of head of the household with full authority, which they did perform despite their dependence on their wives' remittances. Finally, this chapter has tried to give attention to the situation of families in which parents of young married male migrants gain more authority over their daughters-in-law. In the absence of their sons, they feel more responsible for controlling their daughters-in-law so that no doubt may arise in the neighborhood about their good behavior and faithfulness. For such purposes parents-in-law often impose strict rules and demand, for instance, that their daughters-in-law fully fulfill their Islamic duties, but in doing so, they set their own standards. Such power relations between migrant wives and their parents-in-law often result in family disputes that contribute to overall social tensions. The next chapter of this book maintains the discourse of conjugal relationships and calls the attention of its readers to transnational polygamous relations of male migrants from Central Asia in Russia, trying to examine the incentives for establishing such ties across nation-states.

9. Transnational Polygamous Relationships

Mainstream scholarship on migration, much like the previous chapters of this book, calls attention to married male "breadwinners" whose significant others are depicted as recipients of remittances or dependent families in the homeland. One of the unexpected discoveries of the present research has been on male migrants who are involved in multiple conjugal ties. Because the subject of polygamous relationships is mentioned only in the margins of the scholarship on migration, I did not pay much attention to it at first. However, after having become acquainted with several such cases during the fieldwork and observed the phenomenon in the sending countries, I saw a need to address the issue in a separate chapter.

To begin with, there is a scarcity of research that addresses the cases of transnational migrants who are engaged in extramarital or polygamous relationships. When polygamous relationships are mentioned in the scholarship on migration, they usually have the following rationales: first, studies are carried out primarily in the countries of origin and concern the gender imbalance resulting from the mass emigration of men. An in-depth research project conducted in Botswana, for instance, reveals that the out-migration of men caused irregularities in the gender ratio of marriages throughout the 1970s and 1980s.[401] The dynamics of out-migration in sending countries would cause such a demographic surplus that women would see no option other than engaging in a polygamous relationship or concubinage, as in the case of Vietnam in the 1980s. At the same time, the male population working abroad would have difficulty finding spouses from their own country and delay marriage.[402]

Second, polygamous marriages are considered from the perspective of the country of destination such as France or Great Britain, and scholarly debates take place more or less on migration policies of immigration countries and the successes or failures in the assimilation processes of primarily Muslim minorities.[403] When youth riots broke out in several cities in France in the autumn of 2005, they made headlines in the media around the world. Nicolas Sarkozy, then the French Interior Minister, publicly blamed a polygamous family background for the lack of integration among the young immigrants. Migration scholars then noted that France, as a receiving country, provided a legislative framework for family reunions that allowed migrant workers' spouses from polygamous marriages to join their husbands.[404] The family reunion policy was introduced in 1975 but between 1993 and

---

401 Brown, 1983.
402 Goodkind, 1997.
403 Sona, 2005; Coleman, 1995; Sargent and Larchanché-Kim, 2006.
404 *Ibid.*

1997 no more than one wife for every husband was given permission to reunite.[405]

The questions which will be addressed in this chapter differ from the objectives of the research which has been carried out up to now. This chapter will try to follow the socio-cultural traces for the establishment of such conjugal ties at both ends of migration and find answers to the following two questions: what constitutes a transnational polygamous family, and what are the incentives for mobile persons to establish extramarital relationships?

This chapter will be structured as follows: it will first look at the institutional frameworks of both the home and the host countries and discuss the legislation of the Soviet era that was adopted after the countries achieved independence. In a second step, an attempt will be made to trace the factors that condition the emergence of polygamous relationships. These relationships will be linked to conditions at micro-levels, in the frameworks of which examples of polygamous marriages from the data will be discussed together with perspectives of the male and female migrants. Further, in a third step, the transnational social spaces of polygamous families will be discussed. The analysis in this section is expected to reveal societal reconfigurations which are typical of the transnationalizing post-Soviet life-world.

9.1. The Other Wife in Russia: A Typology of Extramarital Relationships of Labor Migrants

During the ethnographic interviews in Russia and Central Asia, in approximately one out of every seven instances, my interlocutors either knew someone from their circle of friends or were closely related to someone who was involved in an extramarital relationship or they were themselves involved in such a relationship. Access to the media and to the social world of the migrants as well as to members of their social networks in the countries of origin and destination enabled me to assess the situation to the extent that polygamous relationships, which often go unnoticed in the research, could no longer be treated in this study as unimportant, unnecessary, or unrepresentative. During the first research trip to Moscow in September 2005, no examples of polygamous relations came out during data collection. I was hosted by a family of Uzbek labor migrants and was in a close contact with them, I participated in social gatherings of Kyrgyz, Tajik, and Uzbek labor migrants, and I conducted ethnographic interviews that revealed a great deal about the transnational social spaces of Central Asians in Moscow. Eventually, as I was collecting data in St. Petersburg a year later in August 2006, my attention was caught by one instance in which a job broker from Tajikistan who had just married a Russian woman allegedly had a wife back in his country of

---

405 Bryceson, 2002:39.

origin. There were rumors in his immediate social environment in St. Petersburg that he had married a Russian citizen to obtain a passport and that everyone knew that he was involved in at least one conjugal relationship in his country of origin. After having collected several instances of polygamous relationships among Central Asian labor migrants during my field trips to St. Petersburg in Russia, Khujand and Kulob in Tajikistan, and again in Astrakhan in Russia, I contacted the very first informants that hosted me in Moscow in September 2005 and interviewed them on the subject. During the interview my host told me the story of her cousin who had a relationship with two women at the two ends of his migrant trajectory. These findings led me to conclude that establishing extramarital relationships is frequently part of the transnationalization process. They fall off the main track of the research because the researcher's focus is often drawn to other aspects of transnational social spaces such as flows of resources and ideas, changes in gender balances, identity construction, collective agency, social interaction on agency, etc.

The ethnographic interviews with male migrants, who turned out to have more than one wife, their spouses in the country of origin or destination, and their family members and informants who were familiar with the aspect of polygamy among migrants point to three categories of causes for these polygamous conjugal relationships. When illustrating each type, I will try to engage both ends of the trajectories in the discussion.

1. A *marriage blanche* of a classic form which migrants admitted as being *tak dlya pasporta* (Rus. 'simply for passport') which is based on a bilateral arrangement between a Central Asian migrant and, most commonly, a Russian female citizen. It can happen that the migrant's wife back home is not aware of such arrangements. The Russian spouse and the Central Asian migrant start sharing an apartment or a room in a communal apartment.[406] The labor migrant can maintain his relationship to his wife in the home country and divorce the Russian spouse after obtaining Russian citizenship. It can also happen, as one of the instances will show, that his relationship with the Russian citizen can last longer and he will remain married to two women. The migrant would commute between two countries and provide for two families.

In one example, during my field research on the outskirts of the town of Kulob (TAJ) I met a returning seasonal migrant. He had been commuting for seven years between Moscow and Kulob (TAJ). He is married in Kulob, has three sons and a daughter. The residents of his village spoke highly of him. I conducted an interview with him and his wife

---

406 Communal apartments comprising several rooms, each allotted to a resident, a couple, a family, or a group of persons were introduced in Russia at the beginning of the 20th century. Especially after the Revolution in 1917, Bolsheviks expropriated large condominiums and houses from affluent urban residents and used them to settle workers.

separately. His wife told me during the interview that her husband had found a Russian woman, his long time co-worker, and he intended to get a license to marry her on his next trip. She said she had confidence in her husband that the marriage was meant for citizenship purposes only. She assured me that having two sons living with him in Russia, her husband would not have a romantic relationship with anyone else. It is not completely clear, however, how men provide the Russian marriage institutions with evidence of their single status. On the other hand, empirical data for this research project has shown that it is, in essence, possible to falsify all types of documents in Russia. The person willing to marry in Russia would not face major obstacles in compiling the necessary documents for the authorities to be able to get a marriage certificate. At the same time, in Tajikistan marriages often take place without registration in town halls. During the Soviet era, the state had more control over every matrimonial procedure and permission for traditional wedding ceremonies had to be requested at administrative offices. Since the collapse of the Soviet regime, however, weddings that take place especially in rural areas often remain unregistered, due to the fact that underpaid state functionaries have lost interest in feeling responsible or exerting control.[407]

2. A *voluntary relationship* that young male married migrants may enter into after several years of bidirectional commutes without cutting off the existing marital ties in their countries of origin. The emergence of this type of extramarital relation in destinations of migration sheds light on the transforming matrimonial traditions and customs in Central Asia, such as arranged marriages, which are widely practiced. In the provinces and rural areas they are indeed more the rule than the exception. Male migrant informants talked more openly with me about their extramarital relationships in the country of destination whereas in the country of origin, given the socio-cultural settings of the environment, they were more taciturn about their private lives as migrants in Russia. Being aware of these conditions I, as a female researcher, had to communicate with them in a very reserved manner. During the inquiries in Russia, male migrants gave me a more or less standard explanation:

---

[407] Having brought up this example, it is necessary to distinguish between Russian citizens of Slavic origin and those who have a non-Slavic (Caucasian or Central Asian) background. For many Central Asian men it is important to marry a so-called Muslim woman. In the Russian Federation, Muslim minority groups include a variety of ethnicities such as Tatars, Bashkir, Chechens, and Avars. Among these minority groups there are those who obtained Russian citizenship based on their refugee status at the beginning of 1990s, that is citizens with Azerbaijani and Tajikistani backgrounds who fled armed conflicts in their regions of birth. While admitting their relationship to Russian women, some of my interlocutors would emphasize, "She is from here, but Muslim...she is Tatar."

Zokirjon: Look, you know our traditions. Put bluntly, the first time I married, I did it for my parents. The second time…all right, it was for me.
Delia: Does your other wife know?
Zokirjon: (looks at his friend and pauses)[408]

In this category, male migrants take advantage of the opportunity of being geographically distant from their spouses, children, and parents. Hence, extramarital relationships can be interpreted as practices that are facilitated through geographical distance. Once away from home, unlike in the first marriage, male migrants would take the initiative and get acquainted with a person of their choice. Although migrants' family ties and sentiments of obligation and responsibility certainly vary, some limit their relationships with their families at home to paying visits and remittances on a yearly basis, while others try to maintain closer connections to their spouses and children at home by making phone calls, sending money, and visiting more often. One such case is that of the head of a diasporic organization of Uzbeks.[409] He married a Tatar woman in Russia during the final years of *perestroika*, officially got divorced, but maintained his relationship with his spouse and children. Moreover, he proudly says that, as a good father, he is taking adequate care of his children. He brought his son and later his daughter and his son-in-law to Russia and provided them with housing and employment. He admitted that his relationship with the Tatar woman did not last long and resulted in separation. At the time of the interview with him, he was in a relationship with a younger woman from his hometown in Uzbekistan.

Both male and female labor migrants confirmed in various contexts that they feel a certain level of independence in Russia, and it is in this context that the category of a migrant engaging in a *voluntary relationship* should be understood. Interestingly, although control of identity documents, work permits, and registrations and humiliation and extortion by the law enforcement agents limit the mobility of Central Asian migrants, they told me that they feel freedom in making their own decisions such as spending their earnings, planning their day, going out or gathering with friends, changing employment, etc. In their homeland all these decisions have to take into consideration the opinion of hierarchically superior kinship members and often require their approval or permission.

3. An *arranged affair* is the relationship that is arranged by the migrant's close kin or friends in the country of destination. Unlike the category of voluntary relationship, the migrant does not take the initiative of getting acquainted with a woman but rather an intermediary person chooses

---

408 Interview with Zokirjon from Osh, Kyrgyzstan.
409 His name and the name of the city where the diaspora is located cannot be revealed due to the fact that he is a person of high respect not only among migrants but also at the administrative level in the Russian city in which this study took place.

someone for him. In a communal apartment of migrants in St. Petersburg I was introduced to a large family from Xorazm (UZB) where the *kelin* (*Uzbek* 'bride' and 'daughter-in-law') was introduced as being from Samarqand (UZB).[410] I had an interview with this woman who was at home as she was on maternity leave with her six-month-old baby. She told me that her husband had been introduced to her by her sister-in-law with whom she used to work at a supermarket. She was about 35 years old at the time I conducted my field research in St.Petersburg, so I asked if she or her husband had had conjugal relationships prior to their departure. She said that she had a six-year-old son from her previous marriage back in Samarqand. She said she would like to bring her son to Russia. As for her husband, no children had been born from his first marriage with his spouse in Xorazm, so his sisters arranged the second marriage which was not registered. My understanding of their situation was that this migrant was still providing for his first wife in Xorazm and at the same time providing for his second wife's family in Samarqand. She mentioned gratefully, *"Erim o'g'ilchamga, bizga yordam berib turadilar"* (*Uzbek*. 'My husband often helps my little son, he helps us').

Of course this typology does not imply that extramarital relations all belong exclusively to one of the three types. In fact, it can well be that an affair is arranged *and* has a functional purpose of, for example, obtaining citizenship. The following genogram (see Figure 4) represents such a family that I encountered in St. Petersburg. In this genogram the male migrant is shown as having two partners, one at each end of migration. He has two sons and a daughter from his first marriage. He later enters into a liaison and may or may not have a child from the more recent relationship. The dotted line is drawn simply in order to leave the possibility open, as in three out of seven cases only one child was involved. The genogram served this research as a semiotic aid to analyze the transnational character of these ties.

---

410 These cities are situated in Uzbekistan.

Country of Origin   **Country of Destination**

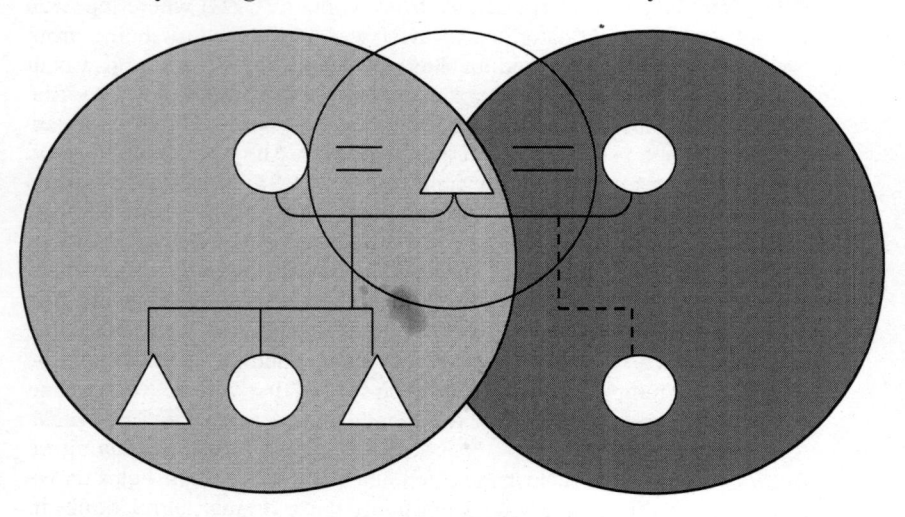

Figure 4: Genogram of a Polygamous Transnational Family

9. 2. The Institutional and Judicial Level

> "Monogamy is the only type of marriage universally recognized, even in societies which prefer other systems. It is probably the most common form of marriage in nearly all societies except the polyandrous, which can be counted on the fingers of one hand. Where monogamy is required, there is obviously no alternative. Where it is optional, as in polygamous societies, most men are too poor to have more than one wife." (Nimkoff M.F. "Comparative Family Systems", p.17).

When seen from the perspective of the sending states in Uzbekistan, Tajikistan, and Kyrgyzstan, a citizen is allowed one spouse at a time, which implies that polygamy is prohibited by law.[411] These three successor states of the USSR took over the Soviet legislation and banned polygamy. Interestingly, between the early years of its foundation in the 1920s and 1944, de facto marriages were tolerated in the entire Soviet Union. Starting from July 1944, a Decree of the Presidium of the Supreme Soviet allowed only civil marriages, whereas de facto cohabitation lost judicial power. To quote Article 19 of the Decree, "Only registered marriage engenders the partners' rights and obligations provided by codes on matrimony, family and guardianship in Soviet Republics."[412] In the section of the legislation on obstacles to entering

---

411   I refer to the citizen as *he*, using the masculine form, as the majority of polygamous relationships are male-headed, i.e. one man having two or more female partners.
412   Matveev, 1985:52.

matrimony, the Code on Matrimony of the Russian Soviet Federative Socialist Republic (RSFSR) states in Article 16 that individuals who are still married will not be allowed to enter into a new marriage.[413] Following the collapse of the USSR, in Kyrgyzstan, Uzbekistan, and Tajikistan Articles 15 and 16 of the Family Code respectively prohibited civil marriage "between those citizens at least one of whom at the time of application is married to another citizen."[414] In addition, all three sending countries in which the present study took place continue the Soviet legislative practice that requires that the marital status of a citizen be marked in the citizenship document by a stamp, which is issued by the city hall upon civil matrimony and which also indicates the name of the spouse. Hence, to highlight the relevance of this issue to migration, only the person whose name is written on the stamp in the migrant's passport is recognized as his or her legal spouse.[415] In the country of destination when migrants settle and find employment, the Russian authorities (usually agents of the police departments or the Federal Migration Service) check only the residence status and work permits of the foreign citizens. Obviously, no legal action would be taken against migrants for engaging in extramarital or polygamous relationships as they could have or would have occurred under the Soviet law. Even if such measures were to be taken, it would be legally quite difficult to prove a husband was involved in polygamous relationships.

In all three sending countries, polygamy is punishable by law. So far, only in two countries, namely Tajikistan and Kyrgyzstan, is the issue currently being raised in the political arena. In Uzbekistan, an independent research institute published the results of a quantitative opinion survey which it conducted in the capital Toshkent, which reveals some positive views of the population on this phenomenon.[416] In March 2007 in Kyrgyzstan, the then Justice Minister Marat Kayipov and government ombudsman Tursunbay Bakir Uulu emphasized that polygamy should be allowed by law. President Bakiev opposed the idea. Interestingly, those Kyrgyz political figures who spoke in favor of the legalization of polygamous relationships linked the issue to labor migration. According to them, an estimated 800,000 men reside in Russia as labor migrants and since some of them do not return to their homeland for many years, "their wives and families would benefit from po-

---

413   Kodeks o brake i sem'e, 1986:9.
414   Code on Matrimony of the republics.
415   Here, one distinction between passport regulations of the three sending countries should be mentioned. In Uzbekistan, the citizenship passport has the same function as the travel passport and citizens are allowed to travel abroad only when they obtain permission in the form of a stamp issued by the Ministry of Internal Affairs (so-called exit visas). Citizens of Tajikistan and Kyrgyzstan are required to obtain travel passports to travel to countries in which visas are mandatory. Since no visa is required from the citizens of Kyrgyzstan, Tajikistan, and Uzbekistan to enter the territory of the Russian Federation, Tajikistani and Kyrgyzstani citizens can travel there with citizenship passports, which are also called internal passports. Both internal and external passports contain pages on which entries about the passport holder's marital status (a stamp from the city hall) and children are made.
416   Pogrebov, 2006.

lygamy." This suggests that the wives of the migrants, referred to in the migration literature as abandoned spouses, could remarry as second wives.[417] This is a significant point, inasmuch as the political figures in Kyrgyzstan do not condone the practice of polygamy simply for purposes of employment beyond the national state borders. In Tajikistan, the debate has taken on similar vigor. Those politicians who have so far spoken in favor of legalizing polygamy in Tajikistan represent political Islam. Tajikistan is the only country in the region to allow a religiously-oriented political party (Party of Islamic Revival of Tajikistan) in opposition, a compromise which resulted from the peace-building negotiations that ended the armed civil conflict of 1992-1997.[418] Discussing the political decision-making in Tajikistan, it is important to refer to the official "Decree (Rus. 'postanovlenie') of the Government" for the country's demographic policy for the period of 2003-2015. This document, which contains a list of the problems and priorities of the demographic development policy for the population of the Republic of Tajikistan, states that out-migration of the young unmarried male population creates a deficit of fiancés, preparing fertile ground for establishing polygamous marriages. Approaching the issue of involving more women in the employment market, the document urges an increase in the marriageable age for both sexes from 17 to 18 and at the same time taking strict measures to combat polygamy.[419]

Neither the surveys in Uzbekistan nor the official document of the government of Tajikistan, both based on quantitative surveys and/or the debates taking place among the Kyrgyz political decision-makers, touch upon polygamous relationships of male migrants who establish extramarital relationships and found families that span territorial state borders. The situation of such polygamous men is, in reality, quite complex. It can be difficult to prove that a man is involved in polygamous relationships, regardless of whether he is an external labor migrant or a rural-urban migrant or a sedentary resident. If, however, he is charged with domestic violence and his polygamous links are revealed, then he can be sentenced to up to three years in prison for violating the family code. This punishment is considered debatable by some Kyrgyz politicians, who argue that absence of the breadwinner of the family

---

417   See further Pribilsky's study on Ecuadorian transnational migrants and their families in the country of origin in which he mentions "esposas abandonadas."
418   Tajik Women Want Polygamy Legalized, Article by Nargiz Zakirova (http://iwpr.net/?p=rca&s=f&o=162938&apc_state=henirca2002). The assessment is also based on the debates which the author attended and co-organized during roundtable dialogues between representatives of political Islam and secular powers in Tajikistan in 2003. Additional source: http://varorud.org/old/analitics/ society/ society 240304.html.
419   Electronic source: Postanovlenie "O programme realizacii koncepcii gosudarstvennoi demograficheskoi politiki Respubliki Tajikistan na 2003-2015 gg." [Decree "On the Program of the Realization of the Conception of the Demographic Policy of the Government of the Republic of Tajikistan for the period of 2003-2015"].

for so long would not alleviate the material situation of his spouses and children.[420]

9. 3. Situational Analysis

After the data collection and the discovery of transnational polygamies, this aspect of transnational migration seemed very complex. It was, however, a challenging task to analyze this phenomenon, not only because it has not yet attracted enough attention in migration research, but also since it was not the primary objective of the present project. It appeared plausible to operate with *situational analysis* as suggested by Clarke. While traditional *grounded theory* focuses more on basic social processes, situational analysis complements it by knitting together the discourses, structures, and conditions of the situation as the situation itself is treated as a unit of analysis.[421] According to Clarke, situational analysis can be applied in a variety of research projects such as interviews, ethnographic, historical, visual materials, and multi-sited research.[422] As the present research is being carried out in adherence to multi-sited research, situational analysis appeared to be feasible for the phenomenon in question; it could assist the researcher in that it requires an analysis of the relations between human, non-human, discursive, and other elements of a given situation.[423] Following Clarke, at a preliminary stage, an abstract situational map was constructed. Reflecting the case of a polygamous family as observed in the country of destination, this map involves a couple in which both partners are from Central Asia. It also comprises places that migrants visit and actions in which the migrants and their close kinship members are involved. Since inclusion of absolutely everything as far as discourses, ideas, concepts, institutions, and interactions are concerned would be both time and space consuming, only those non-human actants and human actors that are of utmost significance for this situation are shown below.[424]

---

420 Kyrgyzstan: Debate on Legalized Polygamy Continues, Article by Bruce Pannier (http://www.rferl.org/featuresarticle/2007/03/d46aefbc-4179-4966-806c-e0d37a9c815c.html).
421 Glaser and Strauss, 2009; Clarke, 2005:xxii.
422 Clarke, 2005:165-167.
423 Clarke, 2005:xxiii, more on multi-sited research see Marcus: 1995.
424 Clarke, 2005:88.

Figure 5: Abstract Situational Map

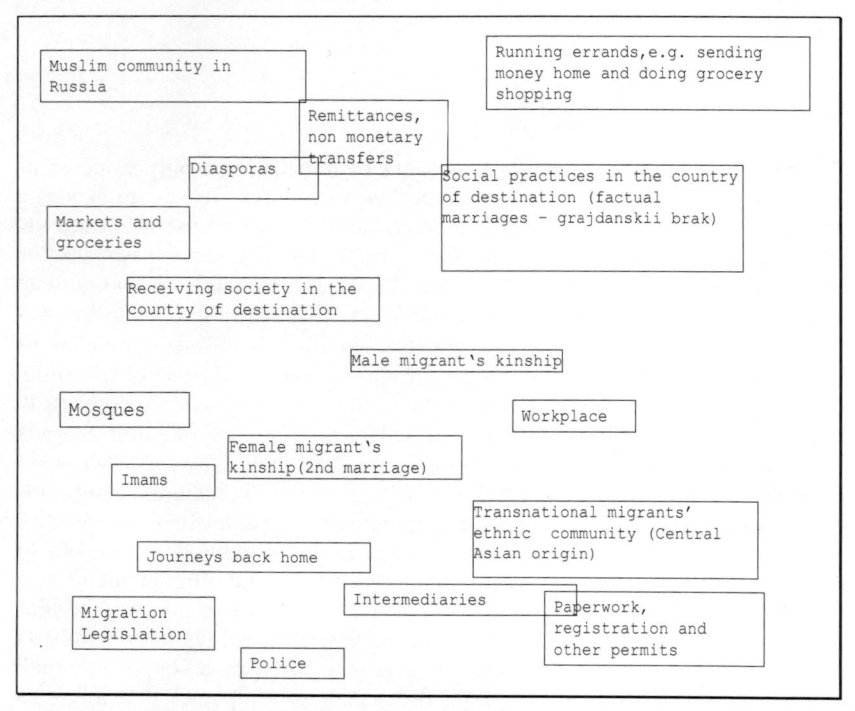

```
┌─────────────────────────────────────────────────────────────────────┐
│  ┌──────────────────────┐         ┌──────────────────────────┐     │
│  │ Muslim community in  │         │ Running errands,e.g.     │     │
│  │ Russia               │         │ sending money home and   │     │
│  └──────────────────────┘         │ doing grocery shopping   │     │
│                  ┌──────────────┐ └──────────────────────────┘     │
│                  │ Remittances, │                                   │
│                  │ non monetary │                                   │
│            ┌─────┤ transfers    │                                   │
│            │Diasporas───────────┘ ┌──────────────────────────┐     │
│            └──────┘                │ Social practices in the  │     │
│  ┌──────────────┐                  │ country of destination   │     │
│  │ Markets and  │                  │ (factual marriages -     │     │
│  │ groceries    │                  │ grajdanskii brak)        │     │
│  └──────────────┘                  └──────────────────────────┘     │
│            ┌──────────────────────┐                                 │
│            │ Receiving society in │                                 │
│            │ the country of       │                                 │
│            │ destination          │                                 │
│            └──────────────────────┘                                 │
│                      ┌────────────────────────┐                     │
│                      │ Male migrant's kinship │                     │
│                      └────────────────────────┘                     │
│  ┌──────────┐                      ┌────────────┐                   │
│  │ Mosques  │                      │ Workplace  │                   │
│  └──────────┘                      └────────────┘                   │
│                ┌─────────────────────┐                              │
│                │ Female migrant's    │                              │
│       ┌────────┤ kinship(2nd marriage)│                             │
│       │ Imams  └─────────────────────┘                              │
│       └────────┘                                                    │
│                                    ┌──────────────────────────┐     │
│                                    │ Transnational migrants'  │     │
│                                    │ ethnic community (Central│     │
│                ┌──────────────────┐│ Asian origin)            │     │
│                │Journeys back home│└──────────────────────────┘     │
│                └──────────────────┘                                 │
│                            ┌────────────────┐                       │
│                            │ Intermediaries │  ┌──────────────┐    │
│  ┌──────────────┐          └────────────────┘  │ Paperwork,   │    │
│  │ Migration    │                               │ registration │    │
│  │ Legislation  │                               │ and other    │    │
│  └──────────────┘     ┌────────┐                │ permits      │    │
│                       │ Police │                └──────────────┘    │
│                       └────────┘                                    │
└─────────────────────────────────────────────────────────────────────┘
```

In constructing this map the following questioned had to be kept in mind: Who and what are important actors and elements in this situation? What additional material and symbolic or discursive features would be relevant to include?

For better comprehension, some of the elements illustrated on this abstract map should be briefly explained. Inverted commas are used for practical reasons.

1. *'Mosques'* – In the cities of Astrakhan (RUS) and St. Petersburg, and to a lesser extent in Moscow, it was observed that Central Asian migrants often attend *mosques*. Depending on their family background, level of education and secularization, and conditions of employment, male migrants attended Friday prayers. At all three sites where the current field research took place, the observations were carried out in and around the mosque sites. These particular buildings had been constructed at the beginning of the 20th century, shortly before the October Revolution of 1917.
2. *'Nikah'* – For many labor migrants intending to get married, it was important to have a religious ritual known as *nikah*. Some of these rituals

took place either at the mosque or wherever it was convenient for *imams* and the marrying couples. One female migrant from Samarqand (UZB) said, during our interview, that one Saturday while she was working at the supermarket, her mediators called her and told her to be ready after work. The family of the bride and the groom set the table for dinner at her workplace. The mullah prayed and after the *nikah*, everyone had dinner and the couple was considered to be married.

3. *'Kinship'* of both parties of the conjugal relationship are important factors in this situation. As it is known from previous research on migration, migrants would rarely find themselves in unfamiliar terrain in solitude but rather rely on kinship networks.[425] If, however, a male migrant finds himself in a network that consists of kinship members belonging to his legitimate spouse in the country of origin, a second marriage, cohabitation, or extramarital relationship would not take place since it would involve a range of conflicts at both ends of the trajectory in the kinship network. In addition, this person would risk losing his employment if it had been arranged by the family of his spouse. The situational map therefore assumes that, for a transnational polygamous family to be established, the social space in the country of destination would not include any members of the male migrant's first spouse.

4. *'Ethnic community'* – Since it is essential for the migrant that his new conjugal relationship be acknowledged by his or her own *ethnic community*, whether it consists of Tajiks, Uzbeks, or Kyrgyz, it is essential to have a celebration, although the religious authorities are not always involved.

5. *'Resources'* and *'Remittances'* – Depending on the male migrant's choice, that is whether the second spouse is a labor migrant of Central Asian or Caucasian background or a local Russian whose family would not be dependent on monetary *'remittances,'* the transfer and distribution of *'resources'* take a crucial position on the situation map.

The abstract map assumes that the migrants are in one way or another connected to *'migrant communities'* or official *'diasporas.'* Having observed the situation of migrants, I decided to add other elements essential to their daily lives such as grocery shopping, sending money home, dealing with the police and migration authorities in Russia, etc.

In a further step, it was essential to define the relations between the elements on the map. In what is known as relational analysis, Clarke suggests focusing on one element and analyzing its relations to others. Considering the

---

425 Pries, 1999:24.

complexity of polygamous relations, a relational analysis that constitutes a web of ties may look as follows:

Figure 6: Relational Analysis Considering Married Migrant Couple in the Center

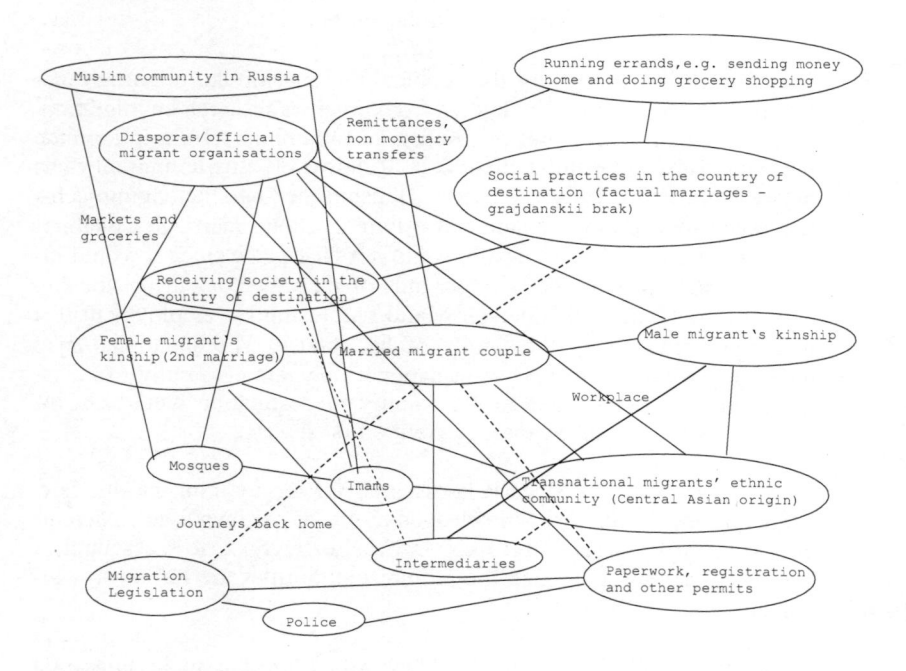

Note that the element '*married migrant couple*' in the country of destination is placed in the center. This relational analysis captures the relationships among the elements. The ties that are drawn between the elements are rather at the beginning stage of the analysis, so as not to make the image look unnecessarily convoluted. This image should by no means imply that '*papers and registrations*' are loosely bound to the '*migrant couple,*' or not tied to '*migrant kinship*' of either side.

Operating with a situational analysis was helpful in analyzing polygamous marriages from entirely different angles. After encoding the data and discovering the seemingly unimportant factor of polygamous relations in the transnational context, any researcher is intuitively tempted to associate polygamy or polygyny with the religious and cultural backgrounds of labor migrants from Central Asia. At first it seemed almost "logical" to associate polygamous relations with Islam that allows men to take up to four spouses. After all, the three sending countries are predominantly Muslim. However, it was imperative to use caution in drawing premature and simplistic inferences and to take a step back from religious explanations for this aspect. Instead, as a vantage point, it had to be considered that employment and sustaining families back home through remittances were the main reasons to migrate, as most of the informants assured me. It then became significant to probe the structure of polygamous families and to find out how resources within such kinship networks were being distributed across the nation-state boundaries. For this reason, before launching the actual discussion of the case of post-Soviet Central Asia, it is essential to take a look at the issue in a broader context and to ponder the conditions and circumstances under which extra-marital relationships are established in countries beyond the Central Asian region. This will be reviewed in the next section. Once this broader picture has been drawn, I shall proceed to bring the region into the post-Soviet context in order to highlight its own characteristics.

9.4. Transnational Polygamies in the Global Context and the Case of Central Asia

Taking a brief look at polygamous relationships in the context of migration, I would like to compare the three Central Asian countries to other examples encountered in the migration literature. Placing Central Asia in a broad geographical and historical context can reveal that polygamous relationships are not too atypical. In addition, in combination with the situational analysis it will assist later on in the analysis of transnational social spaces. In my comparison, I was inspired by George Marcus, who asserts:

> [...] in multi-sited ethnography, comparison emerges from putting questions to an emerging object of study whose contours, sites and relationships are not known beforehand, but are themselves a contribution of making an account that has different, complexly connected real-world sites of investigation. The object of study is ultimately mobile and multiply situated, so any ethnography of such an object will have a comparative dimension that is integral to it[...][426]

Investigation of the migration literature shows that migration patterns of one of the sending Central Asian states, namely Tajikistan, are comparable to Vietnam in the 1980s and 1990s. The reunification war of 1965-1975 in Vietnam that caused a great loss of male population as well as the postwar emigration of men seeking employment abroad resulted in a major deficit in male partners on the marriage market. Studies on Vietnam reveal that economic constraints, particularly the marginalization of women in the job market, as well as the transition to the market economy and the scarcity of the

---

[426] Marcus, 1995:102.

male population, led women to become concubines and second wives.[427] As far as Tajikistan is concerned, scholars and analysts argued in various contexts that in a country in which approximately 25,000 households were reported to have lost their breadwinners during the civil war in the 1990s, becoming a second spouse seemed the only survival strategy for many women. Its legalization still remains a hotly debated issue. Indeed, female spouses of second marriages are known to have asked the authorities in Tajikistan to register their conjugal ties.[428]

One might argue that the comparison to Vietnam with its postwar demographic and economic changes helps to explain emerging phenomenon of polygamy in Tajikistan. It would, however, leave some inferential gaps with respect to two other sending countries, since Uzbekistan and Kyrgyzstan have not fully shared the same conditions in the process of transition following the collapse of the USSR. Investigating further and shifting the comparison to Latin American countries shows different findings. In his study on Ecuadorian transnational migrants in Queens, New York, Pribilsky discovers two instances in the course of his survey where married migrants had gotten involved with other women in the US. Pribilsky makes reference to another study conducted by Guttman in Mexico City.[429] Both Guttman and Pribilsky conclude that the male migrants they surveyed would occasionally take lovers, but in general the macho tendency to *talk* about "cheating on their wives" and the ability to afford prostitutes and lovers did not actually translate into engagement in such affairs.[430] In a personal conversation, an Armenian acquaintance told me that some Armenian male migrant workers who commute between Russia and Armenia were also engaged in extramarital relationships in Russia.[431]

The instances in which Latin American male migrants engage in liaisons once again confirms that migrant extramarital relations occur across many nation-state borders and frequently evolve into polygamous affairs and parallel families. They often go unconsidered in the research because they do not seem important enough or the examples supposedly lack representativeness or are too small in number to discuss. This is surprising considering that extramarital relationships were documented in the scholarship on migration

---

427 Goodkind, 1997:114.
428 See also a report on polygamy at http://www.eurasianet.org/departments/culture/articles/eav102002.shtml.
429 Pribilsky, 2004:321.
430 *Ibid.*
431 I have been told that in the 1970s it was not uncommon for Turkish labor migrants in Germany to engage in extramarital relationships with German women. Unfortunately, apart from Nevim Çil's monograph (2007) in which she marginally treats the subject, I have not been able to find any other sources. In Turkey and among Turkish migrants in Germany, the German first names *Helga* and *Hans* are used to refer to a prototypical German spouse or lover. (I am grateful to Prof. Faist and doctoral seminar participants for their comments on this topic.)

as early as the beginning of the 20th century in W. Thomas and Znaniecki's *The Polish Peasant in Europa in America*.[432]

Transnationalization and Polygamous Relationships in Post-Soviet Central Asia

Bringing polygamous relationships into the transnational context entails inquiries into opportunities and constraints accounted for by the politics, institutions, and social and cultural norms in the countries of origin and destination.[433] The most essential factors conditioning the emergence of polygamous relationships, which can be elicited from the interviews and the relatively scarce literature, are as follows:

(1) France as a host country provided its migrant workers from the sub-Saharan African countries with institutional opportunities which allowed more than one spouse per migrant to join their husbands there.[434] Turning attention to the political opportunity structures in the Russian Federation, it can be deduced that it is the labor migrants who have to come to terms with constraints involving primarily legislative measures for migrants, which, in turn, are closely linked to the development of functioning institutions that are responsible for them. Because migrants face extreme hurdles in becoming documented, they seek alternative opportunities, such as involvement in fictitious marriages.

(2) The economic factors in polygamous relationships are essential. Only economically successful migrants who have been involved in labor migration for at least five years on average can afford an additional spouse. This is especially true if both spouses are of Central Asian origin, since matrimonial festivities involve expenses for dowry and gifts and sustaining families at the two ends of the migration trajectory.[435] One of the migrants I encountered in St. Petersburg worked as a taxi driver and earned 1000 dollars a month, an amount sufficient to support a small second family.

(3) Drawing upon the relational ties of the male migrants and their positions in the networks in the country of destination, it became clear throughout the analysis that polygamous conjugal relationships can only be established under the condition that the social network of the male migrant does not include close kin of the first spouse. This applies even more to the case of those migrants who had been supported by the kinship net-

---

432 The documented records of the Chicago Legal Aid Society reveal cases in which Polish immigrants were charged with bigamy, Thomas and Znaniecki, 1958, v2:1720-1722.
433 Smith, 1999:187, more on opportunity structures, see also Vertovec, 2001.
434 *Cf* introductory notes at the beginning of this chapter
435 For more on matrimonial festivities, see Chapter 6

work throughout the entire process, starting from the initial decision to migrate until settling in Russia and finding employment.

(4) Geographical distance plays an important role, as we have seen in one of the earliest instances. Whether it is independence, being far away from the country of origin and its different social and cultural norms, being separated from the family and authorities in the kinship network, or distance from the responsibility/burden of earning and sending cash, many men claimed that in Russia they led different, freer lifestyles.[436]

(5) Socio-cultural settings in the country of destination are further significant points that should be approached with respect to opportunity structures. Upon their arrival in Russia, male migrants are exposed to social practices with which they have not been familiar in their countries of origin. One of them, which is of particular relevance for this study, is the concept of non-marital cohabitation, known in Russian as *grajdankskii brak*. Translated literally as "civil marriage," a term erroneously or ironically applied for cohabitation, it is becoming popular among the young generation in Russia. In Central Asia, by contrast, it is tolerated or is often ignored only in capital cities.[437]

Having defined these factors, it should be remarked that the order of these points does not imply any strict prioritization and that, depending on each case, some factors can be more relevant than others. It becomes clear that social and economic changes in Russia are reflected in the increase of extramarital affairs and de facto conjugal relationships. While the latter can be seen as a trend, the former is partially a status symbol. Of all the five aforementioned factors, the fifth one deserves particular attention as it underlines the process of cultural transnationalization. Here, it is helpful to extrapolate from the Turkish-German example.[438] In it, the distinction is made among three periods of transnationalization in the cultural realm. In the first period, labor migrants left Turkey in the 1960s and 1970s with a willingness to return after having worked for several years. In many cases their stays lasted longer and their family members joined them in Germany. The second phase is marked by more and more cultural aspects being brought to Germany by Turkish migrants, such as construction of mosques and establishment of cultural organizations. The emergence of religious and political groups within the Turkish community in Germany was observed in this period as well. In

---

[436] These statements are based on interviews with male migrants irrespective of their marital status.
[437] Grajdanksii brak, civil marriage, is a trend that opposes the registration procedure known from the Soviet era as ZAGS, which is an acronym of Otdel Zapisi Aktov Grajdanskogo Sostoyaniya (Rus. Department of Documentation of Records of Marital Status of Citizens).
[438] Faist, 1999:56.

the third period, the transnational social space is characterized by elements from both sending and receiving societies, as migrants "participate in events back in sending countries, but also take advantage of an increasingly 'multicultural' environment and public policies in the receiving polities that recognize 'cultural difference' and 'ethnic diversity.'"[439]

The transnationalization process of Central Asian migrants, regardless of their gender and marital status, encompasses aspects from all three periods of the Turkish-German example. Some labor migrants already settled in Russia in the mid-1990s with the intention of earning a sufficient amount of cash for, for instance, their housing project. They have, meanwhile, obtained Russian citizenship, although some still claim they intend to return. Family reunions occur quite frequently. In this sense, the first period of transnationalization characteristic of the Turkish-German example is not yet over. The mosques, which migrants visit in Russian cities such as Moscow and St. Petersburg in the north and Astrakhan in the south, had been constructed at the beginning of the 20th century, and the first cultural organizations were already founded during the Soviet era, as shall be discussed in a separate chapter. Similar to the third period of transnationalization in the Turkish-German example, elements of sending and receiving societies can also be found in transnational social spaces of Central Asian migrants. What is interesting is that, specifically in the case of polygamous migrants from Central Asia in Russia, there is an interface between cohabitation practices in Russia and matrimonial traditions of the predominantly Muslim home countries. While it may be true that non-marital cohabitation occurs (albeit to a much lesser extent) in the capital cities of the three sending states, such relationships among migrants in Russia should be analyzed in tandem with the reconfigurations of marriage and family practices in modern post-Soviet Russian society. As can be observed, there is a trans-cultural *mélange*[440] of Central Asian polygamous labor migrants and the form in which polygamy is encountered in Russia is rather complex. *Grajdanksii brak*, along with a changing sexuality culture, is itself a trend that "streams" against the strict stipulation of Soviet matrimonial registration regulation in post-Soviet Russia, which in turn has been experiencing a sexual revolution. In Central Asia, especially in the provinces, the changes in marriage and family practices are marked not only by the emerging practice of polygamy, as mentioned at the beginning of this chapter, but above all by a tendency to neglect the state regulations on matrimonial registrations in municipalities.[441]

The trans-cultural *mélange* appears in the language used by migrants. An interviewee in Astrakhan (RUS) from Xorazm (UZB) entered "a civil marriage" with a male migrant two years following her arrival. She fell in

---

439 *Ibid.*
440 A term used also by Faist, 2000a:226.
441 Khegai, 2002.

love with a married man whom, even after their separation, she still referred to as "my husband."

Delia: Did your mother oppose to your marriage at all?
Zukhra: Well, she did, but she knew I would marry him anyway.
Delia: And you say he was married. Did he get divorced?
Zukhra: Actually, he was married but not officially. He had no children from his first but two children from his second marriage. He still had an on-and-off relationship with his first wife. Then his second wife died and he became a widower. We started dating then. Now that we are *divorced*, my husband is living with his first wife and two children from his second marriage.[442]
Delia: You say you were not officially married but did you celebrate your wedding in any ways?
Zukhra: Our marriage was a "civil marriage" (*grajdanksii brak*). We invited people we know from the community and that was our wedding, so to say.

Zukhra's younger sister told me in a separate interview that her sister had not had the Islamic ritual of *nikah*. She had heard about such rituals, but it was important for her that her parents allow her to be together with a person of her choice. During my trip to Astrakhan (RUS) she was dating a young man from Turkmenistan. Towards the end of my trip he proposed to her, to which her mother said "no" since she was only seventeen.

During the interviews, my interlocutors used the same terms as they would in referring to legal marriages. Zukhra was applying the term "divorce" while talking about her separation, so it seems from the perspectives of parties engaged in non-marital relationships, almost no distinction is made between a de facto and a civil marriage.

9. 5. Female Narratives at Both Ends of Migration: From Patience to Tolerance (or the Lack Thereof)

The authors of the *Polish Peasant* provide not only letters written by Polish immigrants' wives from the country of origin that question the whereabouts of their husbands, but also records on abandoned and deceived wives in the United States who filed lawsuits against their husbands.[443] Because I had more access to female interlocutors, more aspects of their conjugal relationships became discernible. It is for this reason that excerpts of female narratives should be briefly documented.

---

442 My italics.
443 Thomas and Znaniecki, 1958, v2:1720-1722.

One such aspect is that of tolerance of polygamous relationships by wives and close family members as far as second wives are concerned. The representative of an advocacy organization in Tajikistan, Nadira, who runs a support program for women, drew attention to the fact that the number of divorces filed by women had increased during the summer of 2006. She said she had looked through the documents of the Konibodom region in the North of Tajikistan and was astonished that, among many reasons, a couple that recurred were the lack of provision and care for the family and the long-term absence of spouses who worked in Russia. While it may be true that more women are willing to get divorced, very few see it as a good option since raising children and providing for a family as a single parent may be extremely difficult, especially due to a lack of education and skills among women.

Despite the tendency of a rising divorce rate in Tajikistan, my experience with migrant wives suggest a certain tolerance of extramarital relationships. In Konibodom (TAJ), where I spent several days with a migrant family, I shared a room with Dilsifat, a young woman whose husband was working in Russia. Her parents-in-law slept in a separate room at the other end of the house, so in the evening before going to bed, Dilsifat took out a photo album and started showing me pictures of her husband in Moscow and telling me more about her life as a labor migrant's wife. Her marriage had been arranged and she said she did not have any feelings for her husband. The photo album contained several pictures of Dilsifat's husband holding a Russian woman tightly in his arms. "Just look at this," she kept saying to me. "I really don't care who he is with, really. Maybe he has a Russian wife, but I am not jealous."

I became interested in the reasons why women were not able to join their husbands. Migrants' wives with whom I met in the sending countries expressed their willingness to work in Russia. While some succeed in reuniting after several years of migration, others stated that their husbands showed concern that without any legal documents they would become a burden. Quite frequently, the husbands would simply avoid the topic.

Delia: And do you think of joining your husband in Russia at some point? Or has your husband offered that you can join him in Russia?
Dilsifat: Actually, I would like to go to Russia and work with him there but he keeps telling me, "This is not a place for you. Or he says, "This is not a place for our women."

There is a case of a mother of a polygamous migrant that should be noted as well. I had an interview with a prominent traditional healer (*tabib*) from Dushanbe (TAJ) in Astrakhan (RUS). The majority of market vendors from ex-Soviet states knew her in this Russian city. The moment she started describing her family situation to me, she proudly said, "I have three sons and oh, I got a daughter-in-law recently. (*Ba nazdiki kelin kardam.*) She is so beautiful, you have to see her." She then took her cell phone out of her purse, called her daughter-in-law, and ordered her to come to the café where were having lunch. Having noted that her son was 30 years old, I inquired curiously, "So, your son was never married before? He married rather late, it seems?" Before her daughter-in-law arrived she told me her son's story.

Marambi: In fact, my son is still married in Dushanbe (TAJ) and has two children. One day he brought this one home and said, "I want to live with her now." I scolded him, sure, but there was nothing I was able to do to prevent him from marrying this woman. But my daughter-in-law is so beautiful. She is nice and beautiful like a fairy (*pari*). She will be here soon and you will see how beautiful she is.
Delia: Does his first wife know?
Marambi: She does...she does. She calls here (in Russia) regularly. She calls and starts a major argument on the phone with my younger one.[444] She called the other day from Dushanbe and yelled at me on the phone, "Call that whore to the phone, I want to talk to her!" This one then took the receiver and yelled, "You are a whore yourself!" Oh, I don't know what I should do. [sighs...] After this my first son does not feel like seeing her any more. I keep trying to persuade him that he should go to her and at least see their two kids.

Marambi lives in Russia with her three sons and husband. The father of her children was murdered during the Civil War in Tajikistan. Having lost the breadwinner of the family, she took her three children and arrived in Russia to make a living by working as a nurse and traditional healer. She remarried several years later, so her eldest son grew up without the control of a strict father. In this situation she sees no other choice than to tolerate her son's polygamous relationship. When I asked if I could take her picture next to her newly-married daughter-in-law, she felt honored.

A factor which was not included in the discussion of opportunity structures in the previous section of this chapter, but which obviously is significant for the case of Central Asia, is that of gender relations. Without being questioned about it, at least one in two married female interviewees mentioned that she was not sure if her husband did not have another wife in Russia. Women's dependence on remittances is closely linked to unemployment or extremely low wages. It was with great nostalgia that many female interviewees mentioned the Soviet government's efforts to educate and emancipate women and, above all, to provide them with employment.

---

444 Meaning younger daughter-in-law.

9.6. Conclusion

The emergence of extramarital relationships creates challenges in manifold ways which I would like to discuss here. First, at the micro level, establishing polygamous families poses challenges to the distribution of capital and resources. Instead of a nuclear family, one would then have to talk about a "polynuclear" family in which one female spouse lives together with the male wage-earner in the country of destination. Second, on a macro level, polygamous relationships emerging in the context of transnational migration challenge the state institutions in sending countries. On the one hand, the state, which bore high responsibility for the well-being of the family, has been losing its role as the defender of the family as an institution. The Soviet state's control of the Soviet family reached its peak in the 1970s, and Matveev's publication on Soviet Family Law testifies to role of the family as a stronghold of the Soviet state.[445] The independent states that came into existence after its collapse in 1991 have, so far, appeared rather weak in idealizing the monogamous family unit as being of high value for the foundation of a strong welfare state.[446] Finally, in the midst of this process of erosion of the state's control, transboundary mobility, especially of the married male population, enables them to escape the social space of hierarchical authority and control within the kinship system in the country of origin. Transnational polygamous marriages challenge the structure of the ideal-typical nuclear family in the country of origin, to which the breadwinner is expected to return in the course of labor migration.

At this point, it is crucial to establish a linkage between this chapter and the general topic of this book. According to Basch *et al.*, transnationalism is a process by which migrants, through their daily life activities, create social fields that cross national boundaries.[447] Further, some scholars such as Sana and Massey argue that while the proponents of the new economic labor migration regard migrant-sending households as the unit of analysis, it "leaves the door open to changing household dynamics."[448] Sana and Massey assume the possibility of the migrant establishing a new household in the country of destination. As a typical example they mention that if a migrant under con-

---

[445] He does not spare the reader citations from "The Origin of Family" by F. Engels in praising the importance of the family. Ironically, while searching for the accurate English translation of citations that Matveev uses for his arguments, the following words by Engels drew my attention: "But if monogamy was the only one of all the known forms of the family through which modern sex love could develop, that does not mean that within monogamy modern sexual love developed exclusively or even chiefly as the love of husband and wife for each other. [...] Among all historically active classes – that is, among all ruling classes – matrimony remained what it had been since the pairing marriage, a matter of convenience arranged by the parents." (Engels, 1972:133).

[446] For more on the relationship of the family and the state in the Soviet Union, see Mace, David and Vera Mace. (1963) *The Soviet Family*. Garden City, New York: Doubleday and Company, Inc.

[447] Basch *et al.* 1994 as sited by Voigt-Graf, 2005:363.

[448] Sana and Massey, 2005:511.

tract by his family in the home country were to found a family of his own, his loyalty would be called into question. The case of emerging polygamous relationships of Central Asian labor migrants may not quite fit into such patterns at the first glance. I argue, however, that it still is one facet of the transnationalization process. We have seen that transnational social spaces of polygamous Central Asian migrants incorporate elements characteristic of transition processes in the societies of the sending as well as the receiving countries.

Part Three

Kinship and Post-Soviet Continuity in Migrant Transnationalism

10. Formalization of Migrant Kinship and Patronages: Emergence of Central Asian Migrant Organizations in Russia

The discussions so far have focused largely on socio-cultural changes in the context of migration in the sending countries of Central Asia. In previous chapters, social, educational, and cultural backgrounds of transnational migrants and their dependent families were explained. Chapters on conjugal relationships and transnational polygamy have elaborated on the families of Central Asian labor migrants in Russia. However, how transnational families come to establish themselves in migrant associations and contribute to the sustaining of labor mobility has not yet been explained.

In this chapter, I focus on Central Asian migrants and discuss how kinship and patronage develop into transnational migrant organizations in Russia. I do so with reference to the concept of fictive kin relationships and patron-client bonds in the context of migration, pointing to two paths for establishing a migrant organization. The first path, which was already mentioned in Chapter 4 on post-Soviet transnationalization, is linked to the Soviet past of the actors who establish a migrant association. These actors take advantage of the resources and networks that they had at their disposal during the Soviet period. In this trajectory, a migrant organization can either be a successor organization of a student association, preexisting during the Soviet period, or can emerge as a new organization with the available resources and ties of its initiator(s). Thus a significant feature remains the emergence of the organizational leadership in Russia during the Soviet period. In the second path, the leader of a formal or informal migrant group is a former (male) labor migrant himself who arrived in Russia in the late 1990s. He has long-existing stable ties with other migrants and develops patron-client bonds with them due to brokerage activities to then formalize or register as a migrant organization.

As Ebaugh and Curry point out, migration scholars emphasize the central role of kinship networks in the process of settling into the new environment. In so doing, they depart, for the most part, from the concept of blood kinship.[449] I too have hitherto applied the concept of kinship in terms of individuals related to one another by blood or marriage. There are, however, pseudo-kinship or fictive kinship ties which are essential for social formations. This is true especially in migration where the majority of the migrant's close relatives remain in the country of origin. In the absence of blood kin networks, migrants have more need to develop friendship ties and fictive relationships that help them to fulfil their social, cultural, and economic needs.

---

449   Ibid.

Fictive kinship ties are understood in anthropology as relationships that are established on the basis of either religious rituals or close friendships, which imitate the reciprocity, rights, and obligations usually practiced in blood kinship.[450] Substantial literature covering the topic of fictive kinship, irrespective of geographic regions and religions, indicates that the main criteria for such ties to be fulfilled are: 1) the rite of passage, 2) the social and/or spiritual ties between the parties involved, and 3) guardianship. To these criteria we could also add reciprocity and obligations since guardianship or sponsorship has the connotation of being unidirectional.

There are many examples of fictive kin relationships. In the Latin American context, there is a pseudo-family relationship of *compadrazgo*. It is connected to the Catholic ritual of baptism and involves godparents and godchildren who fulfil the above mentioned criteria.[451] In their literature review, Ebaugh and Curry draw attention to the existence of fictive kinship beyond Latin American countries, for instance in the Mediterranean region, the Balkans, South Asia, and Southeast Asia.[452] Other research indicates that in Eastern Turkey, similar to the religious fictive bond of *compadrazgo*, it is the ritual of circumcision which forms the basis for the fictive father-son relationship known as *kivrelik*.[453] In the Central Asian context, anthropologist Alessandro Monsutti elaborates on the notion of foster brothers among Afghans, in particular *beradar-e dini* ('brothers in religion') among the Shiites and *beradar-e shiri* ('milk brothers') – male children nursed by the same woman.[454]

The establishment of fictive kinship ties specifically among migrants is essential. I argue that the meaning of socio-cultural and religious rites of passage, which were explained earlier in this chapter as significant criteria for the establishment of fictive kin ties, are redefined in the context of migration. Monsutti contends that while away from their countries of origin, migrants rely on a broader notion of kinship in constructing networks and that their broad kinship comprises neighborhood and friendship ties. In the context of migration between Central Asia and Russia, the concept of a fictive kinship must include the patron-client relationship as well. This is important to note since patron-client ties as fictive kin relationships are essential for the social formation of migrants and the establishment of migrant organizations.

This chapter is structured as follows: at the onset of the discussions I will lay out three examples to illustrate the social formations of migrants.[455] In further sections of this chapter, I shall analyze the patronage of Central Asian migrants in Russia based on three actual patrons with whom I have

---

450 Vichit-Vadakan, 1994:518; Ebaugh and Curry, 2000:189.
451 Carlos, 1973.
452 Ebaugh and Curry, 2000.
453 Magnarella and Türkdoğan, 1973.
454 Monsutti, 2004:223.
455 Names of organizations and persons as well as their ethnic identities have been altered for the purpose of ensuring their personal safety.

either had direct contact, a conversation, or an interview, or about whom I learned through their clients. The discussion will then concentrate on the resource bases of the patrons that are crucial for the establishment of a migration association.

Example A.

When Kanat was recruited into the Soviet Navy in 1968, he was 18 years old and the only Kyrgyz among many Slavs and Caucasians in his unit. He was confident, however, that the three years of service in the Navy would teach him skills that he could employ for the rest of his life. Upon finishing the service, he decided to stay in the Navy and pursue a military career. Having already been an active member of the Union of Young Communists (Komsomol) at school in his native town of Jalalabad, Kanat decided to become a member of the Communist Party. In 1991, when the USSR collapsed, he did not even think of leaving Russia since Kyrgyzstan's economy was worsening. However, Russia too was facing major economic difficulties. It was this economic crisis of the early 1990s that forced him to leave his job in the Navy and open a small restaurant where he could hire his Uzbek brother-in-law from Jalalabad as a chef. He had meanwhile become a Russian citizen. At the end of the 1990s, as he witnessed a growing number of Kyrgyz coming to Russia in search of work, Kanat founded an association of Kyrgyzstanis which would welcome all the people from Kyrgyzstan, regardless of their ethnic backgrounds be they Kyrgyz, Koreans, Uzbeks, Tajiks, or Tatars. Using the entrepreneurial skills he had developed in his restaurant, he developed a plan according to which he would charge labor migrants for the services provided. Adjacent to the building where his organization was located, he soon opened another small café that offered Central Asian food, along with a travel agency where migrants could purchase plane and train tickets. An exchange office and a Western Union booth appeared soon after. Kanat's own daughter became the deputy head of the organization. Similar to many Communist Party members, Kanat later changed to the Putin-led United Russia (Yedinaiia Rossiia) and has been an active member ever since.

Example B.

Qosimsho, from the Tajik SSR, served in the Soviet Army from 1978-1980. Like many other Central Asian recruitees, he was sent to serve in Afghanistan. Upon finishing his service, he was offered a job working for the Soviet Army in Afghanistan as an intelligence officer, as Tajik was his native language and his command of Pashto was meanwhile fair enough to allow him to interpret basic conversations from Russian into Dari, Tajik, and Pashto. Qosimsho came back to his hometown in Tajik SSR in 1982, but only to visit his parents. During his military service, one of his commanders had promised him that he would help him gain admission to one of the most prominent universities in Russia so he could study Persian Language and Literature. Qosimsho soon became a Communist Party member and was elected leader of his university's "Tajik Students Association", which consisted of approximately 50 members. After his studies, he was offered a lecturer's position at the same university and was able to continue his activities in the association. With the growing influx of, first the refugees from Tajikistan at the beginning of the 1990s, then the mass labor migration at the end of the 1990s, Qosimsho founded a migrant organization to help undocumented laborers receive residency permits, find accommodations, and arrange jobs. He appointed his younger brother Olimsho as his deputy. Olimsho was married to a Russian woman. Their daughter Shamsiya, who had grown up in Russia and was now a student, took over the responsibility of the administrative work of her uncle's organization in order to earn some money.

Example C.

Turghunboy left his village in Central Asia in 1998 after a major quarrel with his wife's family. In between his arrival by train and finding the house of his lifelong friend in Russia, the police had stripped him of all his money. His friend gave him enough cash to get by at the beginning of his stay, helped organize his papers, and found him a job at a construction site that had bunks in the basement where he could sleep. Over the course of a couple years, as his wages increased, his Russian employers developed a great deal of confidence in him. He soon became responsible for the entire group of Central Asian construction workers. Turghunboy and his friend Ergash, whom he meanwhile referred to as his brother, decided to engage other young men from their native country, provide them with jobs, and make a profit by withholding part of their wages, similar to many other brokers that come from Central Asia, the Caucasus, Ukraine, and Moldova. Turghunboy's business began to prosper. He had meanwhile made arrangements with the Russian police officers so that they could 'earn their share' from his profits and reciprocate by 'leaving' him and his migrants 'alone.' When Turghunboy's workers started complaining about their low wages and threatened to file a lawsuit against him with the support of private lawyers and advocacy groups, he decided to get registered as a migrant organization. He currently continues his business by working under the umbrella of a migrant association that combines the activities of a job agency and a cultural center.

These examples are representative of many Central Asian migrant organizations. They are based on excerpts from observations in the field and extensive biographic interviews with leaders of informal migrant organizations, legally functioning associations, and labor migrants who either adhered to patronage ties, were members of an association, or had used patronage services while in

Russia. As far their structures are concerned, migrant organizations, as can be seen in these examples, can often be *a)* kin-based from the outset. Over time the leader of such an organization evolves a patron-client relationship with transnational migrants. Establishment of a migration organization can also be *b)* initiated by authoritative persons with patron-like characteristics without said persons necessarily engaging their close kin members in the organization's activities.

Examples A and B deal with two typical Soviet men. They are ambitious young men who joined the Komsomol during the latter years of their secondary school education, enrolled in the military, studied at a higher education institution, and were promoted both by the Communist Party and their employers. Kanat in Example A pursued a career in the Soviet military service and Qosimsho in Example B worked at his university. Unlike Qosimsho, Kanat established his organization after the demise of the Soviet Union without prior experience. Kanat had a vision of his own, which was influenced by the internationalist ideology of the USSR. From the very beginning, his organization was meant to serve all Kyrgyzstanis, regardless of their ethnic backgrounds. During the interview he drew my attention to the fact that his country of origin is home to ethnic minorities that he respects. Qosimsho is different in this way. During the interviews he made nationalist comments and showed sympathy towards President Emomali Rahmon's efforts to revive the Tajik-Persian culture and civilization.

Example B shows a typical post-Soviet development of a student association into a migrant organization.[456] Higher education institutions in Russia (then RSFSR) used to have student associations (*zemliachestvo*) that included members representing a common republic of origin. The (student) association of Tajikistanis (*zemliachestvo tadjikistantsev*), similar to many organizations of students from Soviet republics emerged among other factors as an expression of a multiethnic socialist society. At the same time, it represented the formation of a 'we-group' among Tajikistanis in the larger urban areas of Russia.[457] It is from these associations that migrant organizations arose. They engage in cultural activities such as the celebration of the holiday Navruz. Every year on March 21st, this traditionally Zoroastrian holiday marks the start of the solar calendar and symbolizes spring and the awakening of nature. In the region, particularly in Uzbekistan and Tajikistan, people organize picnics and large meals outdoors accompanied by music and dance. Independence Days of the countries of origin are also celebrated where migrants are invited to share a festive meal. Migrant organizations engage in activities

---

456   A *zemliachestvo* was similar to a *Landsmannschaft* of German immigrants in 19th century America. These are also often known as hometown associations in migration literature. Whether network, association, or organization, a *zemliachestvo*, (Russian word *zemliak* means 'fellow countryman') just as a hometown association points to the region of origin of migrants. (Faist, 2000a:238; 2004:21; 2008:39Ref.).
457   For more on we-groups and transnational communities, see Faist, 2000a:312.

involving the protection of migrants' rights, and assist in paperwork related to employment.

Both Kanat's and Qosimsho's careers in the Communist Party and organizational skills were ideal for their roles as leaders of their respective migrant organizations. Particularly the experience as head of a student organization, where cultural programs were organized and regular reunions took place, was useful for Qosimsho. Then came the disintegration of the USSR, followed by the civil war in Tajikistan. During the interview with me, Qosimsho remembered with bitterness how terrible the start of the civil clashes in the newly independent Tajikistan had been in 1992. He remembered the Western countries and international organizations that had refused to receive refugees from Tajikistan, but that Russia had extended its helping hand. He and his friends assembled to provide support to the newcomers from Tajikistan who were traveling to Russia in their thousands. Under these circumstances he established a migration organization. Moreover, he managed to obtain permission for his organization to be located in the building of the university at which he had studied and was teaching part-time.

The first two examples dealt with internal Soviet migrants who became *transnational* after the fall of the USSR. In both cases they established a kinship-based migrant organization and at the same time developed patron-client ties towards labor migrants. These are organizations existing formally. Example C represents a migrant organization developing out of transnational patronage after the disintegration of the USSR. Having probed into informal transnational patronage ties, I argue that migrant organizations can be a complex mixture of blood and fictive kinship as well as patronage. The section below gives a more detailed illustration.

10.1. Central Asian Transnational Patronages

Anthropologists and political scientists who analyzed patronage in the past did this in so-called agrarian societies in an attempt to explain social and political processes through patron-client ties- 'patrons' typically referring to landowners and 'clients' referring to peasants.[458] Migration scholars such as Massey have drawn attention to patronage ties in considering their roles within migration networks in sustaining international migration flows.[459] Although we are aware of the importance of patronage in migration, scholarship on patron-client ties of transnational migrants is rather limited. Paerregaard who studied the Peruvian diaspora in the United States, Spain, and Japan concluded that livelihoods created by Peruvian transnational migrants depend on three kinds of social relations: 1) patron-client ties in Peru, 2) migrant networks that developed from rural-urban migratory movements

---

458   Wolf, 1966; Weingrod, 1968; Scott 1972, Platteau 1995.
459   Massey, 1986.

there and 3) kinship and marriage ties that are of great significance in the formation of migrant networks across the world.[460] Some attempts have been made to elaborate on Latin American migrants in the United States. Focusing on patron-client ties of Mexican migrants in Dallas, Texas, Adler defines patron-client ties as "vertical, dyadic relationships whereby two individuals of unequal status, power, and/or resources form an alliance with each other for instrumental purposes."[461] I shall bear this definition in mind and, relying on Scott's analyses, inductively derive *relative anonymity* and *pseudoparental authority* as characteristic features of patrons.

10.1.1. Relative Anonymity: Concealed Personal Identities and Activities

Migrant patrons may show clear characteristics of job brokers. Nonetheless, migrant patrons and job brokers should not be confused with one another. A patron may have an additional function as a job broker or a middleman, but this may not necessarily be so as we shall see in this chapter.[462] I also argue that the transnational migrant patronage structure is partially a more complex form of a (fictive) kinship group. Due to their informal activities, patrons are cautious about revealing too much information about their personal identities because they wish to keep their circles of clients closed. Three portraits in this section will illustrate this. The first two male figures who will be introduced are migrant patrons and the third is the leader of a migrant organization, also fulfilling the role of a patron whenever possible. In the first example, I did not have the possibility of meeting with the patron in person and reconstructed his personality from his clients' descriptions. In the second instance, I personally met the patron. However he refused to introduce me to his migrants, so he himself was the sole source of all the information on his activities. In the third case, the person whom I met was the leader of a migrant association who had informal activities in addition to heading a diasporic organization.

---

460   Paerregaard, 2002:127.
461   Adler, 2002:2.
462   This point initially based on my data is also underlined by Scott (1972), who argued that middlemen or brokers are involved as intermediaries in three-party interactions as opposed to patrons and clients who have a bidirectional exchange. This is hard to confirm in the context of migration since in three-party exchanges, the three parties involved often do interact with each other, whereas Scott notes that due to intermediaries, the first and the third parties may not be in direct contact.

Madamin Ota[463]

Excerpts from field notes in St. Petersburg:

On the third day of my observations, I visited the bulk food market located outside of the city of St. Petersburg. There during the summer, hundreds of migrants (mostly women) sorted and packaged fruit and vegetables. The products would then be distributed to grocery stores. At the market I met three women, asked questions about their work at the market, and asked them if I could accompany them home. The two younger ones politely declined my request and reminded me that they had been working the whole day without a break. The third senior member of the group objected to what the younger ones said and agreed. Then the three women discussed in their Xorazm dialect of Uzbek whether my visit would result in sanctioning them from the rest of the group, which meant losing their jobs and at the same time their accommodation. It would, above all, mean betrayal of a certain Madamin Ota to whom they had promised that they would never show their residence to an outsider.

We took the suburban train to the city center. As the train approached the central station, the three women asked me sincerely to come to their place with them. We had to exit the train through the last wagon doors and instead of walking towards the railhead where the main station was, stepped down from the embankment of the platform and walked across a dozen rails. We left the train station compound and took a long passage through hidden back alleys that had no names and where no policemen were to be seen, as my companions told me. They also said that they would pretend that I was just another migrant looking for a place to stay. When we finally got to their place of residence, I hurriedly saw the 80 square meter apartment that was shared by approximately 40 people. It was 7 PM and night-shifters were still asleep. Those who had come home from work earlier in the evening were preparing a communal dinner. The three women I had known from the market were reluctant to tell me more about Madamin Ota. "Above all Jayran would never forgive us," they said. I did not ask them who the woman named Jayran was. I had to leave their place right away since I did not want them to face any difficulties because of me.[464]

Despite the delicateness of the situation, through a different encounter I had the possibility of accessing the close entourage of Madamin Ota. A week after meeting the three women, an interview was planned with Suluv, a 33-year-old female migrant who lived in an entirely different neighborhood of St. Petersburg. The three women whose residence I had visited and Suluv, with whom I had scheduled an interview, were not familiar with each other.

---

463   *Ota*, translated from Uzbek means *father* and is an honorific title for middle-aged men particularly in the Province of Xorazm, Uzbekistan.
464   Field notes, St. Petersburg, August 2006.

Suluv had a newborn baby. She was on maternity leave and therefore had sufficient time for an interview. I visited her in a seven-room communal apartment (*kommunalka*) where she lived with 28 other people. At the beginning of the interview I simply asked my informant whether any person was responsible for the apartment. I was curious about how migrant *kommunalka*s were managed. In answering my questions she said that Madamin Ota was both the owner and the manager. This person turned out to be the same Madamin Ota, whose other apartment I had viewed with three female migrants the previous week. I discovered this unexpectedly when the woman, after naming the owner, also listed the number of other places that belonged to the same owner with precise locations. Because her husband had known Madamin Ota for a long time and was on good terms with him, she had sufficient confidence to tell me more about him.

Madamin Ota is an authoritative patron of migrant workers and owns five apartments in the city of St. Petersburg where he accommodates them. His apartments range in size from two rooms to seven rooms. I found out from Suluv that the migrants are selected in Uzbekistan and transported in smaller groups by vans by his sister Jayran. These vans, usually known by their brand name, e.g. *Gazel*, are made in Russia. Running with natural gas (hence *gazel'*, Russian for 'gazelle') and accommodating twelve passengers, *Gazel*s are fairly profitable means of transportation in the former Soviet countries. Madamin Ota's source of profit besides his support to labor migrants is from repairing foreign brand automobiles that were severely damaged after accidents and renting them for approximately $10 a day.

It turned out to be impossible to meet with Madamin Ota in person. People under his protection told me that he was about 60 years old. In 1966 at the age of 19 when he was a student at a technical institute in Toshkent, a strong earthquake damaged the city.[465] All the students of his university were distributed to other parts of the Soviet Union to continue their studies. Madamin Ota came to St. Petersburg. He stayed in this city and married a Russian woman. His Russian wife's ancestors were German. She left him and emigrated to Germany through the German *Aussiedler* repatriation program.[466]

Madamin Ota's migrants (or clients), spoke fondly of him, emphasizing that he was a person who had gone through many hardships throughout his entire life. Several years after his wife left him for Germany, his younger brother died in Uzbekistan. Madamin Ota, in accordance with societal expec-

---

[465] The earthquake of 1966 was claimed by the Soviet regime to have devastated Toshkent, allegedly reducing the capital of the Uzbek SSR to rubble. Critics raise doubts about the real damage of this natural disaster and argue that the Soviet state in fact took advantage of it to implement rigorous modernization measures such as erecting concrete buildings. According to official reports, humanitarian aid was delivered from all other 14 member-countries of the USSR, which led Toshkent to be known as the city of 'friendship of nations.'

[466] Because ethnic Germans spoke Russian, they were often perceived as Russian in Central Asia. 'Russian' was often a general way to describe anyone whose appearance was European and/or who spoke Russian.

tations and the demands of his mother in Uzbekistan, was forced to marry his deceased brother's widow. He then moved back to St. Petersburg to live with her. He had no children from his first marriage and only one daughter from his second, so being a son-less father seemed to arouse his clients' sympathy.[467]

Faridun

I met Faridun in person. It was one of the rare occasions in which a personal meeting had been arranged with him. I had assumed that he was a job-broker in an ideal-typical sense. His agreeing to speak with me was in exchange, as he said, for "not meeting or interviewing the people who worked for (him)." Faridun arrived in his vehicle whose windows were shaded on all sides. The interview was to take place in the vehicle and upon his request my recorder was turned off.

Faridun took out a professionally-made album of photos and began describing his small construction business. He came to Russia after the disintegration of the Soviet Union and started his career as a mere construction worker. He was now building villas for affluent Russians. Whether demolishing dilapidated country cottages, known as *dacha*s, or constructing entirely new residences, Faridun was able to mobilize his migrants regardless of the stage, difficulty or architectural style of the houses, and/or the urgency with which his business clients wanted him to fulfill their demands. He dominated our conversation. Moreover, he recited the details relevant to his business as if he had learned them by heart and as if he was speaking to one of his business clients.

> Here, look at this picture, this is what this little hut looked like before, and here – what me and my people turned it into. We don't only build houses, we can put in a brand new lawn, put in a nice little well and cobbles. We turned the place into a beautiful home, look.[468]

Faridun preferred to tell me more about his business than himself and admittedly, it was an unusual case in which I as a researcher did not manage to take control of the interview situation. Faridun had a ready-made information package that he would pull out of his glove compartment to show to anyone who was interested in his business. He had a binder that contained a photo album that had been prepared for just such purposes. It was extremely difficult to go beyond the framework of what he was prepared to tell me. While he concealed his private life, he tried his best to explain that he was treating his workers well. In this context he underlined the multiple skills his migrants

---

467 In Denzin's understanding, these events and experiences, which he defines as *epiphanies*, influence people's characters. Denzin, 1989:70.
468 Interview with Faridun, St. Petersburg, August 2006.

had and the loyalty with which they worked for him. He mentioned that he travelled personally to select his workers not only from Tajikistan but also from Uzbekistan. Talented artisans and craftsmen – not simply handymen – were needed to create the quality of work his Russian clients were willing to pay for.

When asked about his ties to his country of origin, Faridun assured me that he went to visit his family at least once a year. People from the small village community in Russia where Faridun lived mentioned that he lived with his Russian wife whom he had recently married. Faridun had meanwhile obtained a Russian passport but allegedly had a Tajik wife living in the same Russian village as well as in his country of origin. My understanding was that he had three wives. When I asked him questions he had not been prepared for, Faridun said that he was worried about his business and that he bore responsibility for the people he had hired and would therefore like to end the conversation.[469]

Turghunboy[470]

"*Well, I just wound up here in Russia...such is life*," was how Turghunboy started our conversation, which he allowed me to record. We exchanged business cards and ordered tea and lunch in a restaurant serving Central Asian food where our interview took place. Turghunboy, too, brought pictures of his migrant organization. He showed the photos where he was posing with officials from his home country. Another photo showed an exchange of gifts with official guests, where migrants welcomed Central Asian and Russian guests in traditional clothes and folk dances were performed. I became curious and wanted to visit his office. Turghunboy told me about his organization with a great deal of enthusiasm. He quoted from the organization's mission statement and said that he specifically supported labor migrants. Then he took a piece of paper out of his leather folder and started reading from what turned out to be part of an undocumented migrant's lawsuit files. His openness about his activities impressed me. His report from which he was reading described how the plaintiff had been smuggled to Russia. "Upon arrival to Russia, the smuggler arranged employment for the plaintiff, the migrant, took away his identity document, and disappeared," he read out loud in the restaurant in the presence of many other customers. Turghunboy explained that he was trying to help this migrant to get a temporary identity document with which he could return home to have a new document issued.[471]

---

469 His anxiety became even more evident as I watched him drive by me at least twice the day the interview took place. He had observed me and my Russian colleagues. We even met Faridun's Tajik workers once, whom I greeted in Tajik and had wanted to chat with. Faridun passed by us with his car, though, so I did not ask his migrants anything.
470 This is not the same person as introduced at the beginning of this chapter.
471 Consulates of the sending states studied in this research are reluctant to replace the lost passports of their citizens. According to what labor migrants reported to me in Russia, the

When I set up an appointment with Turghunboy to visit the office his organization occupied in town, my intention was to observe him and his colleagues at work for the purpose of getting an impression of how such organizations work. I left the city center where I interviewed Turghunboy and went home to the city outskirts where I frequently bought produce at the district market and chatted with my informants who rent stalls and sell clothes there. The informants told me that they knew Turghunboy, as he often came to their neighborhood to chat with them. They asked me to be careful and not to trust him. They pointed to a large two-storied building with shaded windows that had a café and a casino in it and told me that he was, among other things, the owner of a large number of slot machines in that building. They hinted that Turghunboy had other dubious sources of income.

After several requests, the visit to Turghunboy's office did not take place. Having postponed it a couple of times, Turghunboy apologized and admitted that he had migrants living in the apartment which had initially been arranged as an office for his organization. His office was thus a communal apartment that hosted labor migrants whose number he did not reveal. He would present the apartment as his office during official visits for a number of days a year, yet during the rest of the time he would rent it out to labor migrants.

Looking at these three persons, Madamin Ota, Faridun, and Turghunboy, it can be seen that they were hard to approach and distanced themselves from those who did not belong to their circle of clients. Madamin Ota's clients either said it was not a good idea to meet him personally or agreed using the Uzbek word *mayli*, but in a way did not really mean it.[472] Faridun, by contrast, met with me because our meeting had been arranged through his Russian supervisor. Our interview took place within the framework of cooperation with a small group of students of sociology from the European University in St. Petersburg.[473] As mentioned earlier, his workers whom my Russian research partners and I met in the village refused to talk to us, too. Turghunboy was open about all his activities, but only as long as they were directly linked to his organization – to be more precise, he was open about his formal activities. Heeding the advice of one migrant worker, I once went to the train station on the day on which a train from one of the Central Asian countries was expected to arrive. There I met Turghunboy in his suit, holding a leather folder and waiting on the platform. I had heard from migrants before that he would meet newly-arrived migrants at the train station. He would accost them as they got off the train at their final destination and try to arrange jobs and

---

willingness to support citizens abroad among the sending states can be ranked from most positive to most negative in the following order: Kyrgyzstan, Tajikistan, and Uzbekistan.

472 Depending on the intonation, context, and how this word is pronounced, it can mean "all right" and be equal to a complete agreement, but also something like "sure, why not" and imply "yes, but I'd rather not."

473 This was part of cooperation with a small group of sociologists from the European University in St. Petersburg.

paper registrations for them in exchange for money. This was something he had never mentioned in the interview and the several meetings during the fieldwork.

10.1.2. Authority/Pseudo-Parental Attitude of Patrons

As mentioned at the beginning of this book,[474] in instances where the state and non-government structures are weakest, informal institutions not only fill the gaps but also interfere with the state institutions. They may, for example, demonstrate formality (by founding a migrant organization) and abide by the state regulations. At the same time, they may be involved in activities that lie beyond the legislative boundaries as we have seen in the case of Turghunboy, who was introduced in Example C. The patrons whom I came across in Russia occupied an informal space that an outsider was rarely allowed to approach. Similar to many people, they distrusted scholars, fearing they would report to the Russian security agency (FSB). This was especially true for Faridun. The information that was elicited from him during the interview was relatively superficial. He refused to answer a number of questions I posed and I respected his choice not to respond to them adequately. Metaphorically speaking, he played with a number of pawns. He gave out a great deal of information that, from his perspective, was safe to give. In this way, he protected himself from any information that I could use against him and/or to make his patronage weaker.

It was probably also for similar strategic reasons that during the very first field trip, the deputy head of a prominent migrant organization insisted that he walk with me through the market where he knew many migrants and would introduce me to them personally. It was not possible to get into conversation with the labor migrants employed there since the market was crowded and the migrants were busy selling and carrying goods. In addition, it came as no surprise that some migrants shied away from talking to me as a researcher after having seen me with the deputy head of the migrant organization who probably was, at the same time, their authoritative patron.

Patrons show an authoritarian attitude towards their clients that reminded me of a typical Central Asian father. Clients receive benefits from their patrons that would traditionally be exchanged between members of a family. This type of proximity would lead the clients to feel as if they belonged to their patron's household albeit, at a lower hierarchical level.[475]

> Madamin Ota is so kind-hearted. When my husband and I got married, Madamin Ota made arrangements for our religious ritual (nikoh) to take place. He invited the Turkish imam from the mosque. During the ritual, to the question whether I

---

474 Chapter 2, section 2.1.
475 This point has been emphasized by Platteau, 1995:767.

wanted to marry my fiancé, it was Madamin Ota who answered on my behalf...[476]

The Uzbek word *ota* simply means 'father.' In this context it is an honorific title used to address male seniors in Uzbekistan, particularly in Xorazm. However, there is more to this word than just the honorific title and therefore I opted not to leave it out. In Uzbekistan, the patron's and clients' country of origin, it is usually only the father, or, in his absence, the brother or the uncle of the bride, who is allowed to act as a witness and attend such rituals. The mullah first asks the bridegroom whether he would agree to take the woman in question as his spouse. Then turning to the bride, he asks the same question of her. The bride is expected to delay the answer and show embarrassment and modesty. Often times it is a close male family member who responds on her behalf. This situation is reminiscent of Bourdieu's distinction between "practical kin that make marriages" and "official kin who celebrate them."[477] The practical kinswoman in this case is the elder sister of the bridegroom who had arranged it, as Suluv mentioned in the interview. By playing the role of a close kinsman who gives his blessing during the religious ritual and celebrates with the married couple, Madamin Ota becomes a quasi-official kinsman who enters into the domain of practical, albeit in this example, fictive kinship.

Such quasi-kinship patron-client bonds are not confined to the exchange of goods and services in economically reciprocal terms, but also comprise elements of a symbolic nature.[478] Suluv shares how moved she was when Madamin Ota ushered the newly-married couple, the imam, and close family members and colleagues to a beautifully decorated table. He offered the guests a meal at his own expense.

Patrons can reward and punish migrants according to how they comply with their rules. Before getting married, Suluv used to live in the apartment that I had first visited with the three female seasonal workers. As she worked hard and paid her rent to Madamin Ota on time, their mutual respect increased. He rewarded the newly married couple for their loyalty by allowing them to share a room of their own in another apartment. That is to say, from having 15 other roommates, as labor migrants often do, Suluv was promoted to sharing a room with only one person: her spouse. With the high cost of accommodation that migrants face in Russia, this gesture should be seen as a very generous offer by Madamin Ota. I have visited places where couples have to share a small space with dozens of other couples or single migrants. They often separate their beds from their roommates' with a curtain to distinguish their intimate space. Madamin Ota is described as a compassionate person who would allow his clients to continue living in the crowded residence temporarily if they were unemployed and could not afford the rent.

---

476 Interview with Suluv.
477 Bourdieu, 2007:34.
478 Platteau, 1995:767.

However, if he learned that a resident had found a job and still was not paying the rent, he would make him move out.

As a patron, Faridun organizes a common meal every Tuesday. He and his clients prepare a traditional Central Asian dish called *osh,* which is made with meat, carrots, onions, and rice.[479] To my inquiries about how many people he had under his supervision, Faridun refused to comment. As a father-type, Faridun is not as compassionate as Madamin Ota but supervises his clients in a very strict manner with a paternal authority not uncommon in Central Asia.

> My people are well behaved. Discipline is all that I demand from them. I know every one of them very well. What I don't want is that they drink alcohol and do other immoral things. I bring them here, provide them with jobs, create a great opportunity that helps them sustain their families, so they must obey my rules. I warn them. I say, "Look, if I see that any one of you has been drinking vodka or other alcoholic drinks or sleeping with prostitutes, I kick you out of here. You may not even drink beer." Then there was this guy. I was passing by with my car and saw him holding a can of beer. I confronted him. He said, "Ok, I know what you want to say already. I admit I drank beer. I'll pack my things and go." See? My people know how strict I am.[480]

10.2. Asymmetrical Reciprocity

As has been discussed elsewhere in this study, migration scholarship explains the emergence of transnational phenomena in terms of spaces of flows of people, goods, money, information, and cultural practices that span the countries of origin and destination. Elaborating transnational social spaces, Faist argues that evolving from migratory flows, they constitute "combinations of ties and their contents, positions in networks and organizations, and networks of organizations" between nation-states. He distinguishes among three different forms of transnational social spaces: 1) transnational kinship groups, 2) transnational circuits, and 3) transnational communities. Transnational patronage, as we can see from the descriptions of migrant patrons, is more complex than kinship groups and can be perceived as an intermediary stage towards the formation of a community. Perhaps a more detailed explanation and differentiation of transnational patronages *vis-à-vis* kinship groups would clarify this argument.

Transnational kinship groups maintain, as Faist points out, a *social norm* of equivalence.[481] Migrants uphold bonds with kin members from the same countries of origin and destination. *Reciprocity* is the main resource in

---

479 Giving of food is described as an important attribute of chieftainship in most African tribes (Sahlin, 1972:262).
480 Interview with Faridun.
481 Faist, 2000a:203.

this category of transnational social space. Depending on the density of ties, members contribute financially (e.g., in form of remittances) and/or socially (arranging jobs in the country of destination) and expect the recipients to do their share, commensurate with their abilities. In the context of Central Asian kinship, this also means that there is a degree of obligation that members of the same family are expected to fulfill that may involve exertion of control over others.[482] Celebration of wedding ceremonies and other life-cycle rituals, funded mainly by monetary remittances as illustrated in previous parts of this study, is one of many examples.

Transnational patronage, often consisting of migrant kin members, is an interesting form in which the main resource is an asymmetric type of reciprocity. Unlike kin-based relationships, the parties engaged in a patronage do not share material or financial resources and services equally.[483] Examining the role of patron-client ties in Southeast Asian politics in the late 1960s, James Scott underlines precisely this imbalance in reciprocity between patrons and clients. In such relations the client is not in a position to entirely reciprocate the goods and services he receives from his patron. Scott explains such relations in terms of an informal group that is led by an authoritative person who offers "security and inducements."[484] In the context of labor migration in Russia, patrons' "inducements" mean employment, paperwork, payment, accommodation, and social and cultural support. A part of the patron-client relationship is that in return for these resources, clients must offer loyalty and personal assistance.[485] In Central Asian patron-client ties, respect, loyalty, obedience, and abiding by the patron's rules indeed count among the traits that are expected from a client in exchange for the aforementioned inducements.

A patron and his clients are not involved in pure command terms. Rather, their relationship requires a minimum of reciprocity. Hence, besides the abovementioned resources, the migrant has to agree to work at the price offered by the patron. Theoretically, a client would have few alternatives to contribute to the balance of reciprocity. In exchange for his patron's resources, a client can offer skills and services that only he can offer. A client can also seek resources from other sources. Clients could join forces and make the patron balance the exchange; alternatively they could do without his services altogether.[486] We have seen in the vignette in Example C that migrants may join forces and threaten to file a lawsuit against their patron.

I have encountered one episode in which a client had exclusive skills to offer yet the balance still remained unequal. During our interview, Faridun boasted about discovering a talented mason, as he said "in a place where he was not being paid enough for the extraordinary skill of making ornaments

---

482 Faist, 2000a:203.
483 Wolf, 1966:16.
484 Scott, 1972:92.
485 *Ibid.*
486 *Ibid.*

with baked bricks." The mason whom he had brought to join his team in Russia was from Xorazm, Uzbekistan. It could be argued that with his exceptional talents, the mason could demand a slightly more balanced relationship with Faridun than other clients could. The mason, however, is incapable of changing patrons due to his near-total lack of Russian. As often happens, he might even no longer be in possession of his identity documents and be unable to leave the compound in which the patron demands that his workers live. As a result, with this high degree of dependency that the mason has on Faridun, the patron acquires authority comparable to that of a feudal lord. It is only the mason's advanced age to which Faridun seems to show deference. The mason, instead of garnering more equal terms with Faridun for his skills as one would expect, remains humble:

> Here, look at this mason's work [points to the photos]. He says to me: "Do you want me to make the sculpture of the house-owner's wife out of baked bricks? Just tell me and I can do it. I can carve anything from these baked bricks."[487]

10.3. The Base of Resources of Central Asian Patrons in Russia

What resources do patrons rely on? Scott distinguishes among three types of resources that patrons utilize when engaging clients.[488] These are 1) *skill* and *knowledge*, 2) *direct control of personal real property*, and 3) *indirect control* or *office based property*.[489] Even though these are attributed to the preindustrial Southeast Asian context, we can see that Scott's analysis can be applicable to the example of transnational patronage of Central Asians in Russia. To begin with, *skill* and *knowledge* are extremely valuable and durable resources owned by patrons. In the context of transnational migration, we can argue that it is more precisely knowledge about the geographic locale which is of great value since patrons have the newcomers work in these places.[490] We could emphasize this durability further by assuming that this resource is fundamental for the guarantee of security that a patron offers to his clients. Having lived in Russia for at least a decade, some of these patrons have acquired sufficient experience as Central Asians in Russia and often have excellent knowledge of the Russian language. A further resource is their relatively stable position in a wider informal network in their place of residence. The patrons are involved in strong ties with law enforcement offices or, should these be lacking, they have close bonds with other individuals who have the necessary ties. These ties are crucial to sustain the activities of patronage even after they are formalized into migrant organizations, since they continue engaging in practices that lie in the grey zones of law and order.

---

487 Interview with Faridun, St. Petersburg, August, 2006.
488 Scott, 1972: 97-98.
489 Scott, 1972:98.
490 *Knowledge* as a resource is similar to *information* as discussed by Faist (Faist 2000a:40).

Finally, to this type of resource we can add the patron's knowledge of his potential clients, including their cultural, religious, and linguistic backgrounds.

Just as the owner of a large farm can have only a certain number of tenants in an agricultural context, the amount of physical space that the patron of migrants has at his disposal suffices to accommodate only a certain number of clients; the same can apply to the number of jobs that the patron has or is able to arrange. The resource of *direct control of real property* is about access to and control of certain domains. It can be less durable than the first type of resource. The position of the patron in the geographic location becomes discernible to his client on the very first day of their acquaintance. In each of the three cities in Russia (Moscow, St. Petersburg, and Astrakhan), I was offered a short tour around a small neighborhood or market that the patron perceived as *his* domain. In all three cases, leaders of migrant organizations would tell me about a number of cases in which migrants' rights were being violated by either police officers or employers. They would show reports on the number of cases in which migrant organizations engaging themselves in advocacy activities had helped bring the employer to justice. Employers were either forced to pay the wages or charged with fraud. In some cases police officers faced charges based on rights violations, too. Shortly after our interview, however, organization leaders demonstrated their own high hierarchical positions *vis-à-vis* migrants. Walking from one market stall to another, for instance, I witnessed the respect patrons enjoyed in their own domains, as migrant vendors greeted them far more respectfully than they would greet their customers. I had told these organization leaders that I would also consider taking interviews from migrant workers. While giving me a tour of the market, the leader of the migrant organization would introduce me to *those* migrants whom I *should really get acquainted with* and could talk to. A similar situation occurred in the city of St. Petersburg, where I had not told the migration organization leader about my intention to also interview labor migrants.

The third resource which Scott analyses is *office-based property*, which is a resource base attributed to patrons who hold official positions that they take advantage of, such as village headmen in charge of communal land, politicians or administrative officers in higher positions, or businessmen in private sectors.[491] In Russia, this type of resource becomes valuable when the leader of an informal migrant network, who is referred to as an *organizator* ('organizer'), obtains registration as a migrant organization. Functioning under the aegis of an association or a *diaspora*[492] or cultural center, they succeed in attracting more migrants who are in need of security or assistance with papers or accommodation or employment or all of the above. The degree of durability of this category of resource can also be regarded as lower than

---

491   *Ibid.*
492   This Russian word is used quite regularly as the title of a migrant organization.

in *skills* and *knowledge*. In 2006, the leader of a migrant organization in Astrakhan called "Tajikistan" was officially charged with involvement in the drug trade. Unofficially, according to the hearsay from other migrants, the leader had been involved in the exploitation of low-paid human labor from Tajikistan. As a result, with the involvement of the Embassy of Tajikistan in Moscow, the entire organization was closed. Together with its leader, its key actors lost their positions and reputations in the entire transnational community of Tajikistanis, as well as their access to resources and their influence as patrons upon their clients.[493]

10.4. Conclusion

Transnational patronage often consisting of kinship ties is an interesting phenomenon as it can signify the intermediate stage of the development of transnational kinship to transnational communities. This chapter has looked at the establishment of migrant organizations of Central Asians in Russia on the basis of kinship and patronage with a special focus on fictive kinship. It has shown that the structure of migrant organizations can be kin-based (blood or fictive) from the outset of their establishment, and that their main actors have patron-client ties with transnational migrants. Transnationalism, as this chapter attempted to elucidate, can be interwoven with the Soviet pasts of the migrants. Two trajectories have been illustrated in which Central Asian migrant organizations emerge. In the first path, actors use the resources and networks that they had during the Soviet period. In one instance, leading a student association at a Russian university for fellow students from the same Soviet republic was an incentive to found a migrant organization after the disintegration of the USSR. In other cases, individuals' careers in higher education institutions and in the Communist Party during the Soviet period motivated them to assemble with others to establish an organization afterwards. In the second path, the key actors are post-Soviet labor migrants who arrived in Russia in the 1990s. Being relatively new in Russia, they slowly acquire their resources and ties to formal and informal institutions, so it is not unusual for them to gradually become migrant brokers who then formalize their patron-client ties by registering as a migrant organization. Migrant organization leaders have therefore been conceptualized in terms of patrons vis-à-vis their clients, namely labor migrants.

---

493 I have not been able to find information in the Tajikistani or Russian press and cannot confirm the truthfulness of this information. I had found the name of this organization and its address on a list of migrant organizations on the internet and looked for it while I was in Astrakhan. The office which the organization used to occupy was being rented by Russian entrepreneurs who could not give me any information about their predecessors. During the interview, the former deputy head of this organization said that he would organize jobs for people and work on his own but by no means try to found a migrant organization, even though migrant association leaders of other ethnic minorities were suggesting that he do so.

11. Concluding Remarks

This book has presented an empirical analysis of transnational kinship based on labor migration since the late 1990s between Central Asia and Russia – a geographical zone which is not yet fully explored by migration scholars. Kinship ties, as is argued in migration scholarship, are essential for the formation of transnational ethnic communities. This study has tried to clarify the role of kinship for transnational mobility in the post-Soviet context.

The findings of this research point to two major aspects of migrant transnationalism. *First*, in a broader sense, migrant transnationalism represents intergenerational continuity of ideologies and cultures of migrants. *Second*, and more pertinent to kinship ties, migrant transnationalism is bolstered by a) maintaining life-cycle rituals in the country of origin, b) marriage and transnational conjugal ties, and c) change of citizenship among family members. I will elaborate on these two aspects in more detail.

11.1. Transnationalization and Continuity

At the outset of this research, it was planned to focus only on labor migrants who left Central Asia for Russia in the late 1990s and the beginning of 2000s. At the initial stage of the qualitative research, however, one of the challenging issues with which I was confronted was a type of transnational mobility different from other patterns elaborated in the scholarship on migration. This difference was not simply because the field of research was geographically different, but rather because the research setting was discernibly more embedded in the post-Soviet context than had been previously assumed.

It became clear during the first field trip that there is more than one generation of transnational migrants, namely those who settled in Russia prior to the collapse of the Soviet Union from the 1960s onwards, and then those who arrived starting from the late 1990s and early 2000s. The transnational paradigm of international migration research therefore had to be adjusted to the post-Soviet realities. I have attempted to elaborate a framework for understanding post-Soviet transnationalization that is complementary to other widely analyzed migration patterns such as South Asia – the United Kingdom, Maghreb – France, Latin America – the United States or Turkey – Germany. Unlike these patterns which are either associated with a postcolonial situation, immigration policies of receiving states (especially in North America), or institutionalized engagement of the labor force (Turkey – Germany), post-Soviet transnationalization is closely connected with policies of the Soviet state that distinguish migration taking place in the territory of the former USSR. The fact that internal movements of populations within vast territorial state borders (USSR) turned international upon the demise of the Soviet Union is only one of the many distinctive characteristics. It goes without saying that trans-boundary movements of nation-state borders is a key condition for migration that crosses them to be viewed as international. As touched upon in the chapter on historical background, the Soviet state's strict control over population movements, the central state's Sovietization and modernization efforts, as well as the promotion of education and Russification in the spirit of Communist ideology, without a doubt left its imprint on the cultural and educational backgrounds of generations of migrants born prior to the 1980s. [494]

This research on Central Asian migrants has emphasized that migrant transnationalism is part and parcel of historical continuity.[495] This became evident in a generation of Soviet Central Asian students and Army soldiers that stayed on in Russian cities after graduating from Russian higher education institutions and/or finishing their military service. The social ties that they established with the Slavic population in Russia became useful when the USSR collapsed and people began to migrate to Russia *en masse* in search of employment. Chapter 10 shows that by maintaining dense connections to Central Asia, these Soviet Central Asian migrants in Russia became crucial actors in constructing transnational fictive kinship networks and patronage ties. At the end of the 1990s, this generation of migrants, who were meanwhile holders of Russian passports, got engaged in brokerage activities, established private companies to import cheap labor from home, and founded migrant organizations.[496] It is this continuity and its dynamics that I would like to bring to the foreground as one of the contributions of the present research to migration studies.

11.2 Transnationalization and Kinship

The second main aspect of my insights into migrant transnationalism concerns transnational kinship. Regardless of whether transnational migrants

---

494   We should not exaggerate the importance of the Russian language, however. It should be admitted that while it is still spoken among Sovietized elites and ethnic minorities (Russians, Ukrainians, Tatars, Koreans, Jews, and Caucasians) in the Central Asian region, the population in the provinces and rural areas have limited knowledge of the language. On the other hand, the Russian language has been mainly present through the media and, to a certain extent, language classes that are still part of the secondary school curriculum.

495   On intergenerational and historical continuity, see Smith, 2005:241; Levitt and Jaworsky, 2007: 142.

496   Rogers Brubaker would view them as members of *accidental diasporas*. Brubaker argued that when the USSR fell apart, its ethnic members were dispersed across the borders of the newly established states. Brubaker maintained that in the case of the Soviet Union, similar to Weimar Germany, it is not people who crossed borders but rather borders that moved across people. He coined the term *accidental diasporas* to refer to ethnic minorities (e.g. ethnic Russians in the Baltic states or Central Asia) who found themselves outside of their homeland due to major transformation of political space, such as the fall of the USSR and foundation of newly independent states (Brubaker, 2000).

work on a seasonal basis and visit their home countries once a year or if they are involved in regular trade migration with relatively short stays over the course of several years, their earnings are seen as central for sustaining their families. Migrants provide their families back home with food and clothes and they maintain close relationships with them. Yet if economic incentives were the only driving forces behind this vast mobility, there would be less necessity to consider its additional facets in the research. The transnational approach to migration considers the dense ties between movers and stayers and between the places of origin and destination, calling the attention of scholars to the factors that have much more than just pecuniary significance. Concerning the process of transnationalization vis-à-vis the role of kinship, the present extensive empirical analysis of migrants and their families at the two poles of migration has drawn my attention to three factors that contribute to this phenomenon.

The first factor involves migrant practices such as life-cycle rituals and their financing with remittances that I have described in Chapter 7. Life-cycle rituals, above all weddings, are so significant in Central Asian society that they often lie at the heart of individual migration projects. The 'wedding project' is complementary to the argument of the majority of research in area studies and analytical reports that accentuate labor migration as being purely economic. While I do not deny the financial benefits of labor migration in the families, I argue that life-cycle rituals are a significant factor as well. I have observed two patterns in which life-cycle rituals turn initially short-term projects into linchpins of migrant transnationalism. In the *first* pattern, individuals embark on a journey with the sole intention of earning enough money to be able to finance a wedding party, be it their own or that of a close family member. Once the wedding is over – and its expenditures can range anywhere from $2,000 to $20,000 – the migrant sees no other way of making a living than through continued employment in Russia. In the *second* pattern, migration takes place after an expensive wedding or circumcision party. These family events take place with large sums of money borrowed from family and friends or, not infrequently, from private dealers who make loans with high interest rates. Paying back the wedding debt thus becomes a major goal of the work in Russia and the one-time job evolves into long-term employment there. I have argued that labor migrants could be seen as both catalysts for and victims of traditional celebrations and rituals. The longer they stay abroad, the more they feel responsible to contribute to the good reputation of their families within their neighborhoods back home, and thus struggle to keep up with family rituals and cultural/religious gatherings. They claim that only by working in Russia are they able to finance their life-cycle rituals and celebrations.

Following their wedding celebrations, male migrants often find it difficult to provide for their newly-established families. In addition to taking care of their parents and siblings, they have an additional member in the household, namely their wives, then later their children whom they have to sustain. Cross-border conjugal ties become significant factors in transnationalization, especially when the close relatives of the spouses back home start relying on the labor migrant's help and support, be it through pecuniary means or arrangement for jobs in Russia. Over a period of several years, some married male migrants get involved in extramarital relationships. While I had known of such relationships from conversations or from hearsay, I had several opportunities during the research to either meet the wives of migrants involved in polygamous relationships or interview the male spouses themselves. On the one hand, establishing polygamous relationships means that migrants do not sever ties with their families back home, but rather have found an *additional* relationship in Russia which could be seen as part of the transnationalization process. On the other hand, keeping in mind the Soviet state's efforts to protect family values and prohibit polygamy as it was viewed as a residual of a "backward" feudal system, transnational polygamy is a clear indication of the erosion of the state's control over marriage and family.

The change of citizenship by family members has been a more recent factor that certainly adds to the process of transnationalization. In 2006, the Russian Federation introduced a new law on citizenship which allowed all individuals born in the Soviet Union to apply for Russian citizenship. The introduction of this legislation was welcomed by Russia's labor migrants from the near abroad. With the aim of overcoming administrative burdens and experiencing less discrimination by the law enforcement agents, Central Asian migrants, especially from Tajikistan and Kyrgyzstan, began obtaining Russian passports. Obtaining Russian citizenship among labor migrants, be it at the price of abandonment of their Tajik, Uzbek, or Kyrgyz citizenship or receiving a Russian passport in addition to their original citizenship (which is not lawful in Uzbekistan and Kyrgyzstan), certainly has had implications for membership roles within families. On the one hand, migrants who hold Russian passports are able to stay in Russia permanently, work there on a legal basis, and still maintain dense ties to their families back home. On the other hand, as discussed in Chapter 6, for male family members, abandonment of citizenship means restrictions on the rights to own property. This in turn has left migrants' parents rather perplexed as they risk losing heirs who would inherit their property and above all, male children who are expected in Central Asian societies to care for their parents when they are old.[497]

---

497 "Kyrgyz Abandon Passports Along with Country," a report by Ainagul Abdrakhmanova and Azamat Kachiev for the Institute for War and Peace Reporting, Reporting No. 581, on June 19, 2009. The article also emphasizes that politicians and analysts are worried that a considerable portion of the employable population in Kyrgyzstan might opt to immigrate to Russia and help families in Kyrgyzstan to follow them (www.iwpr.net).

11.3. Relevance to the Migration-Development Paradigm and Transformation Discourse

One of the main contributions of this study pertains to the *migration-development nexus*. The empirical analysis of transnational kinship has been carried out against the backdrop of the on-going debate in development studies that concerns the relationship between migration on the one hand and development of the Central Asian sending states on the other. I have not only observed the economic impact of migrant remittances in terms of the sustaining of families or households, but have also considered development in a broader sense, taking into account societal transformation and norms and expectations within kinship networks and kin members' everyday negotiations of roles in the context of migration. Here it is important to differentiate between two categories of roles: membership-related roles within families and gender-specific roles which I will specify below.

As far as membership roles in families are concerned, in Russia, the country of destination, the eldest of the siblings takes on the role of a parent, which is often the case with eldest sons. In the countries of origin, the tasks and responsibilities of the siblings in relation to their migrant brothers or sisters can shift. Migration of the eldest son can often be a hindrance for the younger son who wants to leave.[498] A further widespread practice in Central Asia is the bringing up of children of migrants by their grandparents. Case studies in the scholarship of migration on this subject abound and cover a variety of sending countries, most examples being from the Philippines and Latin America. Evidence from Central Asia shows that, in families in which the mother has migrated and the eldest child is a teenaged girl, this daughter fulfills the duties of the mother of the family. She is entirely responsible for cooking for the whole family, cleaning the house or distributing chores among other siblings, organizing her younger siblings' daily schedules, cleaning their clothes, and playing the role of a care-giver.

This example should not lead us to believe that there are more migrant women than men and it is in this context that the second category, namely gender-specific role shifting, should be addressed. Labor migration to Russia is still dominated by men and results in a large number of female-headed households back home. In Chapter 7 through the portraits of two women, Gulruh from Tajikistan and Shohistaxon from Kyrgyzstan, I have illustrated household management strategies. As an outsider, one is tempted to think that in Central Asia, migrant wives who are dependent on remittances are too busy managing their households alone and are not employed because their salaries would be much lower than their husbands' earnings in Russia. Through the examples of these two women, it has been shown that wives do not always want to fully depend on remittances and they make efforts to earn

---

498 Chapter 7.

extra income in order to save their husbands' earnings and invest adequately. Especially in rural areas, the absence of men often means that women are forced to fulfil the tasks that were traditionally carried out by men. Physically strenuous household tasks, such as cattle-driving and looking after the plots of land where families grow their own produce, are shifted to the female members of the family. It should be noted that despite the Soviet efforts to *mechanize* agriculture, most of the work is still carried out manually.

In this book I have tried to show how closely transnational labor migration can be linked to the economic and political transformation of migrants' sending states. In this respect, it is a study that could be of interest for scholars working on transformation processes in former Soviet states. The life stories of the subjects interviewed reflect the impact which political events and economic changes in their home country have had on their decisions to migrate. I have taken a closer look at filial relations, namely the ties between parents and their children, and tried to highlight the factors that determined migration patterns. In all three sending countries a typical scenario was the transition to the market economy resulting in the parents' failure to establish a private business. Alternatively, during the process in which state-owned enterprises became privatized, there were increased power struggles between different actors. As a result, competing actors defrauded each other. Those facing great financial debts would send their eldest sons to Russia to solve the family's economic crisis. [499]

A few of the cases which have been described in this work can be considered to be country-specific. In Kyrgyzstan, for instance, as the father of two migrants narrated, the regime change that occurred in March 2005 led to a major shift of power and resources, above all throughout state structures. Young, educated, able-bodied people in their late 20s and early 30s were sometimes forced to interrupt the careers they had begun in state institutions during the presidency of Askar Akaev and had to give up their posts to the proponents of his successor, Kurmanbek Bakiyev. For this category of young state employees, labor migration to Russia seemed the only way to find adequately paid employment. In Uzbekistan, where the government periodically closes down large retail markets, people involved in small trade are forced to look for other sources of income. Many small traders leave the country for places such as Russia or Kazakhstan to work in retail markets there. In Tajikistan, migration to Russia has been a mass phenomenon. Apart from the generation of migrants who fled the country's civil war, the employable population sees opportunities for work only in Russia.

---

[499] 7.2.1. The Eldest Son – The Rescuer of the Family.

Perspectives

So far, I have described a number of findings related to transnational migration and kinship in Central Asia. I do not claim to have examined everything within the scope of this study. Indeed, there is a range of issues which should be considered in future research. What has not been discussed in this book but could be worth treating in a thorough systematic study would be the topic of education in Central Asia in relation to the outflow of the educated population from the region. The situation of brain-drain is indeed alarming. I have already mentioned that political events such as the regime change in Kyrgyzstan can result in an exodus of educated people; brain-drain, however, is by no means limited to such power shifts. The stark differences between salaries in the countries of origin and destination have long been a cause for out-migration by the holders of degrees from higher education institutions. The possibility of obtaining of Russian citizenship since 2006 has certainly added to the permanent loss of human resources in the region. On the other hand, I noticed during my fieldwork in Russia that among young labor migrants there is a growing interest in studying in Russia and receiving a Russian university degree. Initially arriving in Russia without a degree from their home countries, these young labor migrants discover a different niche in the Russian employment market: In many cases employers prefer to hire Central Asians with a degree from Russia and offer them lower pay than they do to natives of Russia.

Islam is another phenomenon that has not been discussed extensively in this book. In my research proposal I did not include any aspects of migration that were related to Islam because I wanted to avoid the research process being predetermined by it. In the course of my observations, I noticed that remittances in the countries of origin are used for religious purposes. For instance, in Southern Kyrgyzstan, my interlocutors drew my attention to mosques that were being constructed with the help of migrants working in Russia. I was also told about Habibxo'ja, one of the most prominent and respectful migrants on the outskirts of Jalalabad.[500] Not only was he considered to be a deeply religious person, who through his hard work supported his family, but he also made *palov* (Central Asian rice dish) every Thursday and brought it to the orphanage nearby. Due to the fact that this migrant drove to the central mosque five times a day, I did not manage to speak with him.

As was mentioned in earlier chapters, automobiles are targets of investment and at the same time convenient means of transport, among other things, for missionary activities. My informant Xolidaxon showed me the construction site where a shopping mall was being built by a group of migrants. Every Friday, returned migrants engaged in the investment of this

---

500 Name of the migrant changed to ensure his anonymity.

mall would meet, buy sheep, rice, and carrots, and drive to the neighboring small towns such as Uzgen for *da'vat* (preaching, mission, outreach).[501]

A further point is that of financing pilgrimages to Mecca of dependent family members by the migrants working in Russia.[502] This support is perceived by the recipients, who are often the parents of labor migrants, as a reward for the many years of care and support for their children. The two women with whom I spoke said that a large number of their fellow travellers had children working in Russia who had covered their transportation costs. Both women had been widows for several years and one of them had been raising all four children of her son for ten years while he and his wife were working in Russia.

It must be added that in Russia the majority of male migrants from Central Asia are caught between two fronts: they see themselves as forced to join the group of male migrants who regularly drink alcohol together with Belorussian, Ukrainian, and other Central Asian co-workers, or they integrate with religious friends and practice Islam more often than they used to in the country of origin. The governments of the sending states have recently noticed the tendency among some migrants to become more religious in Russia, and the trend of fundamentalist ideologies of Islam being 'imported' back with transnational labor migrants.[503] From the researcher's point of view, however, we should not ask whether or not people become more religious through transnational labor migration, but rather what mechanisms are created by migrants as actors for their kin members back home that facilitate religious practices.

In view of the current global economic downturn, the short- and long-term dimensions of transnational migration remain to be seen. In the short run, the most recent surveys indicate that labor migrants who returned to their homelands to "sit out" the economic crisis are leaving again and not waiting for the Russian economy to recover. This is especially true of highly educated, skilled, and experienced labor migrants. According to the latest quantitative data, among those who have returned to Central Asia and intend to settle permanently, the majority are unskilled, with lower levels of education,

---

501   Uzgen is located in the south of Kyrgyzstan, in the Ferghana Valley of Central Asia which is also known as a haven for Islamic activists. In June 2009, one year after my fieldwork, Kyrgyz special forces carried out a raid near this town during which they killed a group of several armed Islamists.
502   Section 7.3 Chapter 7.
503   One of the most prominent cases was the persecution of Uzbek labor migrants in the city of Ivanovo, Russia, in 2005-2006 in which the government of Uzbekistan demanded that they be extradited to Uzbekistan. These migrants were accused of planning and financing the mass protests in Andijon in May 2005 that resulted in the deaths of hundreds of people at the hands of the special forces. The government of Uzbekistan has maintained that among those who organized the protests were Islamic extremist forces that had aimed to cause a coup and establish an Islamic state.

and on average 24 years and younger.[504] In the long run what is certain is that, similar to Turkish labor migrants (*Gastarbeiter*) in the 1970s, who were expected to return permanently to their countries of origin but in many cases stayed in Germany, an entire generation of Central Asian labor migrants is not likely to return permanently. This is especially true for those who have, meanwhile, become Russian citizens. In fact, when we observe the bidirectional movements of population between Central Asia and Russia today, we notice that the two regions have become more interconnected than they were during the Soviet period.

---

504 *Tajikistan: No Jobs For Returning Migrants. Many Plan To Go Back to Russia Despite Declining Job Prospects There.* An article published on July 14, 2009 by Institute for War and Peace Reporting. Reporting No. 583. (available at www.iwpr.net).

Appendix

Selected List of Informants

Moscow (RUS), September 2005

Firuz –	restaurant chef, male, born in 1976 in Uzbekistan[505]
Nasiba –	kitchen assistant, female, born in 1971 in Uzbekistan
Saida –	kitchen assistant, female, born in 1982 in Uzbekistan and married to Firuz
Toshpo'lat –	Nasiba's husband, porter at a market for construction materials, born in 1970 in Uzbekistan
Umar –	Nasiba's brother, helper at a retail market, born in 1973 in Uzbekistan

St. Petersburg (RUS), August-September 2006

Faridun –	construction manager and broker, male, born in 1968 in Tajikistan
Mahmud –	street sweeper, male, born in 1986 in Tajikistan
Nargiza –	bakery worker, female, born in 1979 in Uzbekistan
Sohib –	street sweeper, male born in 1987 in Tajikistan
Sobira –	kitchen helper, female, born in 1980 in Uzbekistan
Sotvoldi –	construction worker, male, born in 1956 in Uzbekistan
Shahodat –	vendor at a retail market, born in 1964 in Uzbekistan
Shohida Opa –	helper at a restaurant, born in 1949 in Uzbekistan
Suluv –	supermarket worker, female, about 32 years old from Uzbekistan
Zokirjon –	construction worker, male, 28 years old from Kyrgyzstan

Sughd (formerly Leninobod) Province, September-October 2006

Dilsifat –	female, born in 1985
Dilangez –	female, about 25 years old
Komil –	male, born in 1966, head of an NGO
Mavjuda –	female, about 48 years old
Nozima –	female, approximately 38 years old
Sohib's parents,	about 50 years old, their son was interviewed in St. Petersburg

---

[505] Place of birth of the informants are indicated only in the case of interviews that took place in Russia in order to show their country of origin.

Khatlon Province (TAJ), April – May 2007

Ayub –	male, about 48 years old
Gulruh –	female, about 48 years old, married to Ayub
Shirinmo –	female, born in 1960
Saidali –	female, born in 1978
Saidali's mother	born in 1951
Shamigul –	female, born in 1972
Zulfiya –	female, born in 1990

Astrakhan (RUS), June 2007

Amirxuja –	male, broker, born in 1966 in Tajikistan and has lived in Astrakhan since 1984
Mansurjon –	male, owner of a small shop, born in 1976 in Kyrgyzstan
Marambi –	female, therapist, born in 1958 in Tajikistan
Murodillo –	male, head of an informal migrant organization, born in 1967 in Tajikistan
Ozoda –	female, market worker, Zulxumor's younger daughter, born in 1992 in Uzbekistan
Mumin Aka –	male, retired, born in 1938 in Uzbekistan and has lived in Astrakhan since 1957
Muhabbatxon –	female, worker at an Uzbek café, born in Kyrgyzstan in 1969
Turghunboy –	male, head of a migrant organization, born in Uzbekistan in 1958 and has lived in Asrakhan since 1988
Zulxumor –	female, market worker, born in 1957 in Uzbekistan
Zukhra –	female, market worker, Zulxumor's elder daughter, born in 1989 in Uzbekistan

Osh and Jalalabad (KYR), February-March 2008

Almaz –	male, about 25 years old
Anara –	female, about 50 years old
Cholpon –	female, born in 1956
Ghayrat –	male, born in 1966
Marghubaxon Opa –	female, born in 1951
Masturaxon Opa –	female, born in 1950
Muruvat Opa –	female, born in 1941
Munojotxon Opa –	female, born in 1951
Orolbay –	male, born in 1954
Shohidaxon –	female, born in 1965

Shohistaxon –	female, born in 1971
Tursunoy –	female, born in 1948
Urmat –	male, about 48 years old
Xolmurod –	male, born in 1956

Official Migrant Organizations in Russia[506]

Abdygany Shakirov – Head of the Interregional Association of Kyrgyzstanis "Kyrgyz Birimdigi" ("Unity of Kyrgyz"), Moscow, Russia

Alijon Haydarov – Head of "Umid" ("Hope") Association of Patriots of Uzbekistan, St. Petersburg, Russia

Bahodir Aminov – Head of the Association of Uzbeks, Astrakhan, Russia

Gavhar Juraeva – Head of the Russian Fund for Assistance of Refugees and Settlers and Head of the Information and Resource Center "Migration and Law", Moscow, Russia

Karomat Sharipov – Head of the Fund for the Support of Migrants of Tajikistani Origin and Tajik Diaspora in the Russian Federation "Tojik Diaspor", Moscow, Russia

Qosim – Head of the Astrakhan Branch Office of "Payvand", Association of Tajiks in Russia, under the Aegis of the Embassy of the Republic of Tajikistan, Russia

Maksat – Deputy Head of the Association of Kyrgyztanis in St. Peterburg

Muhammadnazar Mirzoda – Head of the Society of Friendship between Russian and Tajik Peoples "Somonion" ("Samanid"), St. Petersburg, Russia

---

[506] The names of the organizations are literal translations from Russian. Due to the official status and prominence of these organizations, the names of the informants have not been changed.

References

Abazov, Rafiz (2000). Migration of Population, the Labor Market and Economic Changes in Kirghizstan. In: Komatsu et al. (eds), *Migration in Central Asia: Its History and Current Problems*. JCAS Symposium Series 9. Osaka: Japan Center for Area Studies, National Museum of Ethnology.

Adler, Rachel H. (2002). Patron-Client Ties, Ethnic Entrepreneurship and Transnational Migration: The Case of Yucatecans in Dallas, Texas. *Urban Anthropology and Studies of Cultural Systems and World Economic Development*. 31.2 (Summer 2002): 129(33).

Alba, Richard, and Victor Nee. 1997. "Rethinking Assimilation Theory for a New Era of Immigration." *International Migration Review*, 31:826-75.

Alfieri, Allessandra, Ivo Havinga and Vetle Hvidsen (2005). Issue Paper *Definition of Remittances and Relevant BPM5 Flows*. United Nations Department of Economic and Social Affairs Statistics Division (at http://millenniumindicators.un.org/unsd/trade serv/TSG%2002-05-Paris/tsg0502-16.pdf)..

Amuedo-Dorantes, Catalina and Suzan Pozo (2005). On the Use of Differing Money Transmission Methods by Mexican Immigrants. *International Migration Review*. Vol. 39, No. 3, pp. 554-576.

Amuedo-Dorantes, Catalina and Cynthia Bansak (2006). Money Transfers Among Banked and Unbanked Mexican Immigrants. *Southern Economic Journal*, Vol. 73 No.2, pp. 374-401.

Anderson, Bridget and Bianca Hacilova (2008). Migrant Labour in Kazakhstan. A Cause for Concern? Center on Migration Policy and Society. *Working Paper* No. 69. Oxford University. Available at http://www.compas.ox.ac.uk/fileadmin/files/pdfs/WP0969%20Bridget%20Anderson-Blanka%20Hancilova.pdf.

Arce, Alberto and Norman Long (2000). Reconfiguring Modernity and Development from an Anthropological Perspective. In: Arce, Alberto and Norman Long (eds) *Anthropology, Development and Modernities. Exploring Discourses, Counter-Tendencies and Violence*. London and New York: Routledge, pp. 1-30.

Atkinson, Paul and Martyn Hammersley (1994). Ethnography and Participant Observation. Chapter 15. In: Denzin, Norman K. and Yvonna S. Lincoln (eds) *Handbook of Qualitative Research*. Thousand Oaks, CA: Sage Publications, pp. 248-261.

Balci, Bayram (2003). *Missionaires de l'Islam en Asie centrale. Les écoles turques de Fethullah Gülen*. Institut Français d'Etudes Anatoliennes. Paris: Masonneuve & Larose.

Baldassar, Loretta, Cora V. Baldock and Raelene Wilding (2007). *Families Caring Across Borders: Migration, Ageing and Transnational Caregiving*. Basingstoke [England] and New York: Palgrave Macmillan.

Ballard, Roger (1982). Southasian Families. In: Rapoport, Fogarty and Rapoport (eds) *Families in Britain*. Chapter 8. London: Routledge and Kegan Paul (also available at http://archiv.ub.uni-heidelberg.de/savifadok/volltexte/2009/295/pdf/families.pdf).

Ballard, Roger (1990). Migration and Kinship. The Differential Effects of Marriage Rules on the Processes of Punjabi Migration to Britain. In : Clarke, Peach C. and Steven Vertovec (eds) *Southasian Overseas, Contexts and Communities*.

Cambridge : Cambridge University Press. http://www.arts.manchester.ac.uk/casas/papers/pdfpapers/marriagerules.pdf.
Bakewell, Oliver (2007). *Keeping Them in Their Place. The Ambivalent Relationship Between Migration and Development in Africa.* Working Paper 8. International Migration Institute, University of Oxford.
Baraulina, Tatiana and Oksana Karpenko (2004). *Migraciia i nacional'noe gosudarstvo. [Migration and the Nation State].* Joint publication of the Center for German and European Studies and Center for Independent Social Research (CISR). St.Petersburg: CISR.
Basch, Linda, Nina Glick Schiller and Cristina Szanton Blanc (1994). *Nations Unbound. Transnational Projects, Postcolonial Predicamets and Deterritorialized Nation-States.* Amsterdam: Gordon and Breach Publishers.
Berdinskikh, Viktor (2005). *Spetsposelentsy. Politicheskaia ssylka narodov sovetskoi Rossii.* [Special Settlers. Political Exile of the Peoples of Soviet Russia.] Moscow: Novoe Literaturnoe Obozrenie.
Berthomiere, William (2003), Immigration from the Former Soviet Union. Measure of the Impacts on Jerusalem and on the Settlements of the West Bank and Gaza. *The Arab World Geographer*, 6(2), pp.249-264
Bommes, Michael (2004). Der Mythos des transnationalen Raumes. Oder: Worin besteht die Herausforderung des Transnationalismus für die Migrationsforschung? In: Thränhardt, Dietrich und Uwe Hunger (eds). *Migration im Spannungsfeld von Globalisierung und Nationalstaat.* Sonderhelft 22/2003. Opladen:Westdeutscher Verlag, pp. 90-116.
Bommes, Michael and Ewa Morawka (eds) (2005). *International Migration Research.Constructions, Omissions and the Promises of Interdisciplinarity.* Aldershot, Hants: Ashgate.
Bourdieu, Pierre (2007). *Outline of a Theory of Practice.* Cambridge Studies in Social and Cultural Anthropology. Cambridge, England and New York: Cambridge University Press.
Boyd, Monica (1989). Family and Personal Networks in International Migration: Recent Developments and New Agendas. *International Migration Review*, Vol. 23, No. 3, pp. 638-670.
Böcker, Anita (1994). Chain Migration Over Legally Closed Borders: Settled Immigrants as Bridgeheads and Gatekeepers. *The Netherlands' Journal of Social Sciences*, Vol. 30, pp. 87-106.
Bönker, Klaus, Klaus Müller and Andreas Pickel (2002). (eds) *Postcommunist Transformation and Social Sciences. Cross-Disciplinary Approaches.* Lanham, Boulder: Rowman and Littlefield Publishers.
Brown, Barbara (1983). The Impact of Male Labor Migration on Women in Botswana. *African Affairs*, Vol. 82, No. 328, pp. 367-388.
Brubaker, Rogers (2000). *Accidental Diasporas and External "Homelands" in Central and Eastern Europe: Past and Present.* Political Science Series 71. Institute for Advanced Studies, Vienna, Austria.
Brusina, Olga (2008). Migranty iz Sredney Azii v Rossii: etapy i prichiny priezda, social'nye tipy i organizacii diaspor. [Central Asian Migrants in Russia. Migration Stages and Reasons for Arrival, Social Typology and Organization of Diasporas]. *Vestnik Evrazii*, No. 2 (66).
Bryceson, Deborah F. and Ulla Vuorela (eds) (2002). *The Transnational Family. New European Frontiers and Global Networks.* Oxford and New York: Berg.

Bryceson, Debora F. (2002). Europe's Transnational Families and Migration: Past and Present. In: Bryceson, Debora and Ulla Vuorela (eds) *The Transnational Family. New European Frontiers and Global Networks*. Oxford and New York: Berg.

Buckley, Cynthia (1995). The Myth of Managed Migration. Migration Control and Market in the Soviet Period. *Slavic Review*. Vol. 54. No. 4. pp. 896-916.

X Buckley, Cynthia J. and Blair A. Ruble (eds) (2008). *Migration, Homeland and Belonging in Eurasia*. Baltimore: Johns Hopkins University Press.

Bugai, N.F. and A.N. Kotsonis (1999). *"Obiazat' NKVD SSSR...vyselit' grekov"*. "Assign the NKVD of the USSR to relocate the Greeks". Moscow: Insan.

Burawoy, Michael (2000). Introduction. Reaching for the Global. In: Burawoy, Michael, Joseph A. Blum, Sheba George, Zsuzsa Gille, Teresa Gowan, Lynne Haney, Maren Klawitter, Steven H. Lopez, Seàn ò Riain, Millie Thayer (eds). *Global Ethnography. Forces, Connections and Imaginations in a Postmodern World*. Berkeley, Los Angeles and London: University of California Press.

Burgess, Katrina (2005). Migrant Philanthropy and Local Governance in Mexico. In: Merz, Barbara (ed) *New Patterns in Mexico: Observations in Remittances, Philanthropic Giving and Equitable Development*, Cambridge, Mass.: Harvard University Press, pp. 99-125.

Bushkov, Valentin I. (2000). Population Migration in Tajikistan: Past and Present. In: Komatsu *et al.* (eds), *Migration in Central Asia: Its History and Current Problems*. JCAS Symposium Series 9. Osaka: Japan Center for Area Studies, National Museum of Ethnology.

Buwalda, Petrus (1997). *They Did not Dwell Alone. Jewish Emigration from the Soviet Union 1967-1990*. Washington D.C.: The Woodrow Wilson Center Press; Baltimor and London: The Johns Hopkins University Press.

Carlos, Manuel L. (1973). Fictive Kinship and Modernization in Mexico. A Comparative Analysis. *Anthropological Quarterly*, Vol. 42, No. 2, pp. 71-91/

Chamberlain, Mary (1997). *Narratives of Exile and Return*. London: Macmillan.

Chamberlain, Mary and Selma Leydesdorff (2004). Transnational Families: Families and Narratives. *Global Networks*, Vol. 4, No. 3, 224-241.

Charsley, Katharine (2005). Unhappy Husbands: Masculinity and Migration in Traditional Pakistani Marriages. *Journal of Royal Anthropological Institute*, No. 11, pp. 85-108.

Charsley, Katharine and Alison Shaw (2006). South Asian Transnational Marriages in Comparative Perspective. *Global Networks*, Vol. 6, No. 4, pp. 331-344.

Castles, Stephen and Mark Miller (1993). *The Age of Migration. International Population Movements in the Modern World*. London: Macmillan.

Choldin, Harvey M. (1973). Kinship Networks in the Migration Processes. *International Migration Review*, Vol. 7, No. 2, pp. 163-175.

Çil, Nevim (2007). *Topographie des Außenseiters. Türkische Generationen und der deutsch-deutsche Wiedervereinigungsprozess*. Schriftenreihe Politik und Kultur, 9. Berlin: Verlag Hans Schiler.

Cohen, Jeffrey H., Alicia Sylvia Gijón-Cruz, Rafael G. Reyes-Morales and Garry Chick (2003). Understanding Transnational Processes: Modeling Migration Outcomes in the Central Valleys of Oaxaca Mexico. *Field Methods*, Vol.15, No.4, pp.366-385.

Coleman, D.A. (1995) International Migration: Demographic and Socioeconomic Consequences in the United Kingdom and Europe. *International Migration Review*, Vol. 29, No. 1, pp. 155-206.
Coles, Anne and Anne-Meike Fechter (eds) (2007). *Gender and Family Among Transnational Professionals*. London and New York: Routledge.
Collins, Kathleen (2004). The Logic of Clan Politics. Evidence from the Central Asian Trajectories. *World Politics* 56, pp. 224-261.
Collins, Kathleen (2006). *Clan Politics and Regime Change in Central Asia*. Cambridge, New York: Cambridge University Press.
Cooper, Frederick (2005). *Colonialism in Question. Theory, Knowledge, History*. Berkeley: University of California Press.
Dannecker, Petra (2005) Transnational Migration and the Transformation of Gender Relations: The Case of Bangladeshi Labor Migrants. *Current Sociology*, Vol. 53, No. 4, pp.655-674.
Darieva, Tsypylma (2005). Recruiting for the Nation: Post-Soviet Transnational Migrants in Germany and Kazakhstan. *Siberian Studies*. (available at http://www.siberian-studies.org/publications/PDF/ridarieva.pdf).
de Haan, Arjan (2006). *Migration in the Development Studies Literature: Has It Come Out of Its Marginality?* Research Paper 2006/19, World Institute for Development Economics Research, United Nations University (UNU-WIDER) (available at http://62.237.131.23/publications/rps/rps2006/rp2006-19.pdf).
de Haas, Hein (2006a). *Engaging Diasporas. How Governments and Development Agencies can Support Diaspora Involvement*. A Study for Oxfam Novib. International Migration Institute. University of Oxford.
de Haas, Hein (2006b). Migration, Remittances and Regional Development in Southern Morocco, *Geoforum* 37, 4: 565-580.
de Haas, Hein and Roald Plug (2006). Cherishing the Goose with the Golden Eggs: Trends in Migrant Remittances from Europe to Morocco 1970-2004, *International Migration Review*, Vol. 30., No. 3, pp. 603-634.
DeJong, Gordon F., Brenda Davis Root and Ricardo G. Abad (1986). Family Reunification and Philippine Migration to the United States: The Immigrants' Perspective. *International Migration Review*, Vol. 20, No. 3, pp. 598-611.
Denzau, Arhur T. and Douglass C. North (1994). Shared Mental Models: Ideologies and Institutions. *Kyklos*, Vol. 47, Issue 1.
Denzin, Norman K. and Yvonna S. Lincoln (eds) (1994). *Handbook of Qualitative Research*. Thousand Oaks, CA: Sage Publications.
Dey, Ian (1999). *Grounding Grounded Theory: Guidelines For Qualitative Inquiry*. San Diego: Academic Press.
Dietz, Barbara (2000). German and Jewish migration from the former Soviet Union to Germany: background, trends and implications. *Journal of Ethnic and Migration Studies*. Vol. 26, No.4: 635-652.
Dostàl, Petr and Hans Knippenberg (1979). The "Russification" of Ethnic Minorities in the USSR. *Soviet Geography*. Vol. 20 (4), pp. 197-219.
Dragadze, Tamara (1987). Fieldwork at Home. The USSR. In: Jackson, Anthony (ed) *Anthropology at Home*. ASA Monograph 25.
Dubois, Laurant (2000). La République Métissée: Citizenship, Colonialism and the Borders of French History. *Cultural Studies*, Vol. 14, Issue 1.
Duranti, Alessandro (1997). *Linguistic Anthropology*. Cambridge, New York: Cambridge University Press.

Ebaugh, Helen R. and Mary Curry (2000). Fictive Kin as Social Capital in New Immigrant Communities. *Sociological Perspectives*, Vol. 43, No. 2, pp. 189-209.

El Qorchi, Mohammed, Samuel M. Maimbo and John Wilson (2003). *Informal Funds Transfer Systems. An Analysis of the Informal Hawala System.* International Monetary Fund. Occasional Paper. Washington D.C.

Eckstein, Susan (2003). Diasporas and Dollars: Transnational Ties and the Transformation of Cuba, *Rosemarie Rogers Workings Paper Series*. No. 16. Cambridge, MA: MIT (available at http://web.mit.edu/cis/wwww/migration/pubs/rrwp/16_eckstein.html).

Engels, Frederick (1972). *The Origin of the Family, Private Property and the State. In the Light of the Researches of Lewis H. Morgan.* New York: International Publishers.

Ewing, Catharine, Vaughan (1977). *Socioeconomic Modernization and the Linguistic Russification of National Minorities in the USSR.* Ph D Thesis at the University of Oklahoma.

Faist, Thomas (1999). Developing Transnational Social Spaces: The Turkish-German Example. In: Pries, Ludger (ed) *Migration and Transnational Social Spaces.* Aldershot: Ashgate.

Faist, Thomas (2000a). *The Volume and Dynamics of International Migration and Transnational Social Spaces.* Clarendon Press: Oxford.

Faist, Thomas (2000b). Transnationalization in International Migration: Implications for the Study of Citizenship and Culture. *Ethnic and Racial Studies*. Vol. 23, No. 2, pp- 189-222.

Faist, Thomas (2004). Towards a Political Sociology of Transnationalization. The State of the Art of Migration Research. *Arch.europ.sociol.*, XLV 2004, pp.331-336.

Faist, Thomas (2006). The Transnational Social Spaces of Migration. *Working Paper 10.* Center On Migration, Citizenship and Development (COMCAD).

Faist, Thomas (2007). Transstate Social Spaces and Development. Exploring the Changing Balance Between Communities, States and Markets. *Working Paper 10.* Center On Migration, Citizenship and Development (COMCAD).

Faist, Thomas and Peter Kivisto (2007). *Citizenship: Discourse, Theory and Transnational Prospects.* Malden, MA: Blackwell.

Faist, Thomas (2008). Migrants as Transnational Development Agents: An Inquiry into the Newest Round of Migration-Development Nexus. *Population, Space and Place,* 14, pp. 21-42.

Fitzgerald, David (2006). Toward a Theoretical Ethnography of Migration.*Qualitative Sociology*, Vol. 29, No. 1.

Fleming, Judith L. (1975). Soviet Policies of 'Russification' in Uzbekistan Since the World War II. M.A. Thesis at the University of Washington.

Flick, Uwe (2006). *An Introduction to Qualitative Research.* 3rd Edition. London, Thousand Oaks: Sage Publications.

Freund, Caroline L. and Nikola Spatafora (2005). *Remittances: Transaction Costs, Determinants and Informal Flows.* World Bank Policy Research Working Paper No. 3704. Available at SSRN: http://ssrn.com/abstract=803667.

Fouron, George and Nina Glick-Schiller (2001). All in the Family: Gender, Transnational Migration and the Nation-State. *Identities*, Vol. 7, no. 4, pp. 539-582.

Ganga, Deianira and Sam Scott (2006). Cultural Insiders and the Issue of Positionality in Qualitative Migration Research: Moving "Across" and Moving "Along" Researcher-Participant Divides, *Forum Qualitative Social Research*, Vol. 7. No.7. Art. 7.

Garcelon, Marc (2001). Colonizing the Subject: The Genealogy and Legacy of the Soviet Internal Passport. In: Caplan, Jane and John Torpey (eds) *Documenting Individual Identity. The Development of State Practices in the Modern World.* Princeton and Oxford: Princeton University Press.

Gibson, James R. (1991). Interregional Migration in the USSR., 1981-1985 and 1971-1975. *The Canadian Geographer / Le Géographe canadien,* Volume 35, No 2 (1991) 142-156.

Gibson, James, L. (2000). Social Networks, Civil Society and the Prospects for Consolidating Russia's Democratic Transition. American Journal of Political Science. Vol. 45, No. 1, pp. 51-68.

Giddens, Anthony (1984). *The Constitution of Society.* Cambridge: Polity Press.

Glaser, Barney and Anselm Strauss (2009). *The Discovery of Grounded Theory: Strategies for Qualitative Research.* Fourth Paperpack Edition. Chicago: Aldine.

Glick Schiller, Linda Basch and Cristina Szanton Blanc (1992a). Towards a Transnational Perspective on Migration: Race, Class, Ethnicity and Nationalism Reconsidered. New York: *Annales of the New York Academy of Sciences* 645.

Glick Schiller, Nina, Linda Basch and Cristina Szanton Blanc (1992b). Towards a Definition of Transnationalism. Introductory Remarks and Research Questions. In: Glick Schiller, Nina, Linda Basch and Cristina Szanton Blanc (eds) *Towards a Transnational Perspective on Migration. Race, Class, Ethnicity and Transnationalism Reconsidered.* Annals of the New York Academy of Sviences, Vol. 645.

Glick Schiller, Nina, Linda Basch and Cristina Szanton Blanc (1995). From Immigrant to Transmigrant. Theorizing Transnatinoal Migration. *Anthropology Quarterly.* VOl, 68, No.1, pp.48-36.

Glick Schiller, Nina (1999). Transmigrants and Nation-States. Something Old and Something New in the U.S. immigrant experience. In: Hirschman, Charles, Philip Kasinitz and Josh De wind (eds) *The Handbook of International Migration.* New York: The Russel Sage Foundation.

Glick Schiller, Nina (2007). Beyond the Nation-State and Its Units of Analysis. Towards a New Reseach Agenda for Migration Studies. *Wokring Paper* 33/2007. Bielefeld: Center on Migration, Citizenship and Development (COMCAD), University of Bielefeld.

Goldring, Luin (2004). Family and Collective Remittances: A Multi-dimensional Typology. *Development and Change,* Vol. 35, No. 4, pp. 799-840.

Goodkind, Daniel (1997). The Vietnamese Double Marriage Squeeze. *International Migration Review,* Vol. 31, No. 1, pp. 108-127.

Gosewinkel, Dieter (2008). The Dominance of Nationality? Nation and Citizenship from the Late Nineteenth Century Onwards: A Comparative European Perspective. *German History,* Vol. 26, No. 1, pp. 92-108.

Goss, Jon and Bruce Lindquist (1995). Conceptualizing International Labor Migration: A Structuration Perspective. *International Migration Review,* Vol. 29, No.2, pp. 317-351.

Gowan, Teresa and Seàn ò Rian (2000). Preface. At Home with a Global Ethnographer. In: Burawoy, Michael, Joseph A. Blum, Sheba George, Zsuzsa Gille,

Teresa Gowan, Lynne Haney, Maren Klawitter, Steven H. Lopez, Seàn ò Riain, Millie Thayer (eds) *Global Ethnography. Forces, Connections and Imaginations in a Postmodern World.* Berkeley, Los Angeles and London: University of California Press.

Grillo, Ralph D. (1997). Discourses of Development. The View from Anthropology. In: Grillo, Ralph D. and Roderick Stirrat (eds) *Discourses of Development. Anthropological Perspectives.* Oxford and New York: Berg pp. 1-33.

Gullette, David. (2007). Theories on Central Asian factionalism: the debate in political science and its wider implications. *Central Asian Survey.* Vol. 23, No. 6, pp. 373-387.

Held, David, Anthony G. McGrew, David Goldblatt and Jonathan Perraton (1999). *Global Transformations: Politics, Economics and Culture.* Stanford, CA: Standford University Press.

Helmke, Gretchen and Steven Levitsky (2003). Informal Institutions and Comparative Politics: A Research Agenda. Helen Kellog Institute, Notre Dame University. *Working Paper No. 307.* (available at http://kellogg.nd.edu/publications/workingpapers/WPS/307.pdf)

Hernández-Coss, Raúl (2005). The U.S.-Mexico Remittance-Corridor. Lessons on Shifting from Informal to Formal Transfer Systems. *World Bank Working Paper 43.*

Hirsch, Francine (2003). Getting to Know the Peoples of the USSR: Ethnographic Exhibits as Soviet Virtual Tourism, 1923-1934. *Slavic Review*, Vol. 62, No. 4, Tourism and Travel in Russia and the Soviet Union, pp. 683-709.

Hirsch, Francine (2005). *Empire of the Nations. Ethnographic Knowledge and the Making of the Soviet Union.* Ithaca and London: Cornell University Press.

Hunger, Uwe (2003). Brain drain oder brain gain: Migration und Entwicklung. In: Thränhardt, Dietrich und Uwe Hunger (eds) *Migration im Spannungsfeld von Globalisierung und Nationalstaat.* Sonderhelft 22/2003. Opladen: Westdeutscher Verlag, pp. 58-75.

IOM International Organization for Migration (1999), *Migration in the CIS 1997-1998,* IOM Publications, 215 p.

IOM International Organization for Migration (2008), *Migration in the Russian Federation. A Country Profile 2008*, IOM Publications, 104 p.

Islamov, Bakhtior (2000), Migration of Population in Independent States of Central Asia, in Hisao Komatsu, Chika Obiya and John S. Schoeberlein (Eds) *Migration in Central Asia: Its History and Current Problems,* JCAS Symposium Series 9. Osaka, Japan Center for Area Studies, National Museum of Ethnology, pp. 179-197.

Itzigsohn, Jose (1995). Migrant Remittances, Labor Markets and Household Strategies: A Comparative Analysis of Low-Income Household Strategies in the Caribbean Basin. *Social Forces*, Vol. 72. No. 2. pp. 633-655.

Jones-Luong (ed) (2004). *The Transformation of Central Asia. States and Societies from Soviet Rule to Independence.* Ithaca: Cornell University Press.

Joppke, Christian (1996). Multiculturalism and immigration. A comparison of the United States, Germany and Great Britain. *Theory and Society*, Vol. 25, No. 4.

Jorgensen, Danny, L. (1989). *Participant Observation: A Methodology for Human Studies.* Newbury Park, CA: Sage Publications.

Joshi, C.S. (1999). *Sociology of Migration and Kinship.* New Delhi: Anmol Publications.

Kalandarov, Takhir (2008). Pamircy-migranty v Lipeckoi oblasti. [Pamiri Migrants in the Province of Lipetsk]. *Vestnik Evrazii*, No. 2 (66).

Kamp, Marianne (2006). *The New Woman in Uzbekistan: Islam, Modernity and Unveiling Under Communism*. Seattle: University of Washington Press.

Kandiyoti, Deniz (1999). Poverty in Transition: An Ethnographic Critique of Household Surveys on Central Asia. *Development and Change*, Vol. 30, Issue 3.

Kandiyoti, Deniz and Nadira Azimova (2004). The Communal and the Sacred: Women's World of Ritual in Uzbekistan. *The Journal of the Royal Anthropological Institute*, Vol. 10, No. 2, pp. 320-349.

Kapur, Devesh (2004). *Remittances: The New Development Mantra?* G-24 Discussion Paper Series. Paper 29. United Nations Conference on Trade and Development.

Kaspersen, Lars Bo (2000). *Anthony Giddens: An Introduction to a Social Theorist*. Oxford, UK and Malden, Mass: Blackwell Publishers.

Khadria, Binod (2004). *Migration of Highly Skilled Indians. Case Studies of the IT and the Health Professionals*. OSCD Science, Technology and Industry Working Papers 2004/6.

Khegai, Margarita (2002). *Polygamy Research in Tajikistan*. A Report for Swiss Cooperation Office in Tajikistan.

Kivisto, Peter (2001). Theorizing Transnational Immigration: A Critical Review of Current Efforts. *Ethnic and Racial Studies*, Vol. 24, no. 4, pp. 549-577.

Kivisto, Peter and Thomas Faist (2009). Chapter 5. Transnationalism and Persistence of Homeland Ties. In: Kivisto, Peter and Thomas Faist (2009). *Beyond a Border. The Causes and Consequences of Contemporary Immigration* (forthcoming).

Kluge, Susann (2000). Empirically Grounded Construction of Types and Typologies in Qualitative Social Research, *Forum Qualitative Social Research*, Vol.1, No. 1, Art. 14.

Kodeks o brake i sem'e (1986). [Code on Matrimony and Family.] Moskva: Yuridicheskaia Literatura.

Kofman, Eleonore (2004). Family-Related Migration: A Critical Review of European Studies. *Journal of Ethnic and Migration Studies*, Vol. 3, No. 2, pp. 243-262.

Komatsu, Hisao, Chika Obiya and John S. Schoeberlein (eds) (2000) *Migration in Central Asia: Its History and Current Problems*. JCAS Symposium Series 9. Osaka: Japan Center for Area Studies, National Museum of Ethnology.

Korobkov, Andrei V. (2008) Post-Soviet Migration: New Trends at the Beginning of the Tweny-First Century. In: Buckley, Cynthia J. and Blair A. Ruble (eds) *Migration, Homeland and Belonging in Eurasia*. Baltimore: Johns Hopkins University Press, pp. 69-98.

Kosals, Leonid (2006). Essay on clan capitalism in Russia. *Acta Oeconomica*, Volume 57, No. 1. pp. 67-85.

Krämer, Annette (2002). *Geistliche Autorität und islamische Gesellschaft im Wandel. Studien über Frauenälteste (otin und xalfa) im unabhängigen Usbekistan*. Berlin: Klaus Schwarz Verlag.

Kuehnast, Kathleen R. and Nora Dudwick (2004). *Better a Hundred Friends than a Hundred Rubles?: Social Networks in Transition – Kyrgyz Republic*. World Bank Working Paper No. 39. Washington D.C.: World Bank.

Lachenmann, Gudrun and Petra Dannecker (eds) (2008). *Negotiating Development in Muslim Societies: Gendered Spaces and Translocal Connections*. Lanham, MD: Lexington Books.

Lahav, Gallya (1997). International Versus National Constraints in Familiy Reunification Migration Policies. *Global Governance* 3, pp. 349-372.

Laruelle, Marlène (2007). Central Asian Labor Migrants in Russia: The "Diasporization" of the Central Asian States? *China and Eurasia Forum Quarterly*, Vol. 5, No.3. pp.101-119.

Lacroix, Thoma (2005). *Les réseaux marocains du développement : géographie du transnational et politiques du territorial.* Paris : Presses de la Fondation nationale des sciences politiques.

Ledeneva, Alena V. (2006). *How Russia Really Works. The Informal Practices That Shaped Post-Soviet Politics and Business.* Ithaca, London: Cornell University Press.

Ledeneva, Alena (2008). Blat and guanxi: informal practices in Russia and China. *Comparative Studies in Society and History.* Vol. 50 (1)., pp. 118-144.

Lee, Everett S. (1966). A Theory of Migration. *Demography*, Vol. 3, No. 1, pp. 47-57.

Levitt, Peggy (2001). *The Transnational Villagers.* Berkeley: University of California Press.

Levitt, Peggy and Ninna Nyberg Sørensen (2004). *Global Migration Perspectives: The Transnational Turn in Migration Studies.* Geneva: Global Commission in International Migration.

Levitt, Peggy and B. Nadya Jaworsky (2007). Transnational Migration Developments. Past Developments and Future Trends. *Annual Review of Sociology.* Vol. 33, pp. 129-156.

Lianos, Theodore P. (1997). Factors Determining Migrant Remittances: The Case of Greece. *International Migration Review*, Vol. 31. No.1, pp. 72-87.

Liebert, Saltanat (2008). *Illegal post-Soviet Migration to the United States.* London: Routledge.

Lindholm, Charles (1986). Kinship structure and political authority: the Middle East and Central Asia. *Comparative Study in Society and History*, Vol. 28. No. 2., pp. 334-355.

Litwak, Eugene (1960). *Occupational Mobility and Extended Family Cohesion.* Indianapolis: Bobbs-Merrill.

Louw, Maria Elizabeth (2007) *Everyday Islam in Post-Soviet Central Asia.* London and New York: Routledge.

Lubin, Nancy (1984). *Labor and Nationality in Soviet Central Asia. An Uneasy Compromise.* Hong Kong: MacMillan Press.

Luong, V.H. (1992). *Revolution in the Village. Tradition and Transformation in North Vietnam. 1925-1988.* Honolulu: University of Hawaii Press.

MacDonald, John S and Leatrice MacDonald (1964). Chain Migration: Ethnic Neighborhood Formation and Social Networks. *The Milbank Memorial Fund Quarterly*, Vol. 42, No. 1, pp.82-97.

Mace, David and Vera Mace (1963). *The Soviet Family.* Garden City, New York: Doubleday and Company, Inc.

Magnarella, Paul and Orhan Türkdoğan (1973). Descent, Affinity and Ritual Relations in Turkey. *American Anthropologist*, Vol. 75, No. 5, pp. 1626-1633.

Mahler, Sarah (1998). Theoretical and Empirical Contributions Toward a Research Agenda for Transnationalism. In: Smith, Michael P. and Luis E. Guarnizo (eds) *Transnationalism From Below.* New Brunswick, New Jersey: Transaction Publishers, pp. 64-102.

Maimbo, Samuel M. (2003). The Money Exchange Dealers of Kabul. A Study of the Hawala System in Afghanistan. *World Bank Working Paper*. No. 13. The World Bank. Washington, D.C.

Mandel, Ruth (2008). Germans, Jews or Russians? Diaspora and the Post-Soviet Transnational Experience. In: Buckley, Cynthia J. and Blair A. Ruble (eds) *Migration, Homeland and Belonging in Eurasia*. Baltimore: Johns Hopkins University Press, pp. 303-326.

Manolo, Abella I. (2004). The Role of Recruiters in Labor Migration. In: Massey, Douglas and Edward Taylor. *International Migration. Prospects and Policies in a Global Market*. Oxford: Oxford University University Press, pp. 201-211.

Maphoza, France (2005). The Impact of Remittances from Zimbabweans Working in South Africa on Rural Livelihoods in Southern Districts of Zimbabwe. *Forced Migration Working Paper Series* No. 14. Forced Migration Studies Programme, University of Witwatersrand. (online http://migration.wits.ac.za/Maphosa.pdf).

Marat, Erica (2006). State-Crime Nexus in Central Asia. State Weakness, Organized Crime and Corruption in Kyrgyzstan and Tajikistan. *Silk Road Paper*, October 2006. Central Asia-Caucasus Institute for Silk Road Studies Program.

Marcus, George (1995). Ethnography in/of the World System: The Emergence of Multi-Sited Ethnography. *Annual Review of Anthropology*. Vol. 24, pp. 95-117.

Marcus, George E. (1998). *Ethnography through Thick and Thin*. Princeton: Princeton University Press.

Martínez, Claudia and Dean Yang (2007). Remittances and Poverty in Migrants' Home Areas. Evidence from the Philippines. *Serie Documentos de Trabajo* No. 257. University of Chile Depart of Economics. (available at http://econ.uchile.cl/public/Archivos/aca/Adjuntos/a877ebd4-2866-4d5f-bfed-44fe99adaff3.pdf).

Massey, Douglas S., Rafael Alarcón, Jorge Durand and Umberto González (1987). *Return to Aztlan. The Social Processes of International Migration from Western Mexico*. Berkeley and Los Angeles: University of California Press.

Massey, Douglas S., Joaquín Arango, Graeme Hugo, Ali Kouaouci, Adela Pellegrino, J. Edward Taylor (1993). Theories of International Migration. A Review and Appraisal. *Population and Development Review*. Vol. 19, No. 3, pp. 431-466.

Massey, Douglas S, Luin Goldring and Jorge Durand (1994). Continuities in transnational migration. An analysis of nineteen Mexican communities. *American Journal of Sociology*, Vol. 99, No.6, p. 1492-1533.

Matthews, Mervyn (1993). *The Passport Society. Controlling Movement in Russia and the USSR*. Boulder, San Francisco, Oxford: Westview Press.

Matveev, Gennadiy Konstantinovich (1985). *Sovetskoe semeinoe pravo*. [The Soviet Family Law] Moskva: Yuridicheskaia Literatura.

Megoran Nick (2002), *The borders of eternal friendship? The politics and pain of nationalism and identity along the Uzbekistan-Kyrgyzstan Ferghana Valley boundary, 1999-2000*, PhD Dissertation defended at Sydney Sussex College, Cambridge, UK. (available at http://www.staff.ncl.ac.uk/nick.megoran/pdf/nick_megoran_phd.pdf

Melkonyan, Eduard (2005). Political Parties of the Diaspora and the Processes of Democratization in Armenia. In: Haindrava, Ivlian and Iskandaryan Alexander (eds) *Diaspora, Oil and Roses. What Makes the Countries of the South Caucasus Tick*. Heinrich Böll Stiftung and Caucasus Media Institute, Yerevan (in Russian).

Modenov, V. A and Nosov A.G.(2002). *Rossiia i Migraciia. Istoriia, real'nost' i perspektivy. [Russia and Migration. History, Reality and Perspectivs]*. Moscow: Prometei.
Monsutti, Alessandro (2004). Cooperation, Remittances and Kinship Among the Hazaras. *Iranian Studies*, Vol. 37, No. 2, pp. 219-240.
Mukomel, Vladimir (2005). *Migracionnaia politika Rossii: postsovetskie konteksty. [Russia's Migration Politics: Post-Soviet Contexts]*. Moscow: Dipol'-T.
Mukomel, Vladimir (2006). Immigration und Russlands Migrationspolitik: Streit um die Zukunft [Immigration and Russian Migration Policy: Struggle for the Future], in: *Russlandanalysen* 102/06, at: http://www.russlandanalysen.de.
Nimkoff, M.F. (ed) (1965). *Comparative Family Systems*. Boston: Houghton Mifflin Company.
North, Douglass C. (1990). *Institutions, Institutional Change and Economic Performance*. Cambridge: Cambridge University Press.
Nyberg-Sørensen, Ninna, Nicholas van Hear and Poul Engberg-Pedersen (2002). The Migration-Development Nexus Evidence and Policy Options. State-of-the-Art Overview. Center for Development Research. Copenhagen, Denmark. *International Migration*, Vol. 40, No.5, pp. 3-48.
Olimova Saodat and Igor BoscOlimova (2003). „Trudovaja Migracija iz Tadikistana" [„Arbeitsmigration aus Tadschikistan"] Duschanbe, Tadschikistan. Meždunarodnaja Organizacija po Migracii v sotrudnichestve s Nauchno – issledovatelskim Centrom «Sharq». [Internationale Organisation für Migration in Zusammenarbeit mit dem Forschungszentrum „Sharq"].
Olimova, Saodat (2005). Strategies for Development and Food Security in Mountainous Areas of Central Asia. Impact of External Migration on Development of Mountainous Regions Tajikistan, Kyrgyzstan, Afghanistan and Pakistan. Fourth Meeting of the Issik-Kul Dialogue on International Migration. Dushanbe, Tajikistan, June 6-10, 2005 (online http://www.akdn.org).
Olwig, Karen Fog (1993). *Global Culture, Island Identity: Continuity and Change in the Afro-Caribbean Community of Nevis*. London: Taylor and Francis.
Orozco, Manuel (2002). Globalization and Migration. The Impact of Family Remittances in Latin America. *Latin American Politics and Society*, Vol. 44, No. 2, pp. 41-66.
Paerregaard, Karsten (2002). Business as Usual. Livelihood Strategies and Migrant Practice in the Peruvian Diaspora. In: Sørensen, Ninna Nyberg and Karen Fog Olwig (eds) *Work and Migration. Life and Livelihoods in a Globalizing World*. ,London and New York: Routledge, Chapter 6, p.126-144.
Palloni, Alberto, Douglas S. Massey, Miguel Ceballos, Kristin Espinosa and Michael Spittel (2001). Social Capital and International Migration: A Test Using Information on Family Networks. *American Journal of Sociology*, Vol. 106, No. 5, pp. 1262-1298.
Parekh, Bhikhu (1996). Minority Practices and Principles of Toleration. *International Migration Review*. Vol. 30, No. 1, pp. 251-284.
Parreñas, Rhacel Salazar (2001). *Servants of Globalization*. Stanford: Stanford University Press.
Parreñas, Rhacel Salazar (2005a). *Children of Globalization*. Stanford: Stanford University Press.

Parreñas, Rhacel Salazar (2005b). Long Distance Intimacy: Class, Intergenerational Relations between Mothers and Children in Filipino Transnational Families. *Global Networks*, Vol. 4, No. 4, pp. 317-336.

Parsons, Talcott (1968). *The Structure of Social Action*. 2 volumes. New York: The Free Press.

Petersen, William (1958). A General Typology of Migration. *American Sociological Review*. Vol, 23, No. 3, pp. 256-266.

Peyrouse, Sébastian (2007). Rückkehr und Aufbruch. Zentralasiatische Migrationsströme. In: *Osteuropa. 8-9/2007. Machtmosaik Zentralasien. Traditionen, Restriktionen, Aspirationen*. Düsseldorf: Gerda Henkel Stiftung.

Pieke, Frank N., Nicholas Van Hear and Anne Lindley (2005). *Synthesis Study. A part of the report on Informal Remittance Systems in Africa, Caribbean and Pacific (ACP) countries*. Center on Migration, Policy and Society (online www.compas.ox.ac.uk).

Piore, Michael J. (1973). *The Role of Immigration in Industrial Growth. A Case Study of the Origin and Character of Puerto Rican Migration to Boston*. Cambridge, Mass: MIT, Department of Economics.

Pleatteau, Jean-Philippe (1995). A Framework for the Analysis of Evolving Patron-Client Ties in Agrarian Economics. *World Development*, Vol. 23, No. 5, pp. 767-786.

Pogrebov, Igor B. (2006). Prevalence and Assessment of Polygamy in Uzbekistan. *Russian Social Science Review*. Vol. 47. No. 6, pp. 57-64.

Poliakov, Sergei P. (1992). Everyday Islam. Religion and Tradition in Rural Central Asia. Armonk, N.Y.: M.E. Sharpe.

Polyan, Pavel (2001). *Ne po svoei vole. Istoriia i geografiia prinuditel'nykh migraciy v SSSR*. [Not by their own will. History and geography of forced migrations in the USSR.]: Publication of the Human Rights Organization *Memorial*.

Portes, Alejandro (1997). Immigration theory for a new century: Some Problems and Opportunities. *International Migration Review*, Vol. 31, No. 4, Special Issue: Immigrant Adaptation and Native-Born Responses in the Making of Americans (Winter, 1997), pp. 799-825.

Portes, Alejandro (1999). Conclusion. Towards a New World – The origins and Effects of of Transnational Activities. *Ethnic and Racial Studies*, Vol 22, No, 2, pp. 217-237.

Portes, Alejandro, Luis Guarnizo and Patricia Landolt (1999). The Study of Transnationalism. Pitfalls and Promise of an Emergent Research Field. *Ethnic and Racial Studies,* VOl, 22, No, 2, pp. 217-237.

Pribilsky, Jason (2004). '*Aprendemos a convivir*': Conjugal Relations, Co-parenting and Family Life Among Ecuadorian Transnational Migrants in New York City and Ecuadorian Andes. *Global Networks*, Vol. 3, No. 4, pp. 313-334.

Pries, Ludger (1999). New Migration in Transnational Spaces. In: Pries, Ludger (ed) *Migration and Transnational Social Spaces*. Aldershot: Ashgate.

Pries, Ludger (2001). *Internationale Migration. Soziologische Themen*. Bielefeld: Transcript Verlag.

Pries, Ludger (2005). Configurations of Geographical and Societal Spaces: A Sociological Proposal between 'Methodological Nationalism' and 'the Spaces of Flows'.Global Networks, Vol.5, No. 2, pp. 167-190.

Rahman, Mizanur (2009). Temporary Migration and Changing Family Dynamics: Implications for Social Development. *Population, Space and Place*, Volume 15, Issue 2, pp. 161-174.

Ratha, Dilip and Sanket Mohapatra (2009). Revised Outlooks for Remittance Flows 2009-2011: Remittances Expected to Fall by 8 to 10 percent in 2009. *Migration and Development Brief,* March 23, 2009. Migration and Remittance Team, Development Prospects Group, World Bank (electronic source).

Ro'i, Yaacov (2000). *Islam in the Soviet Union. From the Second World War to Gorbatchev.* New York: Columbia University Press.

Roman, Meredith (2002). Making Caucasians Black: Moscow Since the Fall of Communism and the Racialization of Non-Russians. *Journal of Communism Studies and Transition Politics.* Vol. 18. No.2, p.1- 17.

Rubin, Barnett R. and Nancy Lubin (eds) (1999). *Calming the Ferghana Valley. Development and Dialogue in the Heart of Central Asia.* Report of the Ferghana Valley Working Group of the Center for Preventive Action. New York: The Century Foundation Press.

Ryvkina, Rozalina V. (1996). *Yevrei v postsovetskoi Rossii – Kto oni? Sotsiologicheskii analiz problem rossiiskogo evereistva.* [Jews in Post-Soviet Russia – Who are They? Sociological Analysis of Problems Related to Russian Jewishness]. (In Russian.) Moskva: URSS.

Sahadeo, Jeff (2007). Druzhba narodov or second class citizenship? Soviet Asian migrants in a post-colonial world. *Central Asian Survey*, Vol. 26, No. 4. Pp. 559-576.

Salih, Ruba (2003). *Gender in Transnationalism. Home, Longing and Belonging Among Moroccan Migrant Women.* Routledge Research in Transnationalism. London and New York: Routledge.

Salt, John (1989). A Comparative Overview of International Trends and Types, 1950-1980. *International Migration Review*, Vol. 23, No. 3, pp. 431-456.

Sana, Mariano and Douglas Massey (2005). Household Composition, Family Migration and Community Context: Migrant Remittances in Four Countries. *Social Science Quarterly,* Volume 86, No.2., pp. 509-528.

Sargent, Carolyn F. and Stéphanie Larchanché-Kim (2006). Liminal Lives, Immigration Status, Gender, and the Construction of Identities Among Malian Migrants in Paris. *American Behavioral Scientist*, Vol. 50, No. 1, pp. 9-26.

Schatz, Edward. (2005). Reconceptualizing clans: kinship networs and statehood in Kazakhstan. *Nationalities Papers.* Vol. 33, No.2.

Schnell, Rainer, Paul B. Hill and Ekle Esser (2005). *Methoden der empirischen Sozialforschung.* 7th Edition. München, Wien: Oldenbourg.

Scott, James (1972). Patron-Client Politics and Political Change in Southeast Asia. *The American Political Science Review*, Vol. 66, No. 1, pp. 91-113.

Scott, James (1985). *Weapons of the Weak. Everyday Forms of Peasant Resistance.* New Haven: Yale University Press.

Silvey, Rachel (2006). Consuming the Transnational Family. Indonesian Migrant Domestic Workers to Saudi Arabia. *Global Networks*, Vol. 6, No. 1, pp. 23-40.

Skeldon, Ronald (2003). Migration and Poverty. Paper presented at the conference on "African Migration and Urbanization in Comparative Perspective", Johannesburg, South Africa, June 4 – 7, 2003. Available online at http://pum.princeton.edu/pumconference/papers/6-Skeldon.pdf (last consulted on 02.01.09).

Smith, Graham (ed) (1996). *The Nationalities Question in the Post-Soviet States.* 2nd Edition. London and New York: Longman.
Smith, Michael P and Luiz E. Guarnizo (eds) (1998). *Transnationalism From Below.* New Brunswick, New Jersey: Transaction Publishers.
Smith, Michael P. and Luis E. Guarnizo (1998). The Locations of Transnationalism. In: Smith, Michael P. and Luis E. Guarnizo (eds) *Transnationalism From Below.* Comparative Urban and Community Research. Volume 6. New Brunswick, New Jersey: Transaction Publishers.
Smith, Michael P. (2005). Transnational Urbanism Revisited. *Journal of Ethnic and Migration Studies.* Vol. 31, No. 2. pp. 235-244.
Smith, Robert (1999). Reflections on Migration, the State and Construction, Durability and Newness of Transnational Life. In: Pries, Ludger (ed) *Migration and Transnational Social Spaces.* Aldershot: Ashgate.
Solchanyk, Roman (1982). Russian language and Soviet politics. *Soviet Studies.* Vol. 34. No. 1. (Jan. 1982) pp. 23-42.
Sona, Federica (2005). *Polygamy in Britain.* Working Paper. Osservatorio delle Libertà ed Istituzioni Religiose. (available at http://www.olir.it/ areetematiche/104/documents/Sona_Polygamy_in_Britain.pdf
Soviet Union (1932). *The Fundamental Law (Constitution) of the USSR together with the Consitution (fundamental law) of the RSFSR.* Moscow: Cooperative Pub. Society of foreign workers in the USSR.
Stahl Charles and Ansanul Habib (1991). Emigration and Development in South and Southeast Asia. In: Papademetriou, Demetrios G. and Philip Martin (eds) *The Unsettled Relationship: Labor Migration and Economic Development.* Contribution in Labor Studies, No. 33. New York: Greenwod Press, pp. 136-179.
Stark, Oded and David E. Bloom (1985). The New Economics of Labor Migration. *The American Economic Review.* Vol. 75. No.3., pp- 173-178.
Stark, Oded (1991). *The Migration of Labor.* Cambridge, Mass.: Basil Blackwell
Strauss, Anselm and Juliet Corbin (1998). *Basics of Qualitative Research: Techniques and Procedures for Developing Grounded Theory.* Thousand Oaks, California: Sage.
Tacoli, Cecilia (1999). International Migration and Restructuring of Gender Assymetries: Continuity and Change Among Filipino Labor Migrants in Rome. *International Migration Review,* Vol. 33, No. 3, pp. 658-682.
Thomas, William and Florian Znaniecki (1927 [1918-1921]). *The Polish Peasant in Europe and America: Monograph of an Immigration Group.* Copyright by Richard G. Badger, Gorham Press: Boston.
Thorez, Julien (2007). Itinéraires du déracinement. L'essor des migrations de travail entre l'Asie centrale et la Russie. In: *Espace, population et sociétés,* 1/2007.
Tilly, Charles and C. Harold Brown (1968). On Uprooting, Kinship and the Auspices of Migration. *International Journal of Comparative Sociology,* Vol. 8, pp.139-164.
Tilly, Charles (1990). Transplanted Networks. In: V. Yans-MacLoughlin (ed) *Immigration Reconsidered.* New York: Oxford University Press, pp. 79-95.
Tishkov, Valery A. (ed) (1996). *Migracii i novye diaspory v postsovetskix gosudarstvax.[Migrations and New Diasporas in Post-Soviet States].* Institute of Ethnology and Anthropology. Moscow: UNHCR and Open Society Institute.
Tishkov, Valery A. (2005). The Population Census and the Construction of Identity. *Anthropology and Archeology of Eurasia,* Vol. 44, No. 2, pp. 10-40.

Trudovaia migraciia v Respublike Uzbekistan. Social'ny, pravovye i gendernye aspekty [Labor Migration in the Uzbek Republic. Social, Legislative and Gender Aspects] (2008). With the support of the United Nations Development Program and Gender Program of the Swiss Embassy in Tashkent (electronic source).

Tursounov, Hamid (2005). *Kyrgyz Women: The Majority-Minority.* Transition Online. February 24 Issue.

Velayutham, Selvaraj and Amanda Wise (2005). Moral Economies of a Translocal Village: Obligation and Shame Among South Indian Transnational Migrants. *Global Networks,* Vol 5, No. 1, pp. 27-47.

Vertovec, Steven (2001). *Transnational Social Formations: Towards Conceptual Cross-Fertilization.* Working Paper WPTC-01-16. Paper Presented at the University of Oxford (available at www.transcomm.ox.ac.uk/working%20 papers /Vertovec2.pdf).

Vertovec, Steven (2004). Migrant Transnationalism and Modes of Transformation. *International Migration Review.* Vol. 38, No. 3, pp. 970-2001.

Vichit-Vadakan, Juree (1994). Women and the Family in Thailand in the Midst of Social Change. *Law and Society Review,* Vol. 28, No. 3. Law and Society in Southeast Asia, pp. 515-524.

Voigt-Graf, Carmen (2005). The Construction of Transnational Spaces by Indian Migrants in Australia. *Journal of Ethnic and Migration Studies.* Vol. 31, No 2. pp. 365-384.

Wallerstein, Immanuel M. (1974). *The Modern World-System.* New York: Academic Press.

Waldinger, Roger and David Fitzgerald (2004). Transnationalism in Question. *American Journal of Sociology,* Vol. 109, No.5, pp. 1777-1795.

Weil, Patrick (2002). Towards a Coherent Policy of Co-Development. *International Migration,* Vol. 40, No. 3, pp. 41-55.

Weingrod, Alex (1968). Patrons, Patronage and Political Parties. *Comparative Studies in Societies and History,* Vol. 10, No. 4, pp. 377-400.

Werner, Oswald (1999). When Recording is Impossible. *Field Methods,* Vol. 11, No. 1 pp. 71-76.

Wimbush, S. Enders and Dmitry Ponomareff (1979). *Alternatives for Mobilizing Soviet Central Asian Labor: Outmigration and Regional Development.* A Project AIR FORCE report prepared for the United States Air Force. Santa Monica, CA: Rand.

Wimmer, Andreas and Nina Glick-Schiller. Methodological Nationalism and the Study of Migration. *Arch.europ.sociol.,* XLIII, 2(202), 217-240.

Wolf, Eric R. (1956). Aspects of Group Relations in a Complex Society: Mexico. *American Anthropologist,* Vol. 58, No. 6, pp. 1065-1078.

Wolf, Eric R. (1966). Kinship, Friendship and Patron-Client Relations. In: Banton (ed) *The Social Anthropology of Complex Societies.* New York: Frederick A. Praeger, p. 1-22.

Wu, Chun-hsu (1967). *Dollars, Dependents and Dogma: Overseas Chinese Remittances to Communist China.* Stanford, CA: Hoover Institute Publications.

Yeoh, B, Graham E. and Boyle (2002). Migration and Family Relations in the Asia Pacific. *Asia and Pacific Migration Journal,* Vol.11, No.1, pp. 1-11.

Yudina, Tatiana Nikolaevna (2004). *Sotsiologiia migratsii. K formirovaniiu novogo nauchnogo napravleniia*. [Sociology of Migration. Towards Formation of a New Direction of Research]. (In Russian) Moscow: Dashkov i K.

Yudina, Tatiana Nikolaevna (2005). Labor Migration to Russia. The Response of State and Society. *Current Sociology*, Vol. 53, No. 4, pp. 583-606.

Zaionchkovskaya, Zhanna A. (1999). *Vnutrenniaia migraciia v Rossii i v SSSR v XX veke kak otrajenie social'noi modernizacii*. [Internal Migration in Russia and the USSR in the 20th Century as the Reflection of Social Modernization]. Electronic paper.

Zaslavsky, Viktor and Robert J. Brym (1983). *Soviet-Jewish Emigration and Soviet Nationality Policy*. Hong Kong: The Macmillan Press.

Zlotnik, Hania (1995). The South-to-North Migration of Women. *International Migration Review*. Vol., 29, No. 1, pp. 229-254.

Zollberg, Aristide (1989). The Next Waves: Migration Theory for a Changing World. *International Migration Review*, Vol. 23, No. 3, pp. 403-430.

Selected Online News and Analytical Sources

www.akipress.kg – Kyrgyzstan News Agency
www.azattyk.org – Radio Free Europe Radio Liberty (Kyrgyz Serve)
www.centrasia.ru – Centrasia News Agency
www.crisisgroup.org – International Crisis Group
www.demoscope.ru – Demoscope Weekly (Electronic Version of the Bulletin Population and Society)
www.eurasianet.org – EurasiaNet Online Service for Information and Analysis
www.ferghana.ru – Ferghana.Ru Information Agency
www.iom.int – International Organization for Migration
www.iwpr.net – Institute for War and Piece Reporting
www.nelegalov.net – All-Russia Migration Forum
www.ng.ru – Russian Online Newspaper "Nezavisimaia Gazeta"
www.ozodi.org – Radio Free Europe Radio Liberty (Tajik Serve)
www.ozodlik.org – Radio Free Europe Radio Liberty (Uzbek Serve)